MW01253423

FLYING HIGH

FLYING HIGH

Inside
Big-Time
Drug
Smuggling

by Wayne Greenhaw

DODD, MEAD & COMPANY   *New York*

Copyright © 1984 by Wayne Greenhaw
All rights reserved
No part of this book may be reproduced in any form
without permission in writing from the publisher.
Published by Dodd, Mead & Company, Inc.
79 Madison Avenue, New York, N.Y. 10016
Distributed in Canada by
McClelland and Stewart Limited, Toronto
Manufactured in the United States of America
Designed by Claire Counihan
First Edition

Library of Congress Cataloging in Publication Data:

Greenhaw, Wayne, 1940–
    Flying high.

    Includes bibliographical references and index.
    1. Narcotics, Control of—United States.   2. Smuggling
—United States.   3. Smugglers—Psychology.   I. Title.
HV5825.G697   1984   363.4'5'0973   84-1468
ISBN 0-396-08360-9

For My Brother
Don
Who Has Always Cared

CONTENTS

FOREWORD

When I began writing this book, collecting information from law enforcement agencies, accompanying agents on drug busts, listening to prosecuting attorneys lambaste the criminals, and hearing defense lawyers state technicalities which might keep their clients free, I wondered about the true preponderance of the problem of illegal drugs being transported into this country. Who smuggles drugs into the United States? Are they organized? Where do they buy the narcotics? How much do they pay? How do the individuals get started in this business? How do they get the drugs into the country? Agents in Los Angeles introduced me to undercover personnel who had kept watch on Burt Reynolds's home. In Washington, D.C. I was told that certain disguised police were watching the cloakrooms of Congress for activity in drugs. I rode with federal agents from Manhattan into Queens on a surveillance stakeout of a warehouse laboratory where the raw product was refined into cocaine and powdered down for distribution on the streets. I witnessed a large plane landing in an abandoned cotton field in south Georgia and a sailing boat riding the high wind into an isolated port in southern Louisiana. The illegal drugs appeared to be everywhere.

Riding in a souped-up Cessna with oversized twin fuel tanks, a prize from an earlier bust at a private airport near Fort Lauderdale, an agent pilot swooped down off the coast of Key West, circled over the glasslike, blue-green waters of the Gulf of Mexico, and said, "I'm going to show you what it feels like to fly into Florida with a doper. You've got to imagine you're tired to the bone. You've flown across 1,000 miles of water on the way down, sat on a hot strip waiting for your dope, and you've returned over the Caribbean and the Gulf. Now you've got to come in low, where you won't be detected by the different radar. You've got to really whizz it. You've got to concentrate. Start dreaming and you might ditch every-thing—including your life."

The plane dropped lower. I closed my eyes as I felt my stomach tighten. When I looked, it seemed as though we were about to fall into the drink. The sea was no longer the calm tabletop I had admired from a distance. The pilot said we were flying at no more than 100 feet. "You've got to stay low. If you don't, you'll be picked up. I've talked to a hundred dope pilots. We know exactly what they do and how they do it." The mist from the water clouded against our windshield, but he did not bring us up. When we crossed the Ten Thousand Islands south of Naples, I thought I could reach out and touch the sand dunes. Then, over the flat swamps of The Everglades, the limbs of the hearty cypress trees shook slightly and made a sheer echo that brought goose bumps to my flesh. Over the flat marshlands honey-colored sage bent low to the ground with the power of our movement.

When we finally landed at an airport south of Miami I felt a quick relief. "What we did was nothing compared to what these guys go through every time they make a run down to Colombia or Venezuela," the agent told me, but it was hard for an outsider to believe.

In the next few months, when I visited several federal pris-ons and talked with convicted smugglers, when I met with others in lounges in St. Louis, Atlanta, New Orleans, and Houston, I discovered over and over again that the agent was not exaggerating. If anything, he had been downplaying the drama.

In my years as a reporter for The *Alabama Journal* in Montgomery, Alabama, and later as a freelance journalist, I had traveled to many places with a varied lot of people. I had walked beside Dr. Martin Luther King, Jr. on several of his marches during the early 1960s. I had camped in the hills with a seventy-year-old prospector who was convinced he had found the mother lode in east Alabama, where New York gold companies owned and operated mines before the rush of 1849. I had played tennis very poorly with Pancho Gonzales. I had stayed up late to drink whiskey with Lieutenant William Laws "Rusty" Calley, Jr. and listened to him pour his heart out about the bloody nightmares of a place called Pinkville in South Vietnam that haunted him in the early 1970s.

I was familiar with unfamiliar surroundings. I enjoyed the reportorial process of going out into the unknown and finding out what is there, why it is there, how it works, and who makes it work. At the *Journal* I had done an eight-part series in 1968 about drugs in Alabama, and it had upset quite a few authority figures and caused a local district attorney to threaten me with jail if I didn't reveal certain sources. The pieces won statewide and regional awards, and The Associated Press Managing Editors Association awarded them a citation in Oklahoma City that year.

In 1982, while conducting my weekly creative writing seminar at Maxwell Federal Prison Camp, I met a tall distinguished-looking man with thinning white hair and a soothingly soft voice. This man, who looked somehow well dressed even in the prison khakis, sat through three classes before he said anything other than his name.

After a while he told me that he was educated as an engineer and in economics; he did not want to take up writing even to pass time in prison. He added, however, that he had a very interesting story that he wished someone would tell.

I smiled and nodded. Sure, I thought, I've heard this before. In fact, I had heard it dozens of times in the three years I had been teaching at Maxwell. And I had heard it more times in the free world, where everybody and his brother thought they had a best seller inside them; they just wanted somebody else to write it.

In the months that followed, Thomas Riley Kimball continued to visit the class. Each time he would remain behind after the others had moved on into the main compound away from the education complex. In bits and pieces, tiny story after tiny story, he told about becoming involved in what was called The Company, a loose-knit group that had banded together to form a corporation with the expressed purpose of making money from the smuggling of marijuana into the United States. At the time more than 150 members had been arrested and convicted. The case was the largest ever in terms of number of defendants, size of forfeitures to the government, and area covered by the covert operation of the law enforcement authorities.

More and more, Tom Kimball's story interested me. I looked into it in depth and found that it was tremendously dramatic.

However, the more I looked into the case of Tom Kimball's Company the more information I discovered about other drug-smuggling cases. One person would lead to three or four others who were involved in drug smuggling either as an active smuggler, an off-loader in Houston, Texas, or Fitzgerald, Georgia, a laboratory technician powdering down strong Turkish products in a warehouse in Queens in New York, a pilot from Marshall, Illinois, an undercover agent in Los Angeles, or a truck driver from Everett, Washington. Drug Enforcement Administration agents, attorneys who specialized in prosecuting narcotics violators, state investigators, sheriffs, and local district attorneys all talked openly. Almost everybody on every Main Street in the United States seemed to be affected by the illegal drug industry. And in the United Kingdom, journalists and law enforcement officials from Fleet Street and Scotland Yard talked about their country being a conduit for the flow of drugs into the United States. On the West Coast DEA (Drug Enforcement Administration) agents and undercover informants spoke about the increasing traffic from the Middle East and Far East. Down in Mexico I talked with some of the most interesting smugglers, middlemen for smugglers, and financiers for illegal drug connections. Nobody was shy about talking. However, many wished to keep their real identities secret. In all cases I have used real names unless otherwise stated. And even when I use fictitious names, they are aliases by which the smugglers and/or undercover police have been known.

Throughout the writing of the book, Tom Kimball introduced me to friends who had been members of The Company. He recalled events that he had personally witnessed. He remembered the tense times and the funny times. He had opinions about many people and decisions that were made by higher-ups in The Company, and he offered them without reservation.

During the months after he was released from Maxwell Federal Prison he continued the missionary work with his church which he had started after being incarcerated. He had met Charles Colson and had been impressed by the former Watergate conspirator's attempt to help prisoners across the country. "I believe that it will help people all over the United States to know what is happening in the smuggling scene," said Tom Kimball. "There is a basic ignorance among most people that smuggling is a romantic, dreamlike way to make a living. In reality, it is tough and dangerous and foolhardy."

I traveled thousands of miles and talked with hundreds of persons involved with drug smuggling. All of it was fascinating, and I hope that you, the reader of this book, will experience that fascination, too.

Very early one morning when I was riding with a plainclothes pilot in pursuit of a DC-4 suspected of being filled with a cargo of marijuana, the man dipped us down into a dark valley between great hills of eastern Tennessee. Two police helicopters topped a ridge to our left and another rode nose-down to the right. It looked like something out of a war. We dipped into another deeper valley and came up again just in time to see the lights of the DC-4 no more than a mile away. The bigger plane, which informants had said was coming in from Colombia, was much closer to the ground. "He's running out of fuel," my pilot said.

We curled toward the starboard side, the two-engine Cessna following the contours of the Appalachians. I gripped the edges of my seat while my heart beat fast and my breath caught. When I glanced at him, I saw that the pilot agent had a grim smile frozen onto his taut face. His shoulders hunched forward slightly, his hands held the steering mechanism expertly. He reached to the panel of dials and turned a knob just as the plane settled flatly upright behind the big bird and a golden sunlight peeked over a far eastern horizon.

Twenty minutes later, after my heart slowed and my breathing became easier, we landed at a small red clay strip cut into the wilderness. We followed within a hundred feet behind the DC-4 while helicopters hovered over the tops of each of his wings and a truck filled with officers in fatigues pulled in front of his nose. As we stepped out and arrests were being made, the police pilot slapped his Australian bush hat against his slender hip and, still grinning, said, "We were both pushing it pretty good back yonder. He and I both were flying high. He's got the same adrenaline in his veins I've got in mine. It takes a special breed of cat to try his kind of stuff and my kind of stuff."

The more smugglers and drug enforcement people I talked with, the more I saw what he was talking about. Whether it was in a plane or on a boat trying to catch the drug smugglers or sneaking past border patrols in southern Mexico or making deals with Central American governments, all of them were flying high.

FLYING HIGH

BOOK ONE:

THE INSIDE TRACK

Chapter One
The Good Old Boys

Once in a great while during the less than one-hundred-year-old history of drug law enforcement in the United States agents have found themselves in a perfect situation to make a case against smugglers. According to former United States Attorney General William French Smith, narcotics trafficking, distribution, and sales to the American people became the country's largest industry. The sales alone in the United States in any single year in the 1980s equaled the combined profits of the five hundred largest industrial corporations, or nearly $100 billion, Smith stated. And in most small towns in America an unemployed person would be able to earn $10,000-plus for one night of illegal work: off-loading an airplane or a boat or driving a truck to and from a distribution location or loading and unloading the truck. Because there is so much money to be made from the deals, trafficking has flourished. Federal, state, and local police work goes on around the clock in an attempt to stop the expanding illegal organizations from Miami to Maine and New York to San Diego. For every successful bust the police make, more than a hundred loads are successfully brought into the country for distribution.

James G. "Jerry" Ward believed he could stop certain groups from bringing drugs into his section of the country. For eighteen years he had considered himself a professional narcotics officer with two law enforcement groups, and he knew he could put on the good-old-boy routine better than most detectives. In Alabama, the name of the game among undercover policemen was, basically, who could be the best good old boy.

Jerry Ward was overweight, with a beer belly which stood out prominently over the big silver buckle that held up his skintight jeans. Already gray, he combed his hair down over his high forehead. He remembered well the days as a narcotics squad detective with the Montgomery City Police Department when he went undercover to spy on teenagers bringing lids of marijuana onto the grounds of the local high schools. And he remembered a later date when he bought pot from country-kid students on Auburn University's loveliest village of the plains campus and nabbed them for trafficking. Ward had experienced hundreds of hours of sitting and waiting for suspects in dozens of drug cases across the state. Now he was an investigator in the narcotics unit of the Department of Public Safety's Alabama Bureau of Investigation, and he walked with a proud swagger characteristic of narc agents across the country.

On Monday morning, February 1, 1982, Ward busied himself with concentrating on a situation that would be coming down that afternoon. The assistant commander of his unit, Lieutenant Louis N. Bradford, had laid out plans for an elaborate operation and had picked Ward to be a major participant. Before Ward and his partner, William Rhegness, who had been in police work for nine years, had left for the weekend on the previous Friday, Bradford had outlined only the nucleus of what might be happening for the next few weeks. He told them to make plans to go undercover and be prepared to stay in the field unrecognized for a lengthy period.

Ward was anxious. An edge of excitement came over him every time he started out into the field undercover. In his mind he went over all the preparations they had made. He and Rhegness knew the lay of the land in and around the small town of Hurtsboro, Alabama, about sixty-five miles east of Montgomery in the heart of flatland farming country known by the investigators to be heavily used by smugglers for landing operations. Four years earlier a farmer had called them from nearby Society Hill, a wide place in the road in Macon County, and the man said, "I found a big plane in my hayfield." When officers from the Alabama Bureau of Investigation arrived, on August 15, 1978, they found a DC-3 that had already been unloaded. The plane was abandoned on the dry red soil, but the fingerprint team covered every inch of the inside and exterior and investigators found residues of marijuana. After a two-year extensive and meticulous investigation, combining efforts with the DEA (Drug Enforcement Administration) and the Georgia Bureau of Investigation, six men from the Atlanta area were indicted and all six were convicted in federal court.

When the call came this Monday afternoon for the investigators to go, Ward and Rhegness, traveling under the names of Bob and Bill respectively, drove to the southwestern section of Montgomery where they were introduced by their informant to a tall, rather handsome, gray-haired man named James Ollis Woodward.

The informant had already spent time with Woodward and convinced him that Ward and Rhegness were on their side: Woodward said he was looking for a sod or dirt airstrip large enough for a DC-6 to land and take off. Ward leaned back in a relaxed pose, knowing that somewhere within the perimeter of their meeting place other members of his investigative team were taking photographs from their hidden positions. He said, "All the land I've got right now is under water. You know, we've been having the winter rains. It does this just about every January. And it makes it hard to find land that's not soaked or under water. A big plane like that would be mired up as soon as it lands," he added.

"I've got to have good hard land," Woodward said.

Ward shook his head.

"When a DC-6 comes in loaded down with 18,000 pounds of stuff, it has to have a solid runway."

Ward leaned forward, appearing very interested. "I know just the place. It's a paved strip about one mile long. It'd be perfect for you. I know the guy who owns it. He lets me use it sometimes. It's a fine strip located behind a chain link fence and has a huge hangar. For what you want to use it for, it'd be perfect. And I could offer you absolutely airtight security."

Woodward frowned. "Are you talking about the strip over there by Hurtsboro, Alabama?" he asked.

Ward nodded. "Yeah, that's the one," he said.

"I know that strip," Woodward said. "But, you know, it's hot right now. The law's watching it. Some smugglers broke into it and landed there back three, four months ago, and ever since, it's been hot. I don't think it'd be a good place. Not now."

Reassuringly, Ward said, "Since those guys broke in, they've put in a very intricate alarm system, connected with a local farmhouse where the superintendent lives, but it can be cut off very easily if you know the combination. And I know the combination. The people out there are friends of mine. If anybody goes onto the land without authorization, the alarm goes off in the manager's house. He knows it immediately. So now, at night, they no longer watch the strip."

Woodward, however, continued to question. He was far from sure about this good old boy who seemed to know what he was talking about.

"I've got the inside track on the place," Ward reiterated. "My buddy and I know all the people over there. We know the place and people. With us on your side, hell, you could land an army and nobody would ever know it."

Woodward laughed to himself and nodded. "Well, we sure would rather have a place like that one at Hurtsboro. It would be much better than having a little strip like the one we've been working down south of here. It's been safe so far. We've brought in twenty-seven loads so far down there."

They drank coffee and passed the time of day before Ward said, "You say twenty-seven loads at one field?"

And Woodward answered, "Yes, sir, twenty-seven loads. We're making that guy down there rich. And if you could do the same for us, I guarantee you, you and your friend will be rich men."

A little later, Woodward said, "My outfit's got two van-type trucks two and a half tons each."

"The kind the airlines use to load and unload cargo?" Ward asked.

Woodward nodded. "They're exactly the kind used by commercial airlines. The rear end lifts up to the door of the large aircraft that we'll be bringing in, and it can be off-loaded straight from the plane onto the truck."

"Sounds like a great operation," Ward commented.

"We do things right," Woodward said. "We're pros. We've been doing it for a long time."

Ward asked how long, but the question slipped past Woodward. His mind was dwelling on something else, and within a minute he asked Ward, "How much do you think you and your friend will be asking to help with the airstrip, to make sure we don't have any problem in that regard, and to be our contacts down there?"

Without hesitating, Ward said, "I'd like to have $15,000 for myself and another $15,000 for my friend."

Smiling, Woodward said, "I don't see any problem with that. I'll talk to my people and get back in touch with you on it. But like I say, I don't see any problem with the figure at all. The only thing is, we don't pay right on the spot when the plane comes in."

"I don't understand," Ward said, appearing worried at the thought of not being able to collect his money immediately after the job.

"Well, it's the system we work under. We have to put money up front down in Colombia, and then after the marijuana gets into this country, we unload it and disperse it, and then three or four days later the funds are channeled back downstream—and that is when you get paid. That way we keep the cash flow steady and everybody is taken care of."

"But I still don't understand," Ward insisted. "If I don't get paid when the stuff comes in, how will I know I'll get paid later? You'll be long gone, and we could be left holding the bag with nothing for our troubles. If you leave us high and dry, we might never see you again and we wouldn't know how in the world to contact you. All I know is, you show up one day and start asking questions, and I answer them; I help you, my friend helps you, and you may skip out and we may have nothing."

"You have nothing to worry about, I guarantee you. If you like, you can hold some of the grass. We'll leave $30,000 worth of the stuff with you, you hold it, and when we pay you three or four days later, you give us the stuff. How's that sound?"

Ward said it sounded better.

"Okay, I'll talk with my people, see what they say, and I'll talk to some of the folks I know over in Hurtsboro. I've got to make sure what you say is the truth."

"It's true," Ward assured him.

They shook hands. The informant and Woodward walked outside, got into a white-top, blue-bottom Cadillac and drove away.

A few days later, Ward and Rhegness drove about fifty miles northeast on I-85 toward Atlanta where they met with three men including a big ex-football player type named Ted Harvey Raulerson. Soon, while drinking coffee at the Opelika Holiday Inn, Ted identified himself as belonging to a group that had been engaged in smuggling marijuana into the United States for approximately three years, working mainly for his brother-in-law, James Ollis Woodward. (This conversation was recorded by the ABI [Alabama Bureau of Investigation] agent on the pages of a legal pad later that night. From the first day on, Ward and Rhegness wrote out every detail they remembered, including word-by-word conversations.)

"Up to now we've only used sod strips," Raulerson told them. "We put driveway reflectors down the length of the strip on each side. We put a pickup truck at one end and another at the other; they're facing each other, see; and when the aircraft approaches, the pickups turn on their lights and also a large Q-beam spotlight shines down the length of the strip where it will reflect off the driveway reflectors. We've never had any trouble with it before."

Relaxing, drinking his coffee, he added, "Sometimes we've used pie pans tacked to wooden stakes that are driven all along the sides of the runway. When you shine the spotlight on them, they reflect just as well as the reflectors."

When Ward said they wouldn't need to worry about reflectors or spotlights at the airstrip at the Sehoy Plantation, Raulerson asked, "How long's the runway?"

"At least a mile," Ward said.

"You've walked it?"

Ward nodded.

"Where's the nearest house?"

"One and a half to two miles away, through a pine thicket; and in the other direction, at least three miles."

"Sounds good. What about law enforcement? Where're the nearest cops?"

"Hurtsboro," Ward said.

"How far's that?"

"Four and a half, five miles," Ward answered.

"How many officers they employ?"

Ward shrugged. "I don't know. Probably two or three. Maybe not that many. Seven hundred fifty people live there."

"How many cops on duty at night?"

Again, Ward said he didn't know. It wasn't a high-crime area, he allowed. They didn't patrol the streets at night the way police did in big cities.

Raulerson continued asking questions: Where was the nearest sheriff's office located? How many deputies were on duty at night? How would they get from their headquarters in Union Springs, about fifteen miles south, to the Sehoy Plantation airstrip? How long would it take if they were notified that a strange plane had landed on the strip? Where was the nearest telephone? What kind of traffic flow moved along Alabama Highway 26 next to the strip? What type of traffic flow moved there—trucks or automobiles?

Ward assured him the strip was very isolated, that it was a secure landing area, that the traffic flow after 8 P.M. was virtually nothing, and the police and sheriff departments were out of touch with current happenings on the drug scene. This was definitely rural countryside.

Raulerson said he had talked with his brother-in-law, and they saw nothing out of the ordinary about the fee asked by Ward and Rhegness. However, he changed the deal slightly. "We'll pay you half when the aircraft has landed, the load has been transferred to the trucks, and we're about to get on our way. And we'll bring you the second half a few days later, after we've got the goods moving in the marketplace."

Seemingly satisfied with the answers the two men had supplied to his barrage of questions, Raulerson said the organization for which he worked was broken down into three main levels of operation. One level, he said, was totally responsible for getting the drugs smuggled into the United States. The second tier was responsible for obtaining an airstrip and refueling the aircraft once it had brought the load into the country. The third element of the organization took delivery of the drugs, dispersed them, sold them, and then paid the other levels.

Expressing interest in the organization, Ward said, "But how do you pay for the stuff all the way down in Colombia, South America?" as though his mind could not comprehend doing business so far from home.

A smile played on Raulerson's lips. "We make sure our money flow takes on a downhill posture," he said knowingly. "First, the marijuana is fronted to persons picking it up down in Colombia, and then it is paid for on the next trip down, after the first load is sold, so there's a never-ending process. They trust us. We've been doing this long enough. They know

us. At first, we had to put money up front, and now we've got
a lot of money invested down there. We've been doing business
for several years and they know we're good for the money."

Back in the States, he said, the local crews, the transportation personnel, the people furnishing the airstrip, and the
wholesalers involved with the final distribution of the marijuana would all work like Ward and Rhegness. "The money
flows back from the final distributor, back downhill to the
persons in another country where it was originally purchased."

"But what if something happens between the time you take
it off the plane and it gets to the streets? What if somebody
gets caught and the stuff is destroyed or something?"

Raulerson shook his head. "You have no worries. None
whatsoever. Our man Boynton keeps $1 million to $3 million
in ready assets all the time. We don't worry about where the
next load is coming from. We've got everything fixed on that
score," he said.

(Later that night, when they were making notes about what
had happened and what had been said during the day, Ward
and Rhegness noted that this was the first time they had heard
the name Boynton.)

And in the next breath, Raulerson added, "You fellows stick
with us. Everybody in our organization has gotten rich, and
they're going to get richer. We work hard at what we do, and
we're good at it."

Before they parted, Raulerson warned that if Ward or Rhegness were arrested for any reason, they should keep their mouths
shut, say nothing, go to jail, and lawyers would be supplied
immediately and their bonds would be made.

Early in March, Ward telephoned Raulerson, told him the
airstrip at Sehoy would be available for the next two weeks,
and on Monday, March 8, Raulerson called and told Ward to
meet him at the Mariner Inn in Opelika at 11 A.M. the next
day. However, at 8:15 the next morning, Raulerson telephoned
again, said the meeting had been changed, and Ward was to

meet him at Franklin Field outside Union Springs on U.S. Highway 110 at 11 A.M.

When the two agents turned into the small airfield in the wide-open rural sage field, they spotted a sleek Beech Baron twin-engine aircraft sitting on the ramp. Three men were near the nose, resting on the asphalt. The men were Raulerson, Woodward, and a man introduced to them as "J," who turned out to be William James Boynton III, a multimillionaire's son who, Ward learned later, had received a gift of about $1.5 million upon his graduation from the University of Florida. About thirty-five years old, handsome, wearing a tailor-made western-cut shirt open at the neck to reveal a gold chain and large nugget, he had lived a privileged life that had become boring until he went into business for himself and joined Woodward and Raulerson in a partnership.

Woodward walked up to their car, a confiscated three-year-old yellow-bottomed and white-topped Lincoln Continental which added to the ambitious redneck image they portrayed. "What do you say about us riding over with you boys and checking out the airstrip?" Woodward asked.

Ward's voice caught in the top edge of his throat with the excitement of actually taking them over to the stage area where he and Rhegness hoped to make the bust of a lifetime go down. After a fraction of a second, Ward said, "Sure, let's go!"

Ward drove through Union Springs, the seat of Bullock County, where a black sheriff and predominantly black governing officials had taken over for the first time since Reconstruction. This was the eastern edge of the Black Belt, where deep rich soil historically yielded a heavy crop of cotton and where most of the population today was descended from slaves of pre-Civil War days. Nobody noticed the five men as they rode slowly through the town of huge frame houses with great banks of pink and crimson azaleas blooming in the first brightness of premature springtime.

Turning from the four-lane U.S. Highway 82 north onto Alabama 26, they shot directly up the straight-and-narrow road through the thick stand of pine trees and through the middle of rich green flat pastureland.

About one and a half miles past a rustic sign reading *Sehoy Plantation*, Ward pulled the Continental onto a small side road and said, "There it is."

All three of the men in the back seat craned their necks to see the sophisticated landing strip in the middle of the rural farmland. The wealthy owner of Sehoy had built a magnificent 5,000-foot cement runway with six-foot asphalt aprons on each side. It was a lighted strip, complete with directional guide lights and a dimmer switch. A wide ramp ran adjacent to a very large hangar made of metal, with all of the latest equipment for tending to airplanes. A smaller hangar at the northern end of the area, all of which was enclosed by an eight-foot-high chain link fence, was a cutdown version of the larger hangar.

Woodward, leaning over the back of the front seat, said, "We want to walk the strip."

Raulerson added, "We want to make sure a DC-6 can land and turn around out there."

Rhegness, looking up and down the lonely stretch of highway, said, "I don't know if I'd do that right in broad open daylight. If anybody sees us, it sure would create suspicion."

"We don't want anybody to get jumpy with us looking over things," said Ward.

Thinking quickly, Ward said, "What if I take y'all over here to a little side road? Maybe we can see from over there." He backed out without waiting for an answer. He drove down what he said was called the Cemetery Road because it wound around an old cemetery, and as he topped a small knoll the car became hidden from the main highway.

From the rise they could look out onto the southern end of the runway and see exactly how a plane could come down the runway and turn around. Raulerson said that Cemetery Road would be a good place to park an escape vehicle on the night the aircraft would be coming in.

Standing next to the car, Woodward asked if Ward and Rhegness could locate a fuel truck or fuel tanks.

"What size do you need?" asked Rhegness.

"We'll need something that will hold at least 2,500 gallons of aviation gasoline," Boynton said.

"That's pretty big," Ward said.

"We need at least that much," said Woodward. He added that they would need 2,000 gallons to fuel the plane for its return trip to South America. And after it got back down to South America, he said, and picked up a second load, it would need an additional 500 gallons to get it back to the home base. He didn't pinpoint the home base.

On the next trip to the rural area several days later, Woodward brought with him a man he first introduced as "T." Arriving at the strip after dark, they drove in and parked in front of the big hangar. Ward went inside and punched out a four-digit sequence into the alarm system to deactivate it. Then he opened the doors and drove his car inside. Rhegness, whom he had let out at the gate, had closed it and had caught up with them. One of the men paced the width of the hangar several times before he announced that it was just a few feet short of being wide enough to hold a DC-6. If it had been wider, he said, they could drive the plane into the hangar on the night it arrived for even safer unloading.

Walking out onto the strip, they said the pilot would be very happy with the fact that he would be landing on pavement because they had always used dirt or sod strips before.

Ward said, "I never have done anything like this."

"Yeah," Rhegness added, "I'm afraid something will happen. I don't want to get caught."

The man who had been introduced as "T," who was later referred to as The Boss and became known to them as Thomas

Warren Shea, said, "We have been doing it a long time. Stick with us, and we'll show you how."

Pacing all the way to the end of the 5,000-foot-plus runway, Shea said he would sit at this spot on the night the airplane would arrive. He told them he would be in his black Chevrolet Blazer that also had black windows. His powerful radio equipment in the vehicle would allow him to talk with the plane as far away as Colombia, South America.

Walking back, Shea said, "After we get the plane off-loaded, we'll need industrial-type vacuum cleaners to get all of the marijuana residue out before the return trip to South America."

Woodward mentioned that he thought it would be a good idea to keep the trucks in the big hangar until the plane arrived.

Shea nodded. He added that the plane would remain on the strip until about 4:30 A.M., when it would depart again for Colombia, ensuring its proper arrival time back in South America.

Moving in front of Ward and Rhegness, the men spoke of having dinner a few nights earlier with members of the Santo Trafficante family in Tampa and "Everything looks like it's been taken care of for the next few days." Later the agents made careful notes of the pieces of conversation they had picked up.

While driving back to Montgomery that night, Woodward asked if the agents would have dinner with them at a downtown restaurant. Later Ward recalled, "I had to think fast to say something. We didn't want to meet out in public with them because some other policeman or some friend might spot us and say, 'Hey, Jerry, how are things going with the narc unit?' or something like that and would blow the whole thing. So I said, 'I've got to go to the hospital,' and Woodward asked what was wrong, and I said, 'My wife's dying of cancer, and I want to stay by her side as much as possible.' They were very kind and sympathetic toward me after that."

When Ward pulled into the motel parking lot to let them out, Woodward handed them two one-hundred-dollar bills. "There's a little something for you all to eat supper on tonight," he said.

Woodward called from his home in Moore Haven, Florida, several times during the next week. Each time he asked how the weather was. In the last conversation he added that Ted Raulerson would be traveling to Montgomery and he would be followed by Woodward "to get the horses together," which was his term for starting the operation.

A few days later Woodward met the investigators and took them to a rural south Montgomery restaurant, the Red Bird Inn, famous for its fried chicken, where they could eat in a small private room. After they had eaten, with the sound of a jukebox playing in another part of the restaurant that had been converted from an old frame house, Woodward told them, "I'm very, very concerned."

"What's wrong?" they asked.

"I've got three questions I've got to know the answers to," he said.

They said they would be glad to answer them, if they could.

"The first is about the alarm," Woodward said. "When it goes off, you told me it sounds in the manager's farmhouse. Doesn't it, in fact, sound at the police headquarters in Hurtsboro?"

They both shook their heads. "No way," Ward said. "It sounds at the manager's house on Sehoy. We've checked that out."

"All right," he said. "Now, if somebody happens to spot us, see the plane, think something is going on out there, who would they call?"

"They'd call the manager, the superintendent of the Sehoy Plantation," Rhegness said.

"Everybody in that area knows he's in charge of the airstrip," Ward chimed in.

"Last," Woodward said, "I want you to know that I've checked you out, and at least one person told me that one—and maybe both of you—are narcotics agents. What do you say to that?"

Rhegness laughed shortly. "That's crazy," he said, and added, "All you have to do is check us out with anybody and everybody. We're glad for you to."

"If we're narcotics agents," Ward said, looking Woodward directly in the eyes, "I hope the good Lord will strike my wife dead this very night."

Woodward did not hesitate. "That's all I can ask," he said. He reached out and shook their hands.

"That's good enough by me," Woodward said. Totally convinced by their superb acting jobs, he added, "Now, I want you to know that if everything goes according to plan, you'll receive a bonus. Instead of the agreed-on $30,000, you'll get an additional $20,000, making yours a total of $50,000 for the deal."

Relaxing, Woodward told them that he was very proud of the organization. He said they were professional through and through, would make the two of them a lot of money, and everything would go just great.

He patted his coat pocket and took out a small address book. "You know, this would be worth a million dollars to some law enforcement people," he said. He flipped open the book and flashed numbers written on the pages. "These are radio frequencies of the Drug Enforcement Administration, and with it I can hear anything they say. We know ahead of time any move they make." Moments later he added that he paid a DEA employee in Washington, D.C. $50,000 for the information.

Obviously very comfortable now with Ward and Rhegness, who talked and asked questions and acted very friendly, he said his organization had deep political and financial roots in the South American community. He said it had spent a great deal of money on political elections in several countries, including Colombia and Venezuela.

When they went back to the motel south of Montgomery

where the agents had met him, Woodward gave each of them fifty dollars and said, "This is a little something to help you get by."

On March 20, Woodward called again and asked how everything looked at Sehoy.

Ward said everything looked fine and asked if the plane might come in the next night.

Every evening for the past four days members of DEA, FBI, and Customs, along with the Alabama Bureau of Investigation's narcotic unit, had kept a watch on Sehoy Plantation. "Every night we timed it and watched every blink of every lightning bug," recalled Assistant Unit Commander Louis Bradford. "We knew that it could be any time, the way Ward and Rhegness had reported Woodward's conversation to us."

Woodward told Ward, "Stand by the telephone; the plane could come tomorrow."

At 7:50 P.M. the same day, Woodward called again and asked if everything was clear.

Ward wondered if Woodward had not seen the field unit wandering around the fields near Sehoy. But he told Woodward that he had talked with the man at Sehoy during the afternoon and the man had said everything was definitely all clear. Woodward said, "Get in touch with him again and make sure everything is clear over there. I'll be back in touch with you tomorrow." He added that his men had been tied up working on one of the fuel trucks because something had happened to it.

Ward and Rhegness discovered later that Raulerson had been driving a Ford pickup into Montgomery with a fuel bladder in the bed filled with aviation gasoline. On the interstate, the right front wheel bearing on the pickup overheated, and caught fire. He had to pull off the highway quickly, leap out, run down into a ditch, grab handfuls of mud, bring it back and pack it onto the tires to put out the fire. Tired, discouraged, sickened, and scared, he walked away, called a taxi, went back to his motel, and arranged for a wrecker to pick up the truck and haul it in.

On the morning of March 21, Raulerson called and said the green light was on, the plane had taken off and was heading for Colombia. He said he would be back in touch by noon.

At 2:50 P.M., Woodward called and said the deal was off for another twenty-four hours.

"What's wrong?" Ward asked.

When the plane was preparing to land in South America, a government plane came in and landed in front of them. The organization's plane turned aside, landed at an alternate spot, but would definitely be going in the following day.

On Monday, March 22, Woodward called and told them to meet the others in Room 500 of the Holiday Inn East.

At 1:45 P.M., Raulerson greeted them at the motel room. "Everything looks good," he said. "The plane is on its way and should be here in about ten hours."

As they entered, they saw a scanner sitting on the table near the front door. It was operating, a small red light moving from frequency to frequency, while a man they did not know sat in front of it and adjusted knobs. Ward and Rhegness knew that the man was attempting to program the scanner into a UHF, VHF, or low band frequency to pick up police, aircraft, or some other channel.

"What's happening?" Ward said, trying to appear nonchalant.

"We're programming into the local police frequencies," Woodward said. "We'll be able to hear what's going on all over this area."

Boxes strewn across the floor contained more radio equipment, walkie-talkies, spotlights, motorcycle batteries, antennas, and several new industrial-type vacuum cleaners.

After they ate hamburgers at a fast food restaurant close to the motel, Boynton joined the group. Woodward and Boynton asked the agents to draw a rough map of the area around Sehoy in order that they might know exactly where to put counter-surveillance personnel.

Raulerson sat in a chair amid the activity while the radio-man moved outside and began checking out radio units in various vehicles.

Raulerson told them the story of his misfortune while driving the pickup with the aviation fuel in the rear. They all laughed nervously when he finished, and Ward said, "I thought you had to report what you're going to use it for when you buy aviation fuel."

"If anybody asks," Raulerson said, "we tell them we use it in racing cars down in south Florida where we live."

Boynton and a new man, Jacques Armand Tremblay, brought large fuel bladders and three-by-six nylon bags into the room.

Rhegness and Ward, who were sitting on the bed smoking, felt uneasy when the sudden fuel odor from the bladders overwhelmed the room.

Rhegness stabbed out his butt into an ashtray and Ward stood up and walked outside where he saw the radioman continuing to work with the units.

A few minutes later it was explained that Robert Autry and Jacques Armand Tremblay were about to leave. They were the alternate field personnel. Their job was to go to an airstrip about fifty miles southeast, near Troy, where they would be in radio contact and would watch the plane closely as it moved over them. If they detected a chase plane anywhere near their plane, they would shine spotlights up to him, and he would divert his route from Sehoy and would land at Troy. The pilot and copilot would jump from the plane as soon as it had landed, get into the car with Tremblay and Autry, and they would abandon the plane and load there.

It was decided that Woodward would ride to Sehoy Plantation with Ward. Rhegness would travel with the others. Before they left, Woodward stepped away from the car to speak to someone back in the motel room. The unnamed radioman handed Ward a walkie-talkie and said, "When J.W. gets back, tell him that you all will be Sugar Gate. That's your call sign. And our call sign will be Sugar Base. Okay?" Ward nodded.

On the hour-plus trip to Sehoy, Woodward talked profusely. He told Ward that he was an independent contractor on jobs like this. "I've got a good reputation with these people. They know that if they've got a plane to bring into the country, all they have to do is contact me; I'll make all the arrangements and bring it in for them," he said.

He said he worked for several different groups and had done many different loads. He said he had worked for Boynton for five years and had made a lot of money for him.

"Now and in the future," he said, "we've got to stay out of Florida. It's too hot down there now with the task force [Vice President George Bush's] keeping a close watch on everything."

He said he knew Sehoy would not always be available, and added, "All we need up here is a good sod strip well off of any traveled road. It needs to be at least a mile long, nice and level and packed hard. If you and your man could find a place like that for us, I'll send Ted [Raulerson] up to help you with the construction, and we'll make you boys millionaires," he added.

They arrived at the Sehoy strip about twenty minutes before sunset. It was quiet. No one stirred. They drove south down Alabama Highway 26 toward Union Springs for at least five miles, Woodward saying he needed to find a place for Raulerson to set up countersurveillance in his El Camino Chevrolet. Woodward decided on a spot near Mile Marker 7 where Raulerson could drive into a thicket of pine saplings and hide.

They sat at the edge of the highway for a few minutes while the sun went down behind them. Finally, Woodward said, "I think it's dark enough. Let's go."

Ward drove to the strip. He handed Woodward the key to the gate. While Woodward stepped out and opened the gate, Ward drove to the large hangar and deactivated the alarm system. Woodward met him at the front and they opened the huge doors wide enough for Ward to drive the Continental inside.

Later Ward opened the hangar doors for two two-and-one-half-ton white van-type trucks with a large fuel tank in the rear where it was also outfitted with a gasoline-powered pump and a refueling hose.

With Thomas Warren Shea was the unnamed radioman working with an air-to-ground aviation-type radio with a magnetic mount antenna which he fastened to the hangar door.

When Shea and the radioman left in the Chevrolet Silverado pickup, Boynton, in the corner of the hangar, kept contact with them on his walkie-talkie.

As time passed, according to Ward, Woodward and Boynton became visibly excited.

Once when Ward walked by and asked, "How long will it be?" Boynton answered, "Five minutes! It'll be here in five minutes." Then he said to tell Rhegness to stand by to turn on the runway lights.

Ward called to Rhegness to get ready, and Rhegness went to the side of the hangar where the electrical switches were located.

Two of the men—John Carl Capasso and George Michael Unitus Jr.—got into the silver Caprice and the maroon Pontiac Bonneville, both of which had Pennsylvania tags. After they found directions to nearby Seale, Alabama, Ward heard Boynton tell them to pick up the return pilots, take them to the Holiday Inn in Opelika, put them in a room registered in the name of Kelly, and feed them.

A few minutes later, Boynton told Ward, "Tell Bill [Rhegness] to turn the lights on."

Rhegness turned them on, brightening the sky with the sudden light.

Several seconds later, Boynton, who was chattering away on the walkie-talkie, looked up and said, "Blink them a couple of times."

And Rhegness blinked them on and off, then left them on.

The moment the lights stopped blinking, they heard the roar of the aircraft overhead.

"It came in on the end of the strip farthest from us, which was Runway 4," remembered Ward. "You could see the exhaust flames spewing from it. Of course, it didn't have the lights on. And immediately on hitting the ground, it began applying the brakes, and there was a loud squalling of the tires, and it came to taxi speed about a third of the way down the strip, maybe a little farther. It continued to taxi on up to the ramp that came into the big hangar. The pilot turned to the left into the ramp, came to the big part of the ramp, the wide area, at which time he turned the aircraft around, went back out the strip, made a right turn, and went and returned to the end of the strip from which he had come. When the plane stopped, its nose wheel was on the grass off the end of Runway 4."

As the DC-4 (a last minute choice) was taxiing back down to the end of the runway, the two two-and-one-half-ton trucks pulled out of the hangar. One was on the left asphalt apron and the other was on the right.

At about the same time, Boynton ordered the lights to be dimmed to 10 percent. And just as the plane neared the end of the runway, someone shouted over the radio, "Tell them to turn the lights off! Tell them to turn the lights off!"

Rhegness pushed the switch to off.

Ward, standing outside the hangar with Boynton and Woodward, held a walkie-talkie and a flare pistol. "We're going down to help," Boynton said. "You and Bill take care of the front gate. If you see anything unusual, give us a call on the walkie-talkie. If you see any law enforcement people whatsoever, fire the flare. That'll give us a chance to run."

As the two men drove down the runway, Rhegness took a state walkie-talkie from the trunk of the Continental. Then the two walked to the gate to wait for their men.

Giving the crews from the trucks enough time to begin off-loading the DC-4 and refueling the plane, Rhegness radioed for his ground crew stationed in the high weeds near the chain link fence to start closing in on the strip.

As they came, the men from ABI, along with officers from the FBI, DEA, and Customs, looked like a small company of soldiers, moving in vehicles down the highway toward the gate.

Although Ward and Rhegness could not see them in the darkness, at the far end of the fenced area, the ground surveillance team of nine officers fired an aerial flare.

At the same instant, the men in the vehicles began moving through the gate. Lieutenant Bradford, with an FBI agent seated next to him, drove onto the ramp. They stopped momentarily and gave an A-OK signal to Ward and Rhegness and then moved with the other vehicles at a rapid speed toward the plane with their blue lights flashing.

Rhegness radioed a Department of Public Safety helicopter in the area to relay a message to the Opelika State Trooper Base: check out Holiday Inn for two men in a room registered to Kelly; the men were suspected of being the return pilots.

When everything was going down as planned, men being arrested, lined up, under control, Ward and Rhegness moved to the DC-4. Near the plane, watching the scene unfold as the officers read Miranda rights to the men they had arrested, Rhegness heard radio traffic coming from the brown and tan Chevrolet Silverado pickup that Shea had driven out of the hangar and parked under the right wing of the plane. "Two voices were communicating with each other," Rhegness recalled. "One was referring to the other as Romeo One and the other was Romeo Two."

Rhegness slipped into the truck, took up the microphone, and spoke into it. He said he was Sugar Gate, using the code name Ward had been given earlier by the radioman.

Each of the others answered, identifying themselves as Romeo One and Romeo Two.

"How does it look, Romeo One?" he asked.

"Everything's quiet on this end. How's it going there?"

"Everything's fine," Rhegness replied. "Where are you? I'll come and pick you up."

As Romeo One said he was located approximately three miles north of the airstrip in a lumber yard, Ward got into the passenger side and two ABI investigators climbed in the back.

They pulled off while Romeo One told Rhegness to pull into the lumber yard and blink his lights.

Over a railroad bridge, Rhegness saw the lumber yard. He again contacted Romeo One. "I'm coming down," he said, and he pulled into a drive and blinked his lights. They waited. The two members of the ground team in the bed of the truck crouched low, their camouflage clothing and the dark chalk on their faces hiding them against the dark background.

A man with a walkie-talkie in his hand stepped from behind a high stack of lumber. The man, Ian Kevin Hopkins, moved to get into the rear of the truck and was arrested by the awaiting officers.

Rhegness, turning around and driving back across the bridge, contacted Romeo Two again. "Everything still okay?" he asked.

"Perfect," the answer came.

Then the truck radio went out. It was dead as the dope deal.

Rhegness stopped the truck and asked the officers in the rear for the walkie-talkie Hopkins had been carrying.

Turning it on, he said, "Where are you, Romeo Two? Can I pick you up?"

"I'm in the woods about three miles south of the airstrip toward Union Springs," Romeo Two said.

"I'll be there in a few minutes," Rhegness said. "You'll know me because I'll be blinking my lights off and on. When you see me, just walk out where I can see you and get in the back."

Rhegness drove to the pine thicket, blinked his lights, and a man with a walkie-talkie walked out. Rhegness picked up the walkie-talkie from the seat and said, "Is that you?" The man put his mouth to the portable radio and said, "Yes it is."

Rhegness stopped the truck, James Michael Doughtery walked to the rear, and he was placed under arrest.

While agents on the scene were discovering that the DC-4 was loaded with 16,960 pounds of top-grade Colombian marijuana with an estimated retail street value of about $8 million, Ward and Rhegness dropped off their two arrests along with the other ABI officers and met a uniformed state trooper at the motel near Opelika. They found the room of William Randall Newbern and Robert Bryan Sheppard and knocked on the door.

As they entered the room, Ward saw Newbern stepping from the bathroom. He also heard the sound of a toilet flushing.

Ward rushed into the bathroom, saw the toilet water whirling and reached down to retrieve pieces of paper, which turned out to be information concerning the airplane that had landed less than an hour earlier at the Sehoy Plantation.

In the first week of June, a little more than two months after the plane landed, eighteen men were brought to trial in the Middle District of Alabama before U.S. Judge Truman M. Hobbs. After two days of testimony from Ward, telling of the incidents involving the defendants from the first meeting at the motel in Montgomery to the late-night arrest of the pilots, and one day of testimony from Rhegness about the same events, sixteen decided to plead guilty. Only Newbern and Sheppard, the pilots arrested in the motel room, claimed innocence.

In December, after all of the others had been sentenced to varying numbers of years in federal prison, the two pilots were tried. Following three days of testimony, most of which repeated the same details Ward and Rhegness gave in the earlier trial, Brian J. McMenimen, a Boston attorney for Newbern, told the jury that the organization importing the marijuana "didn't need two pilots who were part of the conspiracy to fly that plane out, because they had two pilots that had flown the plane in. And if there was any evidence that they were under some disability that would have prevented them flying that plane out, you know what?" He hesitated, his voice giving rise to the dramatic rhetorical question. Then he answered himself, "You would have heard about it from the government, but they don't have an answer to that question. Well, what do you suppose that sixteen coconspirators did need? What do you suppose the organizers did need? I will tell you what they did need. They needed somebody or some people who had nothing to do with this organization, who had nothing to do with this plan, to take that plane after it had been cleaned out. You recall the testimony; one of the things they were going to do with that plane as soon as they off-loaded it was vacuum it out. They needed somebody who had nothing to do with it, somebody that, I suggest to you, was innocent to fly that plane back to whatever base it came from, be it Florida as these tickets seem to indicate—Fort Lauderdale—and walk away from it."

The attorney for Sheppard, Daniel J. O'Connell III, also of Boston, suggested strongly to the jury that his client also was innocent.

Assistant U.S. Attorney W. Broward Segrest, who had prosecuted the case with U.S. Attorney John C. Bell, drew the picture of the multilevel organization that his witnesses said had been described to them. He said that the question was simple: what were the roles of the defendants "in a very sophisticated criminal endeavor, a criminal endeavor that had been planned to the final detail; and it was designed to utilize many, many people in various roles. It's like a play that was put together, with each character selected for a specific role.

"The person that was going to fly the plane back to a safe harbor or to a safe berth, whether in Fort Lauderdale or somewhere else, was not the man that was going to expose himself up here securing the landing strip up here.

"The person that secured the landing strip was not going to be the man that flew the plane in.

"The person that flew the plane in was not going to be the person that flew the plane out.

"Now, they ask: is there any reason that you can think of,

based on the evidence in this case, that the people who flew the plane in from Colombia didn't fly it to the safe harbor?" Segrest showed the jury that he too could add dramatic emphasis with the use of the rhetorical question.

"Ladies and gentlemen of the jury, you know the geography of this great land of ours. You know the distance, approximately, between here and Colombia. And you know that the pilots that flew the plane in from Colombia were probably, reasonably, the pilots that flew down there and back, so you have got a 4,000-mile flight, approximately, and you judge the distance.

"These people had to be exhausted. They came in after flying many, many hours over the ocean, fully loaded with marijuana, over eight tons of marijuana. Surely they needed relief. And surely they weren't the logical selections for the pilots that would fly the plane to a safe harbor."

Segrest continued. He attempted to take any feeling of guilt away from the jurors, stating that the defendants were men who "came down here to join in a criminal venture that is a terrible criminal venture, and they did it for profit.

"Ladies and gentlemen of the jury, you didn't put them in here," he said, repeating an earlier statement. "It was their greed, their avarice, and their desire to get rich quick in an illegal scheme.

"Sure, there are consequences for being in the place they are seated in. There are consequences for being in any of the roles here. But they said, 'Darn the consequences, it's profitable.'

"It's extremely profitable, because the stuff sells for large sums of money. It doesn't matter whether it is one million, two million, eight million, or three million; it was enough to make these people greedy, and for them to come in and participate."

Segrest's argument was effective. After deliberating thirty minutes, the jury returned guilty verdicts on all four counts as charged in the indictments.

Early in 1983, Judge Hobbs sentenced Newbern and Sheppard to five years on count one and four years on count two,
sentences to be served consecutively, and nine years each on
counts three and four, to be served concurrently with the first
two. In essence, it was a nine-year sentence; however, because
of the way it was worded, it would cause the federal parole
board to hesitate before shortening the sentence. If the board
did parole them, Hobbs added a special two-year parole term,
assuring that they would be watched carefully by federal authorities for two extra years, even if they were to be put on
parole prior to finishing their full sentences.

Chapter Two
Bad Bandito

Drug agents are not always as successful as the textbook case of "The Good Old Boys." In fact, they seldom accomplish such an open-and-shut investigation. Many traffickers are sought for years by law enforcement officers. One operator continued his work into the 1980s in Central and South America. The enforcers knew him and where he was but could not put a finger on him as long as he remained in foreign countries where his business was essential to the worldwide underground of the drug smuggling universe.

When he was a boy during the Great Depression, Andrew Starrhill Vallejo lived with his maternal grandparents on a farm in the middle of what was then called The Badlands of North Dakota, within mustang riding distance of the Little Missouri River where he chiseled a form of bituminous coal from its banks when the river froze solid during the long and hard winters.

When World War II broke out, his favorite uncle—his mother's brother, James—entered military service and left the boy behind with his elderly grandparents. A cowboy by the time he was nine, Andy Vallejo was a Mexican-American who had little awareness of his paternal heritage until he became a grown man. Now and then, a roughneck on the mustang drives to Marmath or Medora might refer to him as "Little Mex," but it was all in good-natured fun. When they corralled wild mustangs in the natural rock V's of the canyons, Andy was usually one of the first to volunteer to ride the wild-eyed animals. After a horse was barely halter broken, the small brown-skinned boy with the heavy shock of dark hair hanging over his forehead and eyes would poke his foot into a man's coupled hands and be slung over the sensitive back. He immediately grabbed hold of mane and rein, clasped his heels into the bony sides, and hung on for dear life as the bronco began his rocking motions, swinging from side to side, jerking wildly, doing anything to rid himself of the person who was trying to tame him. Many was the time Andy remembered being vaulted madly through the air, smashing against the ground, hearing the fraternal laughter of the men. One time he felt the sudden blow of the horse's hooves against the side of his face. He remembered little of what happened afterward. His brain went blank. He awakened feeling as though his head was three times its normal size. His eyes blurred as he looked up into his Gram's pale, blue-eyed face. She rubbed a cool, oily mixture over his swollen wound and comforted him with tender words.

Throughout the remainder of Andy Vallejo's life he would carry a heavy, jagged scar across his right cheek. In a quiet way that was uncommon to his jovial personality, he was proud of the scar and seldom talked of how it happened. Usually he let people imagine that he had been in a great fight in some exotic country, for his world was one of constant flight, whispered negotiations, and mumbled money exchanges.

In his fifty-plus years, Andy Vallejo had become one of the most famous of all middleman dealers with South and Central American countries for dope smugglers from other parts of the world.

"Blackie Vallejo is a survivor, a mystery man with more charisma than most of the dictators in the Central American countries, and is smart as a twenty-year-old jungle cat," said a former CIA undercover agent who had followed Vallejo during the better part of a decade from the late 1960s to the middle 1970s. "When you've operated with drug people for that long without being caught and put into prison in the United States, you've got to be a smart cookie," added the agent, now retired in Florida.

Andy Vallejo, also known as Blackie, Wylie, Big Starr, Hombre, and perhaps a half-dozen other aliases, is a slick operator by anybody's standards. Not unlike buccaneers in the days of Captain Kidd or bandits like Billy the Kid, Vallejo runs constantly from the law but manages to remain friendly with the people in power in various governments and the revolutionary leaders of Guatemala, Nicaragua, El Salvador, and numerous South American countries.

The epitome of COOL in capital letters, Vallejo is handsome in a rugged kind of way. He thinks of himself as one of the romantic banditos of yesteryear. He prides himself on his ability to get along with anybody, particularly those who pursue him from country to country and often think he is within their grip. "I think like the tiger from Quintana Roo," Vallejo says, "the province in Mexico bordering the Caribbean, just north of Honduras or Belize, the tiger that is being stalked by the most adept hunter, an animal that has to sneak about through the bush, finding his prey wherever he can—and escaping as soon as he makes the kill."

He stretches lazily, not unlike a cat, and he rubs his right index finger along the pathway of the zigzag scar that crosses the line of his cheekbone.

Set deeply within his brown skin are sea-blue eyes, a strangeness that makes a person slightly nervous in his presence. His voice is mellow and even soft, very persuasive, and his hair is still thick and black. It still falls down over his forehead when his head dips forward to accentuate strong words.

"I want to make it clear to begin with that I am an American, I am not a Latino, my father was of Mexican descent but I never really knew him. I understand he died in a barroom battle, but I won't explain that. It is a simple fact that I picked up from my Grandpa, my mother's father, but he never told me much about it. My father was tough and bad, that I know, but I will not talk about it. I understand it, know it, from my bones, my knowing insides . . . How do you say? Psyche, I believe it is."

Although born in Texas and raised in North Dakota, Andy Vallejo speaks today in an almost broken English. Sometimes he lapses into a stream of fast Spanish. His English words are tinged with a heavy Latin accent.

"I want everyone to know that I am not against the children of the United States. I was a child in the United States. It is my hope that the drugs that I help to escape from this part of the world into the United States will go to the fat rich politicos in Hollywood, New York, Washington, and Kansas City. I believe—deep in my heart, I believe—there is as much dope smoked or sniffed or shot up in Kansas City as there is anywhere else. That is to say, Middle America is spending its money on dope. I don't spend my money on it. I don't fool with it except to negotiate a price, a place, a situation down here in these countries where I now live. When I go back to the United States I am disgusted, because all of these self-righteous people shout about the children getting the drugs. In reality, it is the people who are doing the shouting who are really sniffing and smoking and shooting up. They are the addicts of our time, they have the money to purchase the drugs, and they have created themselves a real drug society. But that is neither here nor there, it is merely my philosophy that comes out of my psyche. But I do wish to say it because it comes from here." He points at his heart, then shrugs and points to his head.

Priding himself on his long history of adventure, he tells about leaving home when he was an adolescent, after hearing the news of the death of his Uncle James in France. Vallejo jumped onto a boxcar and rode west to San Francisco where he lived with a gypsy-like band of burglars who worked their way up and down the West Coast before he slipped away from them in the middle of the night with a sackful of stolen goods and made his way back east as far as Kansas City, Missouri.

"I worked as an apprentice to a printer who taught me that there was a lot of knowledge between the covers of books. That old man gave me Dickens's *Great Expectations* and told me to read it, and I became fascinated with a world I did not know existed before that night behind the little shop, the place where I slept and cooked for myself. After I finished, the old man—his name was Samuel Jenkins—asked me questions about the characters and the way they lived and what they did in their world. I could not answer him, because I didn't read it that closely. He gave the book back to me and said, 'Read it again, and I will ask you more questions about it when you finish,' and that night I read it from cover to cover, absorbing every movement and every detail of the characters. The next morning the old man grilled me, and I answered his questions. Every book that he gave me after that, including Socrates, Plato, *The Odyssey*, Parkman's histories, *The Federalist Papers*, and many, many other books, I always read with the sure knowledge that he would test me afterwards. Because of his grand teaching, I looked at the world around me very closely, trying to take into consideration everything that was happening, how people lied to each other every chance they got—especially if it meant earning an extra dollar here and there. That was when I came to the conclusion that Kansas City was really the center of the universe; everything starts there, you see; and if you want to know the reason behind anything—whether it is the drug culture thing or why Central America is going Communist or why Fidel Castro is now the big daddy of drugs in the Western Hemisphere—you have to go back to Kansas City first."

He laughs deep down in his chest, which is big and dark with black wiry hairs beneath the white silk shirt that is unbuttoned to the top of his hefty stomach. His laugh seems to break something loose down in his throat, and the upper part of his body shakes.

He flips his hair back with the shake of his head, like a dog slinging water from his coat.

He does not apologize for his unusual philosophy, for he is an unusual man in an unusual business. "I have to be tough and wily, like the cat, or like the old bear from The Badlands. Sometimes in the hard cold winter my Uncle James and I tracked bear up past the old lodge Teddy Roosevelt built there on the Elkhorn Ranch; we'd ride horses over frozen rivers and climb up steep canyon walls where the ground itself at twilight looked like a hundred rainbows. We worked and worked, thought we were smart hunters, but we never found the old bear. We found deer and other game, but the old bear always found his way north out of our reach."

In the Navy during the Korean War Andy Vallejo discovered an affinity for the people of Southeast Asia. He liked them and they liked him. After the war he came back to the United States, where both his Gran and Grandpa had grown very old. For several years he cared for them, until his Grandpa died and his Gran was so ill that she had to be placed in a nursing home. "There was no place for me to go but back to the Orient," he says offhandedly. He lived with a Eurasian woman in Hong Kong. "I learned about the drug world from the best traders in that part of China. The families there had been dealing in heroin, cocaine, opium, drugs of all types for centuries. They knew the current market value better than most stockbrokers know Wall Street. I began to make my living running the drugs from one section of Hong Kong to another. I traded with the rich British who frequented the private clubs. I hung around the tennis courts and the fancy nightclubs, and people knew me as somebody they could trust. They knew that there was no danger in dealing with me because I always had good stuff and the right price without a hell of a lot of conversation. I was straight up with them, and we had a *simpatico* arrangement until a big dealer named Tooth Head came into the picture.

"Tooth Head was this guy about this tall, a little squirt of a fellow with an ugly pushed-in face like it had been smushed with a hammer or run over with a truck, and his eyes bugged out like Peter Lorre's eyes, and when he talked it was a lot of jabbering crap. He put some bad dope on the market, slipped it in my bag, and really did me dirty. You got that kind of stuff in the drug business. It's illegal, so the people will do anything that's illegal, including kill.

"In Hong Kong, I thought I'd try to get Tooth Head back and do him in but he had too good a connection. I'm talking millions. And not yen, baby; greenback dollars! I knew I had to split. It was getting really hot for me. Tooth Head had this one big tooth right back here in his jaw like he was some kind of freak dog; it kind of stuck out the side like; real ugly! All those old guys were doing business with him under the table and not telling me anything about it, but I knew it. You can't help but know if you're doing business with them every day. If you don't know, you're stupid."

Vallejo escaped with his woman to Manila, set up a smuggling operation with one of her cousins, traveled through the islands of the East Indies, and learned aspects of the business that he had never known previously. "I discovered a very high grade of *cannibis sativa* in the hills outside Singapore, one of the most active and dangerous narcotics ports in the world. I figured out a way to transport this top-grade hemp from the mainland to Australia via military jets and post office ships. During those days before the war in Vietnam escalated to a full-scale battleground, that part of the world was virtually untouched by law enforcement people. Even today a knowledgeable person who is willing to operate by the underground rules governing the countries in which he does business would be able to transport without the worry of going to jail. Not just anybody. But a person with the right skills and brain power—somebody like me—could make a lot of money. I'm talking two hundred, three hundred thousand a year. That's minimum, after expenses, if the person keeps his nose clean in the countries, paying off the right people, making sure everybody is taken care of. It's very politic!"

With bank accounts in Switzerland and Liechtenstein, and

cash stowed away in several hiding places, Andy Vallejo decided it was time to move on. Why? "I'm lucky, I guess," and he bellows the same deep-down laughter that he belted from the bottom of his throat. His laugh overflows the room. Soberly, he states, "I am lucky. I have always been lucky, if you call having an old man who is a no-account and who never came around after I was born and a mother who hit the streets before I was a year old and an uncle whom I loved but who went off and got killed and grandparents who loved me but didn't know *how* to show their love being lucky, then I'm *magnifico* blessed." And he laughs deeply again. He is a sarcastic man in a cruel, illegal business.

"I am lucky because my woman, Jin Won, got tired of me about the same time I got too hot in the South China Seas and about the same time the Philippine government was closing in on my activities. I moved fast from the murderous banks of Singapore to Bangkok. Once I saw a twelve-year-old boy shot in the back with an American rifle because he was stealing half a kilo of marijuana. Can you believe it?" The thick brows over the Gulf-blue eyes arch high with his rhetorical question. "The boy was making away with this much cured hemp, and a cold-blooded bastard raised a rifle, pointed it, shot—and the boy was dead. Like that!"

Jin Won moved back to Hong Kong with a pouch filled with American dollars, according to Vallejo, and he took a slow freighter through the South Pacific with three trunks packed with clothes, leather belongings, several books, and more than $100,000 in cash tucked away in hidden compartments. "I was in no hurry. I had what I wanted. There was no dope on the ship as far as I knew. I was tired. I was ready for the good life. No more pressure."

On March 18, 1960, Andrew Starrhill Vallejo landed in Acapulco, Mexico. His bags were unloaded with no problem. He checked into the Papagayo Hotel on the beach, relaxed in the sunshine, and moved inland to the old silver mining town of Taxco. For more than a year he made his home in Mexico City's Chinatown, began living with a Chinese woman, and had seemingly left the drug world behind. Later he drove a used MG sports car north to the small art colony of San Miguel de Allende in the province of Guanajuato. He rented a house, sat around the Cucaracha Bar on the *jardin* where the expatriate Americans drank and talked, and after a year he began to get itchy for the excitement he had known in the Orient.

"My life became too commonplace," he recalls. "Everything was too easy. Little bits and pieces about my former life leaked out into the community. The people who live in San Miguel are unusual when you look at them from a North American point of view. Many of them are students, many are retired, many are former servicemen and soldiers of fortune. A segment of the population that is not really underground looks at the Latin American world with a jaundiced eye, sees it for pretty much what it really is: a political playground for America. It has been that for a long time, and it remains so today. At first these people approached me, wanting me to take part in the constant revolutionary atmosphere in Guatemala or El Salvador. Of course, I refused. I told them my morality would not permit me to get involved in such an unholy event." And then he laughs again with the deep guttural tones. His blue eyes sparkle in his brown skin.

In the early 1960s Andy Vallejo traveled south with a companion, met with a wealthy landowner on a coffee plantation, and within days was the guest of the Nicaraguan government in a hotel outside Managua. "On this trip I met with Señor Juan de la Manorez, a member of the cabinet of El Presidente Luis Somoza. This man, who said he was a cousin of the president, was very cordial. He took me to dinner at a delightful Chinese restaurant where we had wonderful heaping platters of food like I had not eaten since I left Hong Kong. I could pay for nothing, and he let it be known in his sullen, quiet sort of manner that the government would appreciate taking any American dollars that I could manage to funnel their way.

He let me know that the government could be very cooperative if I came to them with a plan and a satchel filled with greenback American dollars."

Back in Mexico City, before returning to his home in San Miguel, Vallejo visited some old acquaintances who he knew had been involved in the drug trade. He put out the word that he had "friends in high places" in Central America, that he could arrange "for some sweet deals, if the money was right," and that he could be reached if anyone was interested.

"It was less than six weeks later that a businessman from Los Angeles visited me in San Miguel. We drank good Scotch and talked openly about the drug business. He was into the transportation of marijuana from Colombia into Texas and Louisiana by airplane and into lower California by boat. From the look and the sound of him, the business had been very profitable. There was nothing held back. He was completely up front with me, and from early in the conversation I could tell that we would be able to do business. He was a very professional drug person, very generous in his attitude, not trying to hide the cash from me. Once these people start dealing, if they're smart, they act in this way. They do not lay back and try to play like a restless coyote in a wheat-brush field, they come out in the open like the brave bull. I am the same way. I have to have honesty in the business. If you do not have honesty in the business, you are dealing with sure trouble.

"This man encouraged me to return to Nicaragua, talk to the *numero uno* personally, find my connection in that country, and then talk business again with him. He left me with a sack filled with large dollars—expense money that he knew I would need in the next few months. There was at least $50,000 there—pocket change for my benefit; and, he knew, it would be nice for me to be able to impress upon the El Presidente that I was a serious person with whom he could deal."

Two months later Vallejo was a guest at Anastasio—the

brother of El Presidente—Somoza's cattle ranch in the plains
below Granada near Lake Nicaragua. "It was one of the most
beautiful country sites I have ever beheld," he says, remem-
bering some impressive places from his travels. "The mar-
velous world of grandeur was at my disposal. Somoza was a
great host. The rooms were very large, with a bar and a patio
looking out across the rich pasturelands and the hills in the
distance. In that pleasant atmosphere one would never suspect
that these people would end their lives in the midst of terrible
violence; however, what was now was pure pleasure.

"I talked my way up through the President's lieutenants
and his family assistants. In Nicaragua, as in most of these
countries today and yesterday, you know that the family is
very close at the highest level. The top man—*numero uno*—
is always surrounded by family—brothers, cousins, father, un-
cles, et cetera—and it is through these family members that
you get to the top man, penetrate his walls, and finally are
able to sit down with him and make a real deal. These people
obviously liked me. We had a pleasant talk. I let them know,
without saying so much, that they would become richer people with my help and the help of my clients. Also, I had better
sense than to bring only the money given me by the man from
California. He was generous enough, but not for an entire
ruling family in this part of the world, and when I touched
them I touched them well. I knew that the first impression
was extremely valuable, and if I came on *simpatico* for their
personal pleasure, they would remember me beautifully in the
future. That is the way." He grins and shrugs. A breeze blows
the fragrance of a pungent cologne from his body. He has
sprinkled the liquid onto his closely shaven face.

"It was not long [after four years the Somozas were out of
office] before Anastasio himself became *numero uno*. El Presidente was a big man, and he had a very large, open face with
a high forehead which he told me later was the symbol of
magnificent breeding. He confided that he liked my eyes, and
he said that from my eyes he knew that I had the blood of

kings flowing through my veins. It was then that I was sure
he was a truly great man. His own face showed magnificent
strength, but there was a weakness in his eyes. I did not see
it at first, but I knew it after several visits, after sitting across
the table from him and listening to him talk and knowing his
ways.

"Somoza was a dictator's dictator. Everything of value in
his country was owned by himself or by some other member
of his family. A few people thought they could get away with
owning a factory or a newspaper or something else that might
make money or become powerful; these were disillusioned
people. Soon they discovered that they would eventually lose
their interest in these enterprises, that the sole ownership
would be retained by Anastasio and his family. Knowing this,
I never dealt with anybody outside the family.

"Once when I was returning from Texas I made a deal for
a particularly beautiful three-carat diamond. It had a strange
kind of angular cut, and it caught the light just right and shone
as though it were five or six carats. I had been meeting some
of my North American contacts in San Antonio; we had arranged for some profitable transportation through my part of
the country, and I picked up the diamond and brought it back
down to Nicaragua. I unwrapped it before Anastasio—*El
Grande*—and handed it to him. 'I thought you might like to
present this token of my appreciation to your wife,' I said to
him. You see, I would never be so presumptuous as to offer
the gift to his wife myself. That would be showing ingratitude
and unwelcomed forwardness. But when I gave the diamond
to Somoza himself and said what I said, he felt overwhelming
gratitude; it would make him look good in the eyes of his
wife.

"That evening before dinner he beckoned his wife to his
side, pulled the diamond from his pocket and, before he unwrapped the gift, he made a loud presentation. He said the
gift came from 'our good and dear friend Andy Vallejo,' and
he grinned greatly and hugged me in front of everybody to

show his fantastic friendship with me. And then he unwrapped the diamond. All of the family and friends oohed and ahhed. Everybody patted me on the back and said what a wonderful friend I was.

"The next morning I met with Anastasio in the privacy of his office. I gave to him $250,000 cash—all in one-hundred-dollar bills—and he agreed to allow my clients unencumbered use of three Nicaraguan airports as well as several Pacific ports. We worked out the deal quietly and without argument. Had I not been so thoughtful as to bring his wife such a beautiful gift, we would have spent a great amount of time haggling over time and place—and, of course, money. The way it turned out, we had a deal that was great for him, for me, and for my clients. When I left, there was no misunderstanding of the situation. I would return in a month with more money and a new deal. We were more or less partners. Our business dealings had been sealed."

Absolutely no remorse is shown in Vallejo's features or his voice. As far as he is concerned, he was a businessman making business deals. "I do not look into the morality of my business. That is for the church people, the writers, the philosophers. It is my way of making a living. I am telling you about it with only one request: that it is told truthfully. If you wish to make comments as to its morality, that is your prerogative. I enjoyed working with Anastasio Somoza Debayle for a period of about ten years before he and his family became too greedy and wanted more than their share. For the first ten years, Anastasio Somoza Debayle was a very good business partner. You would have to have known Somoza to appreciate his business acumen. Here is this big man, huge in size as well as in generosity when I first met him in the summer of 1967, within just several months of his election as President. He had already had great wealth, great position; his father, El General Anastasio Somoza Garcia, had first been elected President of Nicaragua when Somoza was just twelve years old. Off and on for three different times, El General was President, and when

Somoza was but thirty-one years old, in 1956, his father was assassinated before his eyes. Later, his brother, Luis, became president of the country, and Anastasio—who was called Tachito—was made chief of all of the armies. Now this came after Somoza had gone to the United States, attended West Point, been indoctrinated not only with our military leadership but the entire free enterprise system. He *believed* in it totally. And when, within days of his becoming the *numero uno* in his country, this man from the north arrives and demonstrates how he can triple, quadruple, even multiply his wealth tenfold, he is interested.

"He told me: 'I have always felt as though I belong to the United States, that my country is a part of the hemisphere which we all share. I think we have more in common than you have with the Europeans or either of us have with the Asians. We must work together to further the great event of twentieth-century capitalism.'

"It was this kind of true believer stance that made him great on one hand and vulnerable on the other. He was intense in this belief. Later, when he grew a mustache, he would reach up and curl the edges when he spoke of his love of the United States and capitalism, and his eyes then would shine brightly. He would say, 'I know my friends in your country will take care of me and my country, if we ever need them badly.' By that time he had become obsessed with the thought that Fidel Castro was attempting to overthrow his government.

"My own dealings with the Somoza government amounted to giving them a total of more than $13.5 million over a period of about ten years. All was paid in cash to Anastasio or Luis, or other family members. Now and then I would give money to one or more of the generals in his government in order to keep them happy, because you never can tell in a country like Nicaragua; you have to make sure that everyone is taken care of. The President also had many cousins. They all needed assistance from time to time, and three of them manned the airports in the highlands. We made our deals man to man, I

always paid in cash, and it was always understood that Somoza's relatives would receive appropriate payoffs commen-
surate with their positions within the government. You see,
you have to realize that toward the end, when it really became
very dangerous indeed to do business with Nicaragua, Somoza's family owned everything that was worth owning. It
was as simple as that. And, of course, when the rebels did
succeed in ousting him, my people had pulled out of Nicaragua. We did not do business there within the last twelve or
fourteen months of his regime. I advised them to withdraw
their interest, not to even attempt to land the planes in a
country where they might be shot down for being traitors.
Generally, smugglers are peace-loving people. They live at a
high intensity, put their own lives on the spot, hate the rats
who squeal, but do not wish to harm anyone while they are
doing their business.

"I moved operations to Guatemala, where I made arrangements with the ruling party bosses. And at this same time
back in Mexico I made deals with two very large landowners
in the upper regions of Guanajuato and Chihuahua. At certain
times of the year when the moon was well hidden and the
night was extremely dark, the pilots could take off from the
fields, fly very high, and come in low over the rural section
of the border between Juárez and Nogales. It was dangerous,
but this is a dangerous business even in the best of circumstances."

Vallejo never saw the hundreds of millions of dollars' worth
of narcotics that he arranged to be transported through the
countries of Central and South America. He was not present
on the night when one of the small planes, which had refueled
from a tank truck on the Chihuahua ranch, faltered in takeoff,
bit the dust, and sent flames licking high into the night while
the pilot's *compadres* raced back across the border to safety.
He was not at the hillside airstrip in the Guatemalan jungle
when a DC-4 touched down and was met by an onslaught of
guerrilla gunfire. The flight was aborted, the pilot and crew

tortured and killed, and the cargo was confiscated by the troop commanders.

"The conservative governments backed by the United States have never had any trouble convincing themselves that they should do business with me or my clients. As long as the money is good, the business is there. What is it to them if we use their little strip of land to touch down, purchase their gasoline, pay real *dineros* to the people manning the strips, leave nothing behind but good will?" He shrugs characteristically. "It is good capitalism, even in pro-U.S. countries like Costa Rica, where we have had *simpatico* arrangements for a long while.

"I know for a fact that in the last year the Salvadoran government supported by our government has built landing strips mainly for our drug operations with funds provided to them by the United States. Sure, they say that it is for military use. Who is truly to question them? Not I. But I know that it is true that the taxpayers' money is being shipped south by the Ronald Reagan government to aid in illegal drug operations while at the same time the same administration is spending more taxpayers' money to wage what they call 'an all-out war' against narcotics smuggling in the United States.

"It is this kind of hypocrisy that makes me believe that the middle-class person in Kansas City is the real dope user and dope abuser in the United States. The government is taking money out of the average taxpayer's pockets day by day to pay the tab of these countries down here to keep them capitalistic. That is the ultra stupidity of this game. It is crazy.

"Because this is happening—and I assure you I am very sure that it has happened and is happening, not only with the governments of Somoza but with the so-called democratic governments of Honduras, Guatemala, Salvador, Costa Rica, and others—we will never have to worry about a shortage of illegal drugs in the United States. I never do business with Communist countries; there is no flow of money in communistic countries. The Soviet Union has no problem with dope because no one, outside of a few higher-up party bosses, has any money with which to buy drugs. A person does not wish to do business in a country like that. In the United States there is no such difficulty; there is a strong flow of money, even among the young. In the United States a person does not have to be filthy rich to buy narcotics. In the U.S.S.R. you have to be very, very rich to have such a luxury; you have to be powerful—very powerful."

When asked, officials of Nicaragua, El Salvador, Honduras, and Costa Rica denied that they had ever used funds from the United States to help in the trade of narcotics. Most vehemently denied being involved in trafficking drugs into North America. However, sources who had worked to police Central America agreed with Andy Vallejo that the countries had built jungle airstrips which had become safety stopping points for aircraft bringing drugs out of Colombia and other South American countries. "The governments that receive funds from the United States say that they build the airstrips for good and honorable reasons. And even the super-conservative guerrillas in Nicaragua—fighting against the Sandinistan government that overthrew Somoza—have cut airstrips in jungle areas, and they have allowed dope planes to land, refuel, and take off," said the former CIA undercover agent no longer operating in the area. "The CIA itself has helped in the construction of some of these strips with the knowledge that the planes from Colombia, bound for Texas or California, will be landing there. It is a part of our hands-off policy. We give money, help with the effort, and then pretend we see nothing, hear nothing, know nothing. It is the way things happen."

And Vallejo agrees. Once, because he did not go along with a road stop situation in the north of Guatemala, where soldiers were detaining highway traffic for as long as three and four hours to search even the old women and children, he was arrested as an unwelcome alien. "They have the right to do it in these countries," he now says matter-of-factly. "For a moment I forgot where I was. For a moment some of the old

Kansas City protestantism came out in me." He laughs heartily again. "I guess it had been buried down in here somewhere but not altogether lost to my soul."

He was placed in detention in a rat and roach infested dungeon-like jail in a small town near the Mexican border. "It was a hellhole, a sewer, even for this country; it was *muy mal*, stank like a gutter, and if one stayed there for more than a week it was truly a life sentence. There was so much disease among the few who lived in the squalor that I could see the germs crawling toward me. This, of course, I imagined, because I was fresh meat and smelled of the outside world; but I knew it could not be for long. I worked very hard, put on my best charm, and spent a quick 20,000 American dollars to become a free man within twenty-four hours. I know my limitations. I know I am too weak to last in places like that."

For Vallejo, life is a series of what to the average man in a wealthy country would be high adventure. Waging war against what he calls "the constant threat of terminal boredom," Vallejo says that he has failed to create happiness. "You can write that I am the great loner from the Wild West, a child of an earlier part of this century when men were men, when individuality actually counted for something, but that would be so much crap. I am a person who lost his way somewhere, whether it was when I was a kid in the Badlands, when I ran away from home, when I got into the business in Hong Kong, I don't know; it doesn't really matter. I'm no great morality story. I am a person who has made much money, who spends it, and who continues to look for the frontier just beyond the next horizon."

Chapter Three
The Money Men

Vic Straus was a nervous man in his middle forties, courting high blood pressure, constantly trying to keep his weight under 200 pounds, beleaguered with piles of bills resulting from two youngsters in college and a third finishing high school, and, although he had been one of the brightest students in the University of Pennsylvania's business school more than twenty years ago, he felt as though modern times were passing him by. During the first fifteen years as a certified public accountant, Victor Herbert Straus (alias) worked diligently, enjoyed his life, and put away a tidy nest egg for the future. But during the hard times of high inflation in the late 1970s and the added expensive responsibility of children attending college in the 1980s, Vic Straus became a vulnerable target for illegal business operators when they walked into his life in late spring, just after backbreaking and eye-straining tax time, in 1981.

Two men in their early thirties called Straus's suburban Philadelphia office, asked for an appointment, and late that afternoon sat down with the CPA. They were no strangers. Vic knew one, Thomas P. Collins, from a civics club they both occasionally attended. They had spoken, knew each other very casually, but their friendship had never blossomed. The other, Edgar Moss, had been a member of the same synagogue where Straus had attended only special religious services for the past few years with his wife and children. Straus never considered himself a devout religious person, although he later discovered a deeper meaning in his Jewishness.

Edgar Moss was the first to speak, after he looked around toward the closed door and, with characteristic paranoid distrust, asked, "Are you sure nobody can hear us?"

The question itself was enough to make Vic Straus tear off a corner of the fingernail he had been twisting nervously.

Edgar Moss stood almost as quickly as he had sat. He walked toward the window and looked through the Venetian blinds toward the street. "We have looked around this town and have decided we might be able to trust you," he said.

"Trust me?" Straus echoed.

Moss went back to the front of Straus's orderly desk, sat down next to Collins, leaned back in the chair, and said, "How would you like to make a lot of money, Straus?"

He didn't have to ponder the question. He knew he needed money in the worst sort of way. He had had a good tax season, had worked into the night seven days a week for more than four months, but he still owed more than he received. He nodded slightly.

"We're in business," Collins said.

Again, Straus nodded.

"Our business is not exactly legal," Moss said.

Straus remembered months later that he was afraid initially to ask exactly what the nature of their business was. Hoping that he had at last found the dream pot of gold at the end of the rainbow, he waited in silence.

"We are making a lot of money," Collins said. He reached over and picked up a small but thick metal suitcase he had brought into the room. While Moss cleared a spot on Straus's desk, Collins placed the suitcase on it, and opened it.

When he looked down onto the neatly stacked one-hundred-dollar bills, Straus's eyes popped. His pulse quickened. He knew his blood pressure was rising.

"This is part of one week's profits," Collins said.

"That . . . that's a lot of money," Straus stammered.

Collins closed the case, snapped the lock, and put it back onto the floor.

In the meantime, while Straus's mind raced to keep everything he was hearing and seeing clear, Moss was saying, "We need somebody with your good reputation and your expertise to be our business manager. We don't want any questions asked. We just want you to help us for a fee. You'll be doing a job."

"But . . ." Straus said later that he did not know what to say, but knew that it would be impossible for him to become a crook. He just wasn't made that way. He had too much to lose. He loved his wife and his children. They loved him. They respected him. He had always been the pillar of their family life, the steady provider, the strong shoulder on which they leaned. Now he was being asked to do something that he felt was totally foreign to his neat and orderly world.

Collins said, "It's a job. Just like you'd be representing a business for a man down the street. We're local people looking for professional help."

"We need somebody with some financial sense, that's why we came to you."

Collins stood. "Now, if you don't feel comfortable with us, we can't go further in our explanation. We don't want any trouble. We don't want to cause you any trouble."

"Let's take the bag and go," said Moss. Staring down into Straus's anxious face, Moss added, "All we ask is that you not say anything to anybody about our visit." He handed an envelope to Straus. "This is for your time."

Glancing inside, Straus saw a small stack of one-hundred-dollar bills. "But . . ."

"That's your fee," Collins said. "No questions asked. No problem for anybody."

"It's no problem," Straus said. He choked out the words. "No problem for me." His hands shook. The paper rattled in the quiet room. "If I don't have to . . ."

"Everything's street clean with us. The money's like dusty, and we need you to clean it up for us." He turned around 360 degrees slowly and sat back down in the chair. "We make a lot of money in our spare time."

"Like doing dishes on the weekends," Moss put in. "We're nice boys out to earn a buck."

"But we can't take it to the banks like this." He motioned toward the suitcase. "You understand."

Straus nodded. He understood that banks would not allow cash transactions of more than $10,000 without reporting it to the Internal Revenue Service. He had read about people having trouble with large amounts of cash, but he had never had the problem.

Within the next few minutes Straus agreed to look into the financial situation for Collins and Moss. At that moment, he realized later, he crossed over the line. Greed overwhelmed him. He took his first step toward becoming a money launderer. Although he knew virtually nothing about the business the younger men were operating, he was aware that it was illegal—or the problem of the money would not have existed.

This is one of the fundamental problems with any smuggling operation. When the fast and illegal money is made, what does a citizen of the United States do with it? If he or she spends the money, using the cash from the illegal deal, the Internal Revenue Service will be on his or her trail almost instantly. In some fashion, the dirty money has to be cleaned or made to appear clean in order that it can be more easily used.

During the next three weeks Straus lived in what he recalled as being the most stressful days of his life. He was left with more than $70,000 in cash, which he kept locked in his office safe and which he looked in on every day—and sometimes three and four times a day—to make sure it was still there. He said he dreamed about the money being burglarized, waking in the middle of the night in a cold sweat, gasping, thinking that he would surely be killed if he let anything happen to the cash.

In the daytime he perused the journals of his trade, thinking he might find something, some clue about what to do and how to go about laundering the money. He was afraid to go to another CPA. He didn't want to spread the word, knowing the more people who knew, the more dangerous his predicament.

More than a month after they left the first case, Collins and Moss came back with another. This one was also filled with one-hundred-dollar bills. And it was larger than the first.

Although the men gave him another envelope, they were disappointed that he had not found a way to clean the money.

Several weeks later, while reading at night in a nearby public library, Straus happened upon a full-page advertisement in a financial magazine. The headlines glared in bold black type: *The Cayman Islands*. And below it in smaller letters he read: International Tax and Investment Seminar.

Of course, Straus had heard of the Cayman Islands being the place to go to launder money, but before this instant he had no idea how he would go about making contact in the country. He began reading the text with interest.

"Why the Cayman Islands?" it asked. "The country is undisputedly one of the leading tax havens in the world.

"There is certainly a lot to recommend the country to the foreign investor. A British colony, it is considered the most stable country in the Caribbean. You won't find strikes, demonstrations, racial conflict, or crime here! It has a small government with minimal powers—and no political parties.

"It levies absolutely no direct taxes whatsoever (except a $10 a year head tax on residents). It has what is considered the strictest secrecy law in the world. And, last year, it completely abolished all remaining exchange controls."

Every word leaped out at Vic Straus. He knew that if the advertisement was true, it was exactly what his clients had been seeking. As he read he was astounded not only by the contents but by the fact that here it was, everything he had been looking for, in a nationally distributed magazine.

The advertisement, placed apparently by three organizations—Bona International, The World Market Perspective, and The First Cayman Bank & Trust Company—continued, "Here the foreign investor can operate in an atmosphere of stability and freedom.

"So it is no wonder that Cayman is booming. Over 300 banks for a population of less than 20,000. More Telex lines per capita than any other country in the world. And a thriving real estate market, with a large resident population of expatriate workers, investors, and retirees.

"That's why we chose the Cayman Islands as the site for our First International Tax and Investment Seminar."

Although the language twisted the out-and-out illegality, never coming straight out and advertising for launderers of soiled cash, it was obvious to Straus that he could find what he and Collins and Moss had been seeking. In a roundabout manner, Straus inquired of several associates if they had had any dealings with investments in the islands. He was told without hesitation by three friends and people he respected that it was perfectly legal to do business in the Cayman Islands. He did not bother to tell them that the money he would be investing was badly in need of laundering.

After meeting next with Collins and Moss, Straus telephoned an attorney's office in the Caymans. Everything seemed on the up and up. In fact, he was surprised by the attorney's businesslike approach to the entire situation. He made an appointment. A week later he was on his way south, carrying with him two suitcases, leaning back in the first class section, enjoying cool chablis and tough lobster. This was Vic Straus's first experience with first class, and he liked it. The night before he had given his wife a thousand dollars in cash, told her he had had a super tax season and this was a bonus from a client, and he had sent the two oldest children gift certificates for one hundred dollars each, and he had purchased the youngest, who still lived at home, a round-trip ticket to Disney World. She had been saying for months that she wanted the trip for her high school graduation. "All of my friends are going after school is finished," she had said and, until his new-found fortune, Vic had failed to listen seriously, knowing that it was out of the question. During this time, it never dawned on him that he was giving his loved ones dirty, illegal money, he said later. While he was working to clean up cash for Collins and Moss, his own sudden wealth did not bother his otherwise orderly mind. "There was so much money with no questions asked that I just seemed drunk with all of it happening so quickly," he recalled.

Now he saw a way to send all three of his children to college at one time without going deeper into debt. In the last few days he placed $10,000 in one-hundred-dollar bills in a shoe box far back in his closet, making sure that it was inconspicuously covered with other boxes of used shoes. He had always told his wife that he wanted to keep all of his old shoes, that he would never give them away or sell them. He put another $10,000 in a metal fireproof container in the far recesses of his personal filing cabinet at his office.

When his plane landed at the Miami airport, Victor Straus clutched the bags to his sides, felt as though hyperventilation was about to set in, breathed deeply in an attempt to ease his nerves. When anyone looked at him for more than one-tenth of a second he looked the other way hurriedly. He convinced himself that Internal Revenue and Customs agents were everywhere and that all of them were searching for him.

Several times he almost dropped the suitcases. Sweat popped out on his forehead and ran down his jowly cheeks and into his eyes beneath the horn-rimmed glasses. "I was as scared as I've ever been, knowing that the police were watching my every move, and when I did see some uniformed guards at a security station I came close to panic," he recalled.

Miraculously, he felt, he made it through the checking-in process, boarded a new plane, and was airborne without incident. "I did not feel safe. I breathed a little easier, but I kept my eyes on the suitcases, wondering if perhaps someone had switched them on me. I had this feeling that if I had made it this far it was because something else had gone wrong. All the time, every second, negative thoughts worked in my mind, and I wanted more than anything to open the bags and find out for sure if they were still filled with the money. I don't know when I'd been so nervous, and I took an extra pill for my blood pressure and the sweat would not quit," he remembered.

When he landed at George Town, he was pleasantly surprised to find the man he had telephoned waiting at the exit. With a big grin, a firm handshake, and a nod toward an official next to the gate, the attorney took the suitcases from Vic Straus. "I know I tried to grasp them stronger, foolishly thinking that he was taking them away from me," he later remembered with amusement. "Actually, this man, Mr. Dennis Fuerago, had taken care of all the details. I had nothing to worry about. But it was difficult for me to switch from being worried silly to being okay."

The dark-skinned Latin with a pencil-thin mustache spoke in soft, reassuring tones as he led Straus to a small foreign car. He said they would go to the bank straight away unless Straus wished to check into a hotel and freshen up. Straus told him he would rather go ahead and finish their transactions. He had a return ticket for the afternoon.

At the bank—a plain white concrete building with small windows in the front and a one-foot by three-foot shingle-like sign next to the door—a pleasant and plain-faced brunette took the suitcases from Señor Fuerago, who explained that she would count the money.

They followed her into a booth where she placed the cases on a table. She took out all of the money, stacked it against the wall, sat down in a chair, and began counting.

Straus was escorted into another office where Fuerago opened his briefcase, extracted papers, and began explaining about setting up corporations in the Cayman Islands.

"It all seemed so simple," Straus said. "There I sat listening to all of his explanations. I hadn't been off the plane thirty minutes. All of the terror of riding down was still draining from my body and my mind. I had hardly looked around at this suddenly bright and sunny country, the dark-skinned policemen like the postcards from Nassau, the white, white buildings, the politeness of Mr. Dennis Fuerago.

"He asked me a series of simple questions. How often I might be coming to his country? How many companies did I wish to start? And when I hesitated, he probed very gently. There was no rush, no harshness like doing business with some banks in the United States. He handled me with kid gloves. He was being of assistance to me, he said, and anything he asked was to aid me in making choices. And as soon as he said this, he said, 'But, of course, you may change your mind at any time. One company may be dissolved and we may start a new one. Nothing is permanent here; we do not expect it; we want only your business.'

"I decided that we would start with three businesses: Empire State Inc., Islands Investment Corp., and Crimson Banner Development Inc. The cash that I brought would be divided equally into three parts and put into each account. Of course, the division would occur after the bank took its percentage off the top and Señor Fuerago took out his fee. Then checks would be drawn on the companies.

"After I was introduced to several officers in the bank, all of them pleasant men who shook my hand and thanked me for my business, Dennis Fuerago and I went to lunch. After a stiff martini, an excellent white fish cooked in a light wine sauce, and singsong conversation about the relaxing life in the islands, I felt much better about everything. I believe that was the first time I really felt good about my new business relationship. I felt comfortable with the entire working arrangement at that point. Things had gone well, Dennis Fuerago was amiable, the bank appeared to have everything under control.

"When we returned from lunch, all the necessary papers were ready to sign. I sat down at a desk in the air-conditioned room, read over the documents, found everything in order, signed them, and within minutes I had nine cashier's checks—three each on each of the corporations.

"Fuerago took me to the airport. There was a short wait; then I made arrangements to meet him again ten days later. We said good-bye, and I got aboard the plane feeling really quite buoyant about the whole thing. I settled back in first class, had a drink, patted the checks inside my pocket, and watched the blue-green water below as we lifted out over the sea."

The checks were marked as expense payoffs for work and/ or services completed for the companies. Vic Straus explained, "There was no way in the world that the IRS could find out about these checks the way we had done our business. On paper, Empire State, Islands Investment, and Crimson Banner Development were all corporations doing business outside the United States. They did not fall into any category of company that could be regulated, controlled, or taxed by the United States. As foreign corporations, the IRS had no power over them."

The checks, he said, "were as good as gold. Maybe better. One might have to explain the possession of gold. These checks could be put into a U.S. bank, could be cashed, and everything was up front. At least, that is the way we felt about the situation."

Back in Pennsylvania, his two clients were extremely happy with his success. And he was given another $10,000 in cash as soon as the checks were deposited into Moss's and Collins's accounts. He was also given a check for $5,000 to go into his business for services rendered.

Ten days later, when Straus traveled to Cayman for his second visit, he was not half as nervous as the first time. However, a Customs official at the Miami airport stepped very close to the line through which he was moving. Straus felt some of the same old anxiety. On this trip his suitcases were new, larger than before, and contained much more money.

After he went through the same process in George Town, he told Fuerago about the suspicious seeming man in Miami. Fuerago suggested that if the trips were to continue on a regular basis and if Straus would like to bring more money and make fewer trips, it might be easier for him to arrange private transportation.

Straus questioned this. He did not think in high-rolling terms.

Fuerago drove past the airport, parked off the highway, and pointed toward several Lear jets sitting on alternate runways. "The people who arrived in these came in from Washington and Houston this morning. Their pilots are waiting to carry them back. It is much easier for them. They load their baggage into the rear, enjoy a nice uninterrupted flight, and leave whenever their business is completed," Fuerago told him.

Back home with the good checks and another fee for his work, Straus told Collins and Moss about Fuerago's advice. The two men agreed and said they might travel with him on the next trip.

Up to this time, according to Straus, he did not know the source of the big money. "They had told me their business was illegal, and I suspected that they might be involved in drugs, but I really didn't know any more than that. It seems ridiculous, I know, looking back on it now, but I was really and truly in the dark. Of course, I knew I was doing wrong by hiding money from the IRS, and it is completely against any type of ethics for an accountant to do what I was doing, but it got to be like a game with me—a very dangerous but exciting game. The only trouble was that I was playing with real live people," he said.

In the first year he carried in excess of $3 million in cash on twenty-two trips to the Caymans. Three more companies were formed, and some money was put into island real estate and insurance ventures. But, Straus insisted, he never let the money get out of sight. "I was always relatively sure where we were, which companies held what, and how we could arrange a quick withdrawal if necessary. In other words, I kept them liquidly solvent; they liked the way I was managing their affairs; and all the while I was becoming a wealthy person in my own right. After the first year, I too put some of my own cash into the Caymans, but I usually left with checks made out to myself, my wife, and even to my children; all were paybacks for expenses incurred for services rendered.

"Everything went well until my wife and children began asking questions. I avoided them for as long as I could, but there came a time when I could no longer turn away. They confronted me, said, 'What are you doing?' and I said, 'Look, it's paying your way through school,' or 'Darling, you are able to buy more than you've ever had in your life.' We had a new car, the kids all had cars, the wife and I took a two-week vacation to Acapulco, and everything was paid for. But when they finally did confront me solidly, demanding to know something, I said, 'I'm involved in something; I've involved you; I'm sorry; I'll get out,' and they accepted my word.

"I went back to Moss and Collins and said, 'I want out. I've had enough.' I didn't tell them I had had checks made out to my children and to my wife. I knew that that had been stupid, that it was unrealistic, that in my eagerness to hide all of my assets I had brought them into the illegality of it all and had tainted them without their even knowing it. I think that that above all else made me feel absolutely lousy. It hurt me that I could not even go to the synagogue and talk to the rabbi, that I didn't even really know him, and because of the family and the religious thing, I felt empty inside.

"Moss and Collins shook their heads. They said, 'No, you can't leave us now. Maybe after several more trips, but not now. Everything is going too good now. You've got us into a great situation, but we can't go to somebody else. Not at this time.' And when they left me with two more big suitcases full of money, I felt as alone as I've ever been in my life. I sat there and I was like in shock, stunned, not knowing what to do or where to go; I was faced with what I knew to be disaster. What do you do? Where do you go? Whom do you talk with?

"At first I thought about running. I actually did. I wanted to hit the road with the money that I had. I could go a long way with the money they had left in the suitcases, but I knew—even as anxious as I was—that they would find me and would kill me if I took their money.

"Next I thought about going to the police, the FBI, somebody. I would tell my wife, then together we'd go to the police. But I had never before really lied to my wife. We had lived together twenty-three years, I had loved her longer than that, and we had a really good relationship most of this time. We *knew* each other, we confided in each other, but now we had grown apart. My deception had alienated me from my wife, my children, and I felt as though my entire world was one of failure."

Victor Straus, a man of order, purpose, attainable goals, respect, and professionalism, wandered through a chaotic maze for more than a month, traveling again to George Town in the Caymans, delivering a packet of cashier's checks to Moss and Collins, and learning to live with fear. He was so consumed by the dread of facing life day to day, he remembered, that "I know every hour I wished that I would be caught, arrested, and put away."

When he was arrested, it was primarily because he became too loose in his own purchasing. He bought a Mercedes convertible for his wife and a new Cadillac for himself and paid cash for both, leading agents to watch him closely. The agents put together visits by Collins and Moss, his visits to them, his renting private jets with cash, and his moving back and forth between the Philadelphia area and the Cayman Islands. His telephone was tapped, and finally he was arrested.

"It came as a relief. When they walked in, I knew who they were and why they were present. It was almost like I could breathe freely for the first time in a great while. I sat back and listened to their words, informing me of my rights, and I know I must have smiled widely. I could not help the relief that consumed me.

"Of course, the rest of it was hell. What was the worst hell was facing my wife and my children, knowing that they now knew that I was a fraud, but they were magnificent. All rallied to my side. All held me close. They gave me what I needed: love. They made me feel good instead of terrible. They said they knew that I had done everything for them, that I was not a selfish person, and that helped me as much as anything. I told them they were wrong, that I was indeed doing it for myself because I had felt bad about not doing as well as I thought I should have. Everything at that time became a big explanation; every hour of every day, I sought some solution. Months later I knew that the solution would be found in the Lord God, in my coming to terms with myself and my world and my religion. My rabbi consoled me with good strong words. The world, I knew, would again become mine.

"In the meantime, however, the agents, the prosecuting attorneys, everyone, it seemed, asked thousands of questions. I answered many of them. Some I did not need to answer. Some merely showed up in the records confiscated from my home and office."

Straus insisted that he did not talk until he was given the go-ahead from Collins and Moss. He said this came about through the actions of his two associates. Once he knew they were out of the country—both took refuge first in Mexico and then in Costa Rica—he said that he was free to tell whatever he knew. His implications of Moss and Collins, who nearly a year later fled Costa Rica for Paraguay, caused prosecutors to charge him with a lesser crime than a stiff organized crime charge. He pleaded guilty to two counts of income tax evasion, was ordered by a federal judge to pay a fine of $50,000, had both of his cars confiscated, and received two sentences of three years each to run concurrently.

*   *   *

In another case on the East Coast in 1982 and 1983, an attorney became involved with his clients—and the U.S. Justice Department prosecutors broke new law when for the first time in recent years a judge allowed investigators to search the office of an attorney.

An assistant U.S. Attorney and investigators convinced the District Judge in Arlington, Virginia, that they had sufficient cause to believe the attorney was acting in a less than professional manner. According to an informant, the attorney for two very successful smugglers in the Washington, D.C., area was not only aware of his clients' business dealings, but he used the money gained by smuggling to invest in legitimate businesses.

Texas-born twenty-nine-year-old Assistant U.S. Attorney Karen Tandy admitted that she had been dragging her heels in the case that DEA agents had been investigating for more than a year. "It was the hardest kind of drug case you can have," she said. "We had no undercover agent (within the suspected drug ring), no informer, no one close to the group who could absolutely and totally confirm our intelligence. The outlook was very bleak, and it took the agent at least six months to persuade me to get moving on the case."

The suspected smugglers were two freewheeling young connoisseurs of the good life, men their friends said were worldly, sophisticated, spent money lavishly, and lived up to one of their favorite ocean-going vessels, *The Free Spirit*.

Julian Pernell was thirty years old, tall, with long black hair and heavy brows. A former short-order cook, he kept his beard trimmed neatly and his mustache curled under at the corners of his mouth.

Barry Toombs was seven years older, several inches shorter, and about fifteen pounds heavier. Usually he was clean-shaven, his light brown hair unruly, and his double chin sagging.

Like most drug smugglers, both liked to live high on the hog. Pernell, who had scrambled eggs in all-night eateries for a living before he became rich through smuggling, became addicted to luxurious $10,000-per-day chartered jet trips. Toombs fancied himself a self-educated art collector, assembling the world's largest privately owned collection of Tiffany glass, valued at $867,000. "Barry Toombs grew up in a middle-class family that was always in pretty good shape financially but never rich," recalled one of his many associates. "Both he and Pernell hit the gold mine when they got into the drug business. They were like two people who had suddenly inherited the family fortune, throwing money this way and that, spending it like there was no tomorrow."

Tandy first learned of the pair from Washington-based DEA agent James Mittica, no slouch when it came to staying with investigations the size of this one.

Mittica informed Tandy that he was sure of two things: First, in the years from 1978 to 1980, five major East Coast drug-related arrests had been made by local and federal authorities in Haiti, Maryland, South Carolina, and Virginia, and in that time the officials had seized nearly ten tons of marijuana; second, Pernell and Toombs both had prior convictions in drug smuggling. Indeed, the case was ongoing throughout those years, although at the time the DEA was not aware of all of the activities.

As usual in such cases, Tandy and prosecutors and Mittica and investigators worked very slowly and very tediously putting a case together. Mittica was determined to connect Pernell, Toombs, and the rest of their group in the business, because he also knew much more marijuana than that seized by agents had actually been distributed in D.C. and the surrounding metropolitan area.

In the quiet, cool, early dawn hours of Sunday, April 29, 1979, a boatload of sheriff's deputies from Charles County, Maryland, alerted to a possible smuggling operation in the area, arrested six men stepping ashore on an isolated beach near Smith Point on the Virginia side of Chesapeake Bay. Onc of these men, none of whom possessed any drug of any form, was Julian Pernell.

When the name appeared on his info sheets the next day, Mittica took notice. He was aware of the fact that U.S. Customs agents searching that area of the Chesapeake later on the same gray Sunday had found a fifty-one-foot sailing yacht named *Centaurus* run ashore near Smith Point. On board the Morgan Out Islander sailboat, which had cost the smugglers $167,000, agents found six-and-one-half tons of marijuana said to have a wholesale value of $5.3 million at the time.

Using the meticulous investigative techniques DEA agents had been honing to a fine edge for almost a decade, Mittica discovered a series of long distance telephone calls charged to the Fairfax County, Virginia, home of Barry Toombs. Exploring the coastline of Virginia on the map, running his finger along the shore of the Potomac River from Washington to Smith Point where the river emptied into the Chesapeake, Mittica discovered all three locations from which the calls had been made were along the route most likely traveled by the crew of the *Centaurus*. Such circumstantial evidence did not in itself tie Pernell and Toombs together in a conspiracy, but it pointed in the direction of guilt, leading the agent to continue his dogged investigation.

Making sure that he checked every occurrence within the area, Mittica made note of the fact that when they boarded the *Centaurus* agents found among the items the license renewal application for a vessel called *The Free Spirit*. Later he learned that *The Free Spirit* was a favorite boat of the two leaders. They had bought it for drug smuggling but used it frequently for a number of pleasure cruises in the Chesapeake and the Atlantic.

For nearly a year, Mittica, Tandy, et al worked over the details of every drug case that occurred within a hundred-mile radius, but nothing appeared that made them suspicious. "We didn't let one piece of evidence escape us while we pushed toward a realization that there did exist the connection which we thought was there," said one of the agents.

The something did hit. It was only slight, but Mittica realized he had another thread of evidence to link the two. Customs agents tracked a light airplane north from the Gulf of Mexico. When it landed at a rural Virginia airstrip, the agents found 703 pounds of marijuana aboard. The agents also seized all of the belongings of the pilot, William Dickerson. And among the personal items was an address book which listed the name "Doc" and a telephone number. Mittica knew that Pernell's nickname was "Doc," and a search of records from telephone company sources showed that Dickerson had also called Toombs more than once.

After each record search, Mittica felt as though the trail was getting warmer. And in June of 1980, when police in Ridgeville, South Carolina, a small town just south of I-26 between Columbia and Charleston, stopped a camper and found 1,320 pounds of marijuana, the owner began throwing away ripped-up pieces of paper. Scrawled on one of the tiny pieces was the telephone number of Julian Pernell in Fort Lauderdale, Florida, where he owned a beachside home.

Exactly ten days later, a boat named *Green Sea* was abandoned off the shore of Ocean City, Maryland, which had been known for several years as a hotbed of drug activity. When the boat was searched by Customs officials and Coast Guardsmen, they found 5,082 pounds of marijuana and in a drawer in a stateroom they discovered the same telephone number that had been on the tiny piece of paper being thrown away in South Carolina.

On close inspection, it was discovered that *Green Sea* was actually a boat of another name. After it became hot, Pernell and Toombs had not ditched *The Free Spirit* as they had other properties that had been spotted by federal law enforcement authorities. The smugglers had the boat's name changed to *Green Sea*, did some cosmetic painting, and kept it in their stable of transports.

Armed with his evidence, Mittica pushed Tandy to prosecute. However, she felt that they should wait for a while longer to make sure they had a case.

On Thursday, June 5, 1980, Customs patrol and a Virginia State Police investigator took up their usual watch of chartered jet flights from the Washington area. A man who called himself Doctor Thompson rented a plane to be flown from Washington to Nassau and back the same day. When the officers filed their report, Mittica noticed that the description of Doctor Thompson matched that of Julian Pernell. Accompanying Doctor Thompson on the trip were two unnamed passengers, all three carried luggage, and Pernell paid $11,000 cash rental fee for the jet.

Two months later, a Washington lobbyist who worked for high-paying clients on Capitol Hill, a man who was known to be a close friend of an associate of Pernell and Toombs, chartered a jet to the Bahamas from National Airport in Virginia. After the trip, which also took only one day, an unnamed informant told Mittica that the lobbyist, Phillip Marinovich, opened a suitcase at Customs in Nassau. The suitcase was packed with U.S. currency in one-hundred-dollar bills which prosecutors later determined totalled at least $800,000.

With the data concerning the two plane trips as evidence, Mittica went to the Internal Revenue Service and asked for help. He unloaded his information, received an okay from the Treasury Department, and IRS Special Agent Patrick Lydon of the Criminal Investigation Division joined the case.

Lydon went to work immediately, searching through tax returns and other information filed with the Service, but federal law prohibited his telling any of this newly found information to anyone, including Mittica, although they were obviously working on the same investigation. This was an old problem with federal law enforcement agencies working the same side of the street. It had been discussed in Congress on several occasions, but no one had ever arrived at an adequate solution.

It was not until a special grand jury convened in February of 1981 in Alexandria that Mittica and Karen Tandy learned of Lydon's findings. He told the jurors that, according to tax returns, Pernell and Toombs had no reasonable and valid explanation for the money they were obviously spending.

With the grand jury in session no more than a month, the FBI received information from a confidential source that large amounts of money from Julian Pernell were flowing in and out of escrow accounts in the office of a former U.S. Justice Department tax attorney in private practice in Annandale, Virginia. The source that expressed "fear for its life if its identity is revealed," according to FBI affidavits, revealed that these "substantial amounts of cash" had been given to Stephen McConnell off and on for a period of more than two years.

The source became the conduit of a wealth of information. Pernell and his family had deposited at least $1 million in cash in the McConnell firm's escrow accounts. Toombs and others had also been and still were clients of McConnell. Once Pernell had delivered some $275,000 in cash in a paper sack to the McConnell office. After giving the details to Mittica and his investigators, the informant drew a layout of the office and told where certain diaries, ledgers, and other records were kept.

This was the big break that Tandy had been waiting for, and she began hard pursuit. Traveling on little-used pathways of the law, she first sought approval from within the Department of Justice for a search warrant to enable the lawmen to enter McConnell's office. Going against the constitutional safeguard protection of attorney-client communications, Tandy asked the director of Justice's criminal division, Lowell Jensen, who agreed that she should go after the warrant.

On July 14, 1981, the U.S. magistrate in Alexandria signed the warrant. Several days later files showing a complex hidden financial empire were taken from McConnell's office. Records revealed that straw companies had been created through banks in the Cayman Islands and the Bahamas to handle the huge profits from the smuggling business. These companies were listed as Atlantic Fidelity Ltd. for Pernell's interests and Pacific Fidelity Ltd. for Toombs.

The records showed that Pernell owned a company in the United States called First Dominion Development Company to which checks were made from Atlantic Fidelity in the Caymans. In turn, First Dominion invested in legitimate northern Virginia development corporations such as South Lakes Joint Venture and Reston Industrial Joint Venture.

As in other such operations, Bahamian and Cayman laws effectively placed the invested drug profit monies beyond the legal grasp of IRS, DEA, Customs, and other U.S. law enforcement agencies. The investigators were stymied by the international laws. If they inquired as to the source of the financing for either of the Joint Venture companies, they could be told "foreign investors," and they knew that would be the end of the trail.

Whereas the Collins and Moss case had been relatively simple transactions, in this case McConnell, apparently acting on instructions from his clients, had attempted to hide the money by making all the financial deals as complicated as possible.

However, since Pernell and Toombs in some instances had taken shortcuts by investing directly into American companies, and these transactions were recorded in the pages of files that the investigators and prosecutors perused, it became obvious that these investments could be the Achilles' heel of the two otherwise supersmart smugglers.

For instance, their attorney, McConnell, had established a centerpiece corporation in Grand Cayman in February of 1980 entitled B.W.I. Joint Venture, which used the combined resources of Pernell, Toombs, and several other participants high in the organization. It was established that the main purpose for this company was to lend $1.8 million to Long Cove Club Associates, a legitimate firm that was developing a section of Hilton Head Island, a luxurious vacation resort off the coast of South Carolina.

The way the legitimate portion of the deal was set up, Toombs, Pernell, and others were scheduled to receive nearly $300,000 in interest from the loan and 50 percent of after tax profits from Long Cove until 1990. Such an operation, it was estimated, would return from $5 million to $12 million in the designated period of time.

While the grand jury was meeting, between February and June of 1981, $1.8 million was to be handed over to Long Cove Club Associates. On June 12 a courier was sent by McConnell to the Caymans where he picked up a cashier's check for $870,000 in laundered money. Eleven days later a courier picked up another check for $211,266 in the Caymans. And other funds were transferred by wire directly from the escrow accounts in McConnell's law office to the developers on Hilton Head.

In a quick conversion of $120,000 in cash to cashier's checks, the group worked sixteen banks in the Washington, D.C. area. They apparently had the mistaken belief that they could not exchange cash in amounts of more than $5,000 into cashier's checks without such transactions being reported to the IRS. They turned the cash into twenty-five different checks. Actually, according to law, banks are required to report transactions above $10,000. It would have been twice as easy if they had not been mistaken about the law, and because they went to several branches of the same bank their transactions appeared on the computer printouts and the number of transactions alone caused suspicion.

But that was not to be their last miscalculation of the law.

Throughout 1981 and into 1982, the grand jury continued its investigation. Lesser members of the group gave testimony against the leaders of the ring after Mittica and his men caught them at stash houses in Virginia. With other contraband in trucks near Alexandria, Pernell and Toombs fled the country.

Thinking that Costa Rica was a perfect place to live because it had been the hideout of fugitive financier Robert Vesco among others, the two men made their home temporarily in a hotel in San José.

After they were indicted in the summer of 1982, Karen

Tandy traveled to the Central American country, discovered the officials were willing to cooperate with the United States in an effort to improve their image, and also found them in a pleasant mood because the Reagan administration had recently given the country several million dollars to do with as it pleased.

In the middle of the sweltering afternoon of Thursday, August 5, the day after Tandy returned from her second trip to Costa Rica, local officers arrested Pernell, Toombs, and two associates. The four lingered in a Costa Rican jail for five months until they were returned to Alexandria to stand trial in January of 1983.

Toombs was given a fifteen-year sentence without parole by a federal judge who found him guilty of racketeering conspiracy and possession of 33,000 pounds of marijuana. Pernell pleaded guilty to being a part of a continuing criminal enterprise, and he was sentenced to ten years in federal prison without parole.

The lawyer whose office had been searched in Annandale was sentenced to eighteen months in prison after pleading guilty to preparing false income tax returns for the members of the ring.

Nineteen associates entered guilty pleas and were given lesser sentences to lesser crimes.

A cocaine dealer in Los Angeles became rich quickly on the West Coast when he brought the white powder up through Salvadoran and Nicaraguan connections. "We have people in the government, good men with good American contacts, and the flow opened wide in 1980 after Ronald Reagan was elected President. Before, [President Jimmy] Carter's position was one of distrust, and the government people down there distrusted us. Now they think we are good people, we pay to use their airports, buy our way through their laws, and it is a good situation," he said.

The smuggler dealer, an Italian-American whose primary

alias in the early 1980s was Benito Lugano, found his own
method of laundering big bucks that piled up from the illegal
profiteering. After four trips across country and into the Caribbean, Lugano said, "It seemed far too risky to me to travel
the long distances, rush through Customs where you may or
may not be spotted, and have the IRS and Customs agents
checking on you. You know the agents are there, you learn to
spot them from hundreds of feet, and even when you don't
spot them, you know they're there. They're always there when
you go through Houston or New Orleans or Miami.

"I scouted the turf in this direction. I could go into the
Pacific. There are dozens of islands out there with banks that
are possible for secret, foreign dealings: the Marianas, the Mar-
shalls, possibly down in New Zealand; but you're talking
thousands of miles, days, and then the possibilities may be
dark. You never know. I moved on something closer, something very sure, something nobody would question."

Benito Lugano's answer lay little more than 200 miles from
his home. He had been to the gambling capital of the world
in Las Vegas many times before, but it had never truly crossed
his mind that the place would be superb for laundering the
hundreds of thousands of dollars he was now forced to hide.

"I talked to my people, and we came to the conclusion that
Las Vegas might be the best place for us. This is a hard-ass
business, we get uptight with the pressure, we need to jump
and stomp, get it out of our bodies and minds. In Vegas we
could turn free, you know," he said with a nervous twitch and
a singsong sound in his voice.

In Las Vegas he found what the big-time gamblers had known
for a long time: nobody cared where his money came from as
long as he lost. They loved losers in Vegas.

"The first time we tried it, we really hung out. My partner,
Joe Kostowski (alias), and I took $300,000 in one-hundred-
dollar bills. We checked one of the big casino hotels on The
Strip, where we had reservations, and we started gambling
before we even got to the room. Joe hung around the crap

table, I hit the blackjack. I bought a stack of black chips (worth $100 each) and placed a black chip out in the marked square. I lost it, busted out with a face card, then put two black boys out there, and this time I hit a jack! Right on the ass! That put me up. Then I played for one again and lost. Then I played for three, and I hit! Bingo! Like that! I was up again!

"Within an hour I was playing for two and upping it to five and six after I had lost two or three times in a row. It was sweet! Really sweet! Like watching a boss chick flipping handstands on a champion roller down a Venice sidewalk. Foxy! I was up. And all the time, I hear Joe in the background, and I see him leaning over the table and throwing dice and screaming, 'Come! Come, baby, come!'

"It was really great winning that first night. Like the pit boss comes over and says, 'For sure, you guys deserve our best suite,' and puts us into a real paradise joint, having our bags moved because they are not unpacked and everything, and here we are with two bedrooms with beds the size of Steve Martin's tennis court and bathtubs like Johnny Carson's swimming pool. We call down and say we want to see a show and have dinner and all that, and the guy at the desk says, 'Yes, sir, Mr. Lugano,' and, 'Sure, Mr. Kostowski,' and we're real big shots. When we go down to the bar and have a cocktail two really knockout dames, like 35-23-34, blond and brunette, dressed like Rodeo Drive, catch our eyes, and we move in. We are really on, really driving, knowing we're in control, and everything is be-u-ti-FUL! We're having the time of our lives, and, of course, the ladies accompany us into the dining room and then to the show, and it's out of sight. I won't even describe the things they did to us on the Hollywood beds. It's not until the next morning that I realize the joint had fixed us with some real first-class hookers, but that was all right too. We weren't questioning their taste or their timing; it was great!

"We gave the girls a thousand each and told 'em to go shopping, buy themselves a bikini or something, and we fell into gambling again. In about four hours, we lose $40,000, $50,000, each! It's all cash, and we discover that the people in the place really do love us. They come over, the pit boss, the woman in charge of the downstairs lounge, the maitre d' in the gourmet dining room, and everybody wants to know if everything was okay the night before. And we're all set again tonight— with new broads, if we want them. We don't! We stick with the originals, hang in there, do some more losing around midnight, and fall back into the sack. It's a wild time. It goes on for four days, we lose a total of $180,000, but in the meantime, we've played with every dime we brought over; we've been through the whole suitcase full of C-notes, and now our money is as clean as a prince's palate. We had a great time, our credit is A-1, we have $120,000 worth of good money, and we're invited back. The manager says, 'Anytime, Mr. Lugano. You don't even have to call, just show up at the front door, and you have our very best suite. If you like, call, and we'll send our jet over to L.A. for you.' It was *really* sweet."

Lugano and Kostowski threw bad money after good. If they started an evening with $500,000 in money from snow they had delivered to California, they put it all in the casino bank, turned all of the money into high-denomination chips, and played with them like madmen. At the end of the night they cashed in the chips that remained in their possession, and all of the new money was relatively clean, laundered money.

During the following three months, Bene Lugano called for the small jet four times. With his partner, Joe Kostowski, they laundered more than a million dollars, losing more than half of it and declaring wins of at least $300,000; of this, the IRS took 50 percent straight off the top, but Lugano and Kostowski couldn't care less. The transactions, signing the forms, and turning over the money to the IRS, made them legitimate. After each trip, they returned to Los Angeles, invested some money in real estate, buying old apartment houses in the Venice area, speculating in land near Bakersfield, and putting some money in high-risk stocks.

After the first year, during which more than $1 million in drug profits were lost at the casinos and about $1 million was washed clean, an attorney friend advised Lugano to move his laundering operation to other methods. "He told me, 'If you persist in making Vegas trips, losing that much money that quickly, the IRS is going to be glued to your ass.' He said that we should go to the offshore islands in the East, and I did make one trip there. It was less expensive but not half the fun of Vegas. When we stayed at the big hotels in the suites the rich Arabs usually reserve, nothing was too good for us. We were kings. Everybody knew us and bowed and scraped to please us. We were their darlings. One of the casinos sent an out of sight doll up to teach me baccarat. She was one of the shills, hired by the house to play with the company's money, to look good sitting at the table and to make sure the action stays hot and heavy. She spent two hours or so going over the rules, showing me about holding the bank, betting for or against the bank, the theories of the cards, and all that. She was really good-looking, and I said, 'How's about going in the bedroom with me?' and she said, 'Fine,' like that; it's cool and calm, like there's nothing to it, and I know she's been told to give me anything I want; right? It really is like being king, getting *anything* we want, being on top. That's what losers are in Las Vegas: they're kings. If you're a big enough loser, you're dictator, or something. That afternoon, after I learned about the game, I go downstairs, sit down in that throne below the croupier, play for a thousand. I lose! I raise it to two thousand! Then up to three! The doll, who I've already given a thousand in cash, sits down across. She plays for 25 to 50, and I know she's playing with house money because she's a shill, see; but I watch her and think I see a glow about her as she takes the bank. I put $5,000 on her. She wins! Like that! Then I double it. She wins again! I double it again, up to $10,000, and they call over the manager, and he smiles at me and touches me lightly on the shoulder like I'm his good friend or something.

She wins! I say, 'What about double again?' and the manager nods, and there's a tenseness in the air that's like coming over the Mexican border with six sacks of albino sugar; it's strong! Everything moves real quiet and slow. All the noise of the floor seems like it's miles away. You're up higher than the others, elevated on that stage where things are unusual. Everybody has their eyes on the cards, and he turns it in slow motion. Again she wins! Now I feel the manager behind me tighten, especially when I say, 'One more time?' What can he do? He has a limit, but generally it's lifted at baccarat. I already know this, because I watched the play the night before and see a guy lose $25,000 on one deal. Now I'm up to $80,000 or nothing, but what the hell? As the gamblers out there say, 'It's easy money; easy come, easy go!' When I look over at her, I see the redheaded shill is less pretty than she was an hour ago; sweat is dripping from her pert nose, mascara is a little smudged around her green eyes, and she no longer looks like the dreamboat I saw in her this morning. She fiddles nervously with her stack of chips, and I know she's thinking: *I've got to get unlucky or the management might think I've not only turned a trick with the guy but am now in business with him.* When the card flips, she breathes softer. Her eyes mellow. I don't even have to look down to know I've lost. There's a team sigh over everybody, and the kibitzers shake their heads. The manager touches my shoulder again and says, 'Sorry,' but I know he's lighting up a new cigar in personal congratulations for sticking in there with me. It's now a new game, the girl looks over at me and smiles, and I wink at her to let her know I'm not angry at her. What the hell?''

As it turned out, Lugano did perhaps too much grandstanding on this trip to Vegas. As before, he lost more than he won; he went through hundreds of thousands, buying chips with cash, playing, turning them in for cash, purchasing $1,000 suits, $500 sport coats, $750 alligator shoes, and a $40,000 diamond ring for his pinkie. Winging home on Monday morn-

ing in the Lear with the possessions, he was unaware that the
IRS had started a full-scale investigation into his financial
dealings.

Nine months later the IRS tightened their clamps, trying
to determine how and where he acquired the money he used
to gamble with such blatant audacity. During the following
year he was indicted, tried, and convicted. He was sentenced
to three years in federal prison. He served almost two years,
was within ten days of being released when his partner, Kostowski, was arrested during a setup cocaine purchase in Beverly Hills. DEA agents, with the assistance of undercover
informants, had infiltrated the operation which Kostowski had
continued in Lugano's absence. They had recorded wiretap
conversations, videotapes of buys and sells, as well as distribution outlets, and had followed associates of the two ring-
leaders on pickups south of the border. They had already arrested
fourteen of the other members who had worked with Lugano
and Kostowski during the past seven years; most of them had
talked, and Lugano was transferred from the federal prison
camp where he had been serving out his last days to the jail
in Los Angeles. Ultimately more than $1 million worth of real
estate, automobiles, jewelry, and other property was confiscated by the government. Lugano and Kostowski were sentenced to fifteen years in prison without parole. The others
received shorter sentences because they cooperated with the
authorities.

Before a congressional hearing, convicted trafficker Harold
Oldham told the Permanent Subcommittee on Investigations
of the U.S. Senate Committee on Governmental Affairs that
as a result of his successful business as a smuggler, "I had
significant amounts of profits which I needed to legitimize. I
contacted an attorney and asked him if he knew of any way
I could account for this money if challenged.

"My primary concern was to hide the fact that the money
was narcotics profits. The first scheme we came up with was

to set up a phony loan agreement which showed that I had borrowed $30,000 from Mideast Overseas Investment. This was later changed to reflect a capital investment instead of a loan.

"My attorney, through his various contacts, was then introduced to the use of Cayman Island shell companies as a better method to wash funds. During my stay in South America, I had also heard of the Cayman opportunities and my attorney's information corroborated my own.

"As my earnings increased and it was obvious that something needed to be done, my attorney went to the Caymans to see if I could discreetly use the services. He spoke with several managers there and selected one. We were surprised to find that the island flourishes on secrecy, and they are very happy to accommodate whatever the needs of the clients might be.

"Subsequently, we formed Esmeraldes y Mariposas and after being assured by my attorney that there would be no problems I made my first trip down with a briefcase bulging with one-hundred-dollar bills. I discovered that the Caymanian customs officials provide curtained booths for examining luggage of those who request privacy.

"On that flight and subsequent flights, I speculated that at least half of the aircraft passengers were evading taxes. I made several other trips, laundering my money and also offering a laundering service to a few associates who needed to disguise their source of income.

"I tried to get paid by my distributors as soon as possible. What money I didn't spend on extravagant living, I hand-carried to the Caymans for laundering or put into my U.S. bank accounts in less than $10,000 amounts. During this period I normally carried $10,000 to $15,000 in pocket money with me though at times I had up to $100,000 on me. I never had a problem with the U.S. currency laws.

"I continued my hash import business for several years during which and after which I spent an extensive amount of time in South America. I traveled to South America at my company's expense, as I was interested in cocaine and was considering setting up an operation similar to my Moroccan operation.

"The minute I got off the plane in South America I was inundated with propositions of cocaine. The busboy wanted to sell me some. The cab driver tried to interest me. Virtually everyone I met wanted to turn me on to cocaine. It got ridiculous. I must have been approached by over a hundred people like this in one week. I even attended a division governor's party in Colombia. He had cocaine available. The supply and usage of cocaine in many circles in Colombia is similar to the supply and usage of alcohol in the United States.

"While in Colombia it became apparent that a significant number of airline stewardesses and pilots trafficked in cocaine. For instance, I was approached by a pilot in Central America who made it no secret that he wanted to get into the business.

"I eventually made a connection with an American in Colombia and set up a deal. I mailed several letters into the United States with small amounts of cocaine in them. These would be mailed to a phony name at a legitimate address. The people at the addresses would not open the letters for several days in case they were suspect. That way, if DEA showed up, they could plead ignorance. This, by the way, is a very common practice.

"It took me weeks of false starts to get my first actual import off the ground. I eventually received a small amount of cocaine that had been brought in by an air-freight pilot. Several weeks later, he was killed in a crash, and I basically gave up on smuggling cocaine as it was not only more trouble than it was worth, but was dangerous."

Showing his ability to wash funds, Oldham provided the investigating subcommittee with a chronology of his Caymanian company. "The method we used to do this, though it sounds involved, was really quite simple," he stated.

He then went through a process very similar to the one used by Victor Straus: contacting a Caymanian manager, establishing a company or companies, negotiating a percentage for laundering with various Caymanian banks, converting cash to cashier's checks, bringing the checks back and depositing them to corporate accounts in the United States. "This substantiated the fact that the funds came from an overseas source, and we documented it with loan agreements and correspondence to make it appear that these were very legitimate loans.

"In this manner, if we ever were challenged, and the great fear was being challenged by IRS, if we were ever challenged by IRS as to how we came by our assets, we could show substantial documentation of the fact that it had been borrowed from an overseas company. This, of course—the Cayman Islands—is a brick wall, that is impenetrable by IRS. They would have had no choice but to accept our documentation. The funds, when they came back into the United States and were deposited into our bank accounts, were used for various normal purchases: salary, expenses, automobiles, these sorts of things. In some cases, they were used as capitalization for companies; in some cases they went specifically for extravagant living or company expense accounts, these sorts of things.

"An integral part of this seemingly elaborate scheme was to ensure that the cover correspondence and documents were accurately prepared.

"For instance, any correspondence coming from our Caymanian contact was actually composed simultaneously along with the entire series of correspondence between the two companies and then his part was prepared by him on Esmeraldes y Mariposas stationery on his typewriter.

"Should the IRS ever go to such lengths, we would have been able to supply typewriter exemplars to corroborate the fact that these were actual loans made from the Caymans. Likewise, any correspondence we sent from our company to the Caymans was prepared in our office on our stationery and mailed to the Caymans.

"Bear in mind that all of this correspondence might be made up on the same day and even mailed on the same day. Again, if we wished to carry the charade to its extreme we could wait several months between mailings and save the envelopes and appropriate postage marks. Some people may feel that all this is necessary but hindsight tends to indicate that it is not necessary at all.

"It is interesting to note in retrospect that we were absolutely paranoid about the Internal Revenue Service. I assumed that they had every single plane going in and out of the Caymans monitored and that they had undercover agents everywhere in the Caymans, in Florida, and in Texas, watching the various flights. I also assumed that they would minutely inspect every piece of paper revolving around any of these transactions. For these reasons, we seemed to perhaps go to extremes in our documentation and in our efforts to wash these funds. Knowing what I know now, I could say that much of what we did was probably unnecessary.

"Once the money gets to the Caymans, it is apparently completely lost to the IRS and only minimal documentation would be necessary to erect the brick wall that exists in the Caymans.

"Later in my dealings, I set up accounts with the Cayman branches of Barclays Bank and the Bank of Nova Scotia. Both of these accounts were in the name of Esmeraldes y Mariposas, though the passbook I received had only an account number on it. Thus, even if I made a large deposit into the U.S. branch of these banks, any currency form filled out would reflect only a number, and not the company name or my name.

"It does not take a very sophisticated person to open up a company like this in the Caymans or to wash funds through the Caymans. Esmeraldes y Mariposas consisted of a stack of stationery and a file folder in our Caymanian representative's office. He had several hundred such file folders representing several hundred such companies at the time we were doing business with him.

"I would assume his business has grown since then. Our Caymanian contact told us of numerous U.S. citizens with whom he did business, though he named no names. He also mentioned that he serviced several major U.S. corporations.

"I might add that he stated in his opinion and in his experience, virtually all the money transiting the Cayman Islands is doing so for tax evasion purposes. His clients were certainly not exclusively narcotics people but also major entertainers, professional people, multinational companies, et cetera, and the same he felt held true of clients of his fellow Caymanian corporate representatives.

"Our Caymanian contact did not hesitate to state that the Caymans were inundated with drug money, organized crime money, money skimmed off legitimate businesses, including large corporations, and other illegally gotten gains. The banks even complained of the problems associated with handling large amounts of cash," he said.

Oldham stated that he entered the United States as many as forty and fifty times each year while he was doing business as a smuggler. "I did a great deal of extensive travel. When they punch your name and number, date of birth or passport number into the computer, their reaction is such that you know you are being detained slightly, and they sort of ring a bell, call somebody over to go through your luggage more thoroughly than normal." Otherwise, however, Oldham never endured hardships in coming and going to and from the United States. "At that time the primary access to the Caymans was through Miami Airport and the flights to the Caymans left out of gate number one. Gate number one was the only gate at the Miami Airport—and to my knowledge almost any airport in the United States—that did not have metal-detecting devices or any security of any kind. I cannot explain this. I only know that at that time it was easy just to walk from the ticket counter onto the aircraft without any examination of any kind."

After DEA agents infiltrated his operations, Oldham furnished them a money laundering service, thinking they were fellow smugglers. He was eventually arrested, fled the country about three months prior to sentencing, and left behind a $10,000 cash bond. Eventually he gave himself up and was sentenced to ten years—after having squandered about $1 million in four years.

Chapter Four
The Glitter Game

One DEA agent on the West Coast wore his bleached hair modishly long, bought clothes from sales shops that sold rejects from Rodeo Drive, and rubbed elbows with not quite millionaire class rock musicians, movie stars, soap opera standins, and bit part players from pornography bonanzas. "He did not simply rub elbows; he became a part of their world. It was like osmosis for him, entering into the wild drug scene of the entertainers and actually changing from a narcotics agent to a person possessed of the same wildness. He moved from becoming an observer to a participant," explained a fellow agent who wished to remain anonymous. "It is a problem for all undercover law enforcement people, particularly when you go after drugs in a very glitter-conscious atmosphere," he added.

When Californian James C. Stuart (alias) became a paid informant for federal law enforcement agencies, he thought that he would be thrust into the middle of the glittering world of film stars and other entertainers. Several years later, after he became one of the outer-edge participants in the John V. DeLorean cocaine case in which the famed automobile entrepreneur was charged with purchasing millions of dollars worth of the white dust in order to turn it over at a huge profit and save his company, Stuart became disillusioned with the game.

In the beginning Stuart fancied himself a spy for the government. He was a straightforward, no-nonsense businessman who had made several highly profitable real estate invest-

ments in the Orange County area south of Los Angeles. He
had lived a more or less quiet life, clipped monthly coupons
from tax-free bonds, read *Reader's Digest* and particularly enjoyed the suspenseful condensed books, and he dreamed of
fulfilling a childhood ambition to be a cop. He had known
Federal Bureau of Investigation agent Harold McLean at least
three years, meeting him at the health spa where the two
worked out with other lunchtime weight lifters Mondays,
Wednesdays, and Fridays. It was over casual after-exercise orange juice that James Stuart began questioning McLean about
the kind of work the FBI "really did." McLean, in a short but
pleasant answer, said that most was "merely administrative
details, following up on bank robberies, checking out leads
from other agencies and mostly bureaucratic duties." When
Stuart persisted, saying that he had been approached more
than once about furnishing up-front money for drug deals,
McLean showed interest. He had been with the Bureau long
enough to know that all dope dealers were not long-haired
types or big daddies driving pimpmobiles.

Within the next two weeks, without McLean pushing or
probing aggressively, Stuart mentioned that a neighbor had
spoken twice about "shipments of coke, nobody handling it
but Japanese couriers, and we could make tons." Both times,
Stuart said, the incidents happened after they had had "a couple of martinis and were by ourselves, completely alone, and
nobody even within viewing range." The neighbor had told
him, he said, that if he put up $10,000 cash it would come
back to him tenfold within a month.

The federal agent showed mild interest, attempting to handle the matter in as professional a manner as possible while
inwardly being excited about the prospect of making a really
big bust.

This was 1981. Times were lean. Since its inception in 1970,
when the Nixon administration made the Drug Enforcement
Administration a separate agency to fight the increasing problem of illegal drugs, every agent knew that a big bust meant

favorable publicity, and such publicity was generally followed by a rash of telephone calls offering information concerning other possible illegal schemes. Now that President Ronald Reagan had put the DEA into the same law enforcement category with the FBI, McLean knew that the hierarchy in Washington liked to know their men were doing their jobs, and a big bust was the best way for them to be aware of that fact. A big bust made all the law enforcement personnel involved, as well as the politicians in power, look good; furthermore, it acted as a deterrent, like a red flag of danger, to other dope dealers—at least for the time being.

So, while agent McLean held back his excitement, James C. Stuart could hardly contain his own eager enthusiasm between meetings, especially after McLean indicated rather subtly that Stuart might be of help in nabbing certain culprits.

The agent spent more and more time with his new friend, asking questions, listening intently to the answers, carrying the details back to his superiors, and finally instructing Stuart in the crafty art of the informant. Stuart was being prepared for duty behind the lines. He would be an espionage agent, a gatherer of information, a spy. McLean would have another mole to turn loose in the underworld in the hope of stopping crime and helping himself and the agency.

In the spring of 1981, the DEA was not faring well against the enemy. Compared to previous years, DEA's seizure records were not holding up statistically. Not one person of substance—politician or movie star or musical performer or industrial tycoon—had been arrested, indicted, convicted, and sentenced, or the kind of bust made that mushroomed into big headlines. In fact, during the first quarter, seizures in nearly every category of drugs were down: marijuana by more than half, heroin and cocaine almost the same. The only drugs that were up in arrests from the previous year were opium, hash, depressants, and hallucinogenics. When everybody knew that drug trafficking was on a rise every year, McLean knew it was not good business when fewer seizures were made by the DEA.

If he could make a headline bust for the FBI, he would make the agency look good against the poor statistics being compiled by the DEA. No matter what the higher-ups in Washington said for public consumption, he knew there was always competition among the various agencies. He was on the alert. He felt as though Stuart would pay off sooner or later; if not on the first try, on the second, third, or fourth.

Stuart's first job was to discover more about his neighbor's business, show interest in his previous proposition, and give the impression that he had plenty of loose money for such an investment. However, before turning Stuart out, McLean stressed that for the present time he should not be specific, talk only in generalities and leave the door open for the neighbor to make a deal when he could be wired with recording equipment.

"Before I knew it, I was sucked into the system," James C. Stuart recalled two years later. "It was all very romantic to me in the beginning. I was an everyday person living in an everyday world. All I knew about the world of dope was what I saw on television or read in the newspaper. I knew one thing: I didn't want my grandchildren being subjected to the cruel tortures of drug addiction, and from what I saw and read, I felt like it was closing in on them in our society. It made me shiver to think about it, and I wanted to do something about this disease being spread all over, but I didn't really think about it—not in those terms—when I started. I guess I really was taken by the glamour, the possibility of doing something good for the good side, helping law enforcement people capture crooks, knowing deep down inside that I was on the *right* side."

Despite his enthusiasm, however, Stuart's first try was a failure. He followed the advice of agent McLean, worked his neighbor into a corner, arranged a final meeting at which he was wired across his upper body with a taping device, was armed with marked money. But his overzealous attitude led to suspicion. When pushed to make the deal, Stuart's neighbor withdrew his original proposal. They made a date for a later meeting, but the neighbor never showed.

"I was very down after that first time. I had felt like such a hero before. I was doing something that was wonderful, but I simply threw it away by pushing too hard," Stuart remembered. "But the agent told me to be patient, that something would come up soon that I could be a part of, that I didn't have to worry about failure. In the meantime, I was paid several thousand dollars cash for my work, told to keep it and spend it and not say anything about it. I thought, what the hell, this is the law talking. I'm fine, I'm okay; it's not really breaking the law; they're letting me have something that should be mine anyway; I pay taxes, don't I?

"In the meantime, the agent met with me at least once a week, sometimes two and three times, and we'd eat lunch out in Griffith Park. He would tell me that something would be going down soon, that part of my job was to be patient and keep my eyes open. He said if I saw anything or heard anything about drugs in my community that I should let him know and we'd start to work on the source. I mean, I was definitely not sophisticated about the operations of the FBI or the DEA or any of that kind of stuff. I felt like I was in the middle of something extremely important, something extremely vital. I remember when I watched "60 Minutes," I'd think: I'm just like those guys, particularly when they showed some undercover agent doing something. It never crossed my mind once that this kind of situation I was in was wrong; I knew it couldn't be *wrong*. I was a law-abiding citizen."

Within the next six months Stuart was introduced to two other men he was told were also working undercover. Both men, he was told, had been working Hollywood and Beverly Hills, which immediately impressed Stuart. Stuart had visions of hillside parties, rambling mansions, and half nude starlets lounging around Olympic-sized swimming pools.

But the reality was that the three men—without the agent—met several times a week at what Stuart later described as "a

more or less fleabag hotel off a seedy section of Sunset Bou-
levard. It was one of those dark, stinking little bars where you
expect floozies and winos to hang out. We always sat in the
back, in the dark, huddled around a little table, and these men
filled me in on what they had been doing: working a dope deal
with a television actor. This actor, they said, actually furnished marijuana, cocaine, and other narcotics to a number
of outlets within the entertainment community. To hear them
talk, it was a really big deal."

Although the surroundings were not what Stuart had imagined, he too became caught up in the hyper-enthusiasm of his
two new partners. He had been called in to assist in a major
bust, or so he was led to believe.

Like the situation with his neighbor, Stuart would truly be
acting, just as though he was on a stage or in front of movie
cameras. They described his role to him in detail.

His name was "Harold Morgantheau" and he hailed from
Ocean City, New Jersey. He owned three dry cleaning estab-
lishments, but he was actually a behind-the-scenes money
man for the organization that backed casinos in Atlantic City.

Listening to the details, Stuart shook his head in disbelief.

"What's wrong?" one of the pair asked.

"This is getting too complicated," Stuart said. "The last
time I was just me, trying to convince a man I'd back him in
a drug scheme. Now you've got me covered up in all of this
crap."

"That's just it," the other man said. "You've got to be covered up so deep he won't suspect anything. In a situation like
this, the outsider has to have plenty of depth; the more com-
plication, the better. It's no good at all if you're just plain Jim
Stuart; he'd never believe that in a thousand years. But if
you're really *somebody*, he'll believe you. These guys got egos,
just like everybody else." He grinned.

Stuart listened.

That evening Stuart went home and studied his part. He
ran it over and over through his mind like a motion picture

projector playing reel after reel until he knew "Harold Morgantheau" backwards and forwards.

In his efforts to perfect his role, feeling the nervousness in
the bottom of his stomach like a child getting ready to step
onto a stage for his fifth-grade recital, Stuart was taking the
last step toward becoming one of the hundreds of cogs in the
large, intricate machinery of the federal law enforcement
crackdown on illegal drugs in the United States—a machine
that had grown larger since President Reagan had combined
FBI and DEA forces in 1981.

During his next two years of working with agent McLean
and others, Stuart played a dozen roles. "It seemed to me that
they should have worked with out-of-work actors in Hollywood. You meet 'em all the time in the places we met and
arranged the setups and became known as part of the scene.
The first time was not very easy; it was tough on me physically
and mentally, but it got a little easier," he said.

He was introduced to the actor in the dark bar; they had
drinks and talked small talk, and later they rode through the
hills in "Morgantheau's" Lincoln Continental convertible. "The
guy fell hook, line, and sinker for the whole story," Stuart
said. And two weeks later they were both arrested when the
actor made a buy of more than a kilo of cocaine from a third
party in "Morgantheau's" presence.

"They took me in but never booked me. I was 'bailed' out,
disappeared back onto the street, and the actor ended up with
a prison sentence. As far as he knew, I guess, my people got
me out and took me back East," Stuart said. "It was far from
the big deal I had been led to expect."

By late 1982, after he became involved in what he termed
"a classic setup" of controversial industrialist John DeLorean,
along with several dozen other paid informants and undercover operators as well as FBI, DEA, and other federal officers,
Stuart believed he had fulfilled his dream, weaving in and out
among the bikinied starlets around the swimming pool of the
Beverly Hills Hotel. And one evening in the Polo Lounge he

sold a bag of coke to a movie producer "in a round booth where he told me David Selznick made the final deal for *Gone with the Wind*. It was all going great, I thought; everything was going faster than it ever had for me before all of this, but somehow I knew the bubble had to burst. We were working everything too loose, I felt. We were trying to make busts where there were no busts. What the hell is the big deal if a wealthy movie producer wants to buy a couple of grams of coke to sniff with his sweetie pie? The agents kept saying we were getting closer and closer to the source, but I just didn't see it. Once we spent three weeks staking out Burt Reynolds's house; the guys with law enforcement told me that Reynolds had some friends who would be transporting him some grass; as it turned out, there was nothing whatsoever to it. I had never seen it like that before. I had never seen where we were doing anything wrong. I didn't think the United States could ever operate a Gestapo, setting people up, screwing 'em just because they were rich and powerful—so rich and powerful that they might have forgotten the difference between good and bad. I didn't think we could do *anything* like that. But here I was a part of it. It made me as sick at my stomach as I had been that first time when I went after that two-bit actor with a sack of coke and a bottle of uppers. I had been working a damn sham for two and a half years, lying to myself and screwing myself all at the same time."

At the moment, according to Stuart and others like him in Seattle, Denver, New York, Atlanta, Miami, and places between, federal agents were infiltrating a society that had become riddled with illicit drugs. Many informants questioned the validity and even legality of many of their own activities. Nevertheless, many, like Stuart, were intrigued with their undercover life, many had been caught up in it, and many were convinced that they were taking the right and legal approach to correcting a society gone wrong. When questioned, DEA authorities denied use of paid informants. The FBI insisted, as did state and local law enforcement personnel, that the network of civilian informants was necessary to control drug traffic. Only a dent in the armor of big-time drug smuggling was made, but the agencies—often working together, although sometimes hampered by the strict rules and regulations imposed on them by their various departments—were attempting to put a halt to this ever-growing crime phenomenon of the twentieth century.

In the 1970s, agents in New York bragged about watching John Lennon of Beatles fame like a hawk when he and his wife, Yoko Ono, traveled back and forth from Europe. The FBI agents who kept investigative eyes on the Lennons stated, "We were on official business, but you won't find it on any roster. That's the kind of thing we keep hush-hush. But after Paul McCartney was arrested in Japan, the Japanese police and criminal justice system got all the credit. In reality, we let them know he was on his way with a cache of marijuana and dangerous drugs. We are not after a small bag of grass or a few pills. We want them if they are truly trafficking, and as far as we could tell they were not. They traveled as VIPs, but we still had opportunities to put the dogs on their luggage and test it with ultrasensitive X-ray devices."

The agents said that in the early 1970s they were positive that super entertainer Elvis Presley's musicians were moving "a great amount of drugs from Middle East connections in Europe into the United States. We halted them four or five times, after informants assured us they had picked up quantities of pills in Germany and Britain, but we were never able to make anything stick. We don't know what they did with the drugs, but we were relatively sure on all occasions that they made pickups in Frankfurt and London. We were never able to find the drugs—except for a handful of barbiturates and amphetamines once.

"We were told by insiders that Presley's group had the same connections that the Rolling Stones had, and we also kept a sharp eye out for them. We were told on numerous occasions that members of the Stones provided drugs to the scene in some of the biggest and fanciest disco clubs in New York. However, after watching them for months and months, we decided that the opposite was true; that if the Stones were doing drugs, which our sources said was positive and which they did little to hide, connections within the clubs were providing them with narcotics and not the other way around.

"It is interesting, being a celebrity watcher; they do things differently from others. Once we did grab a nightclub singer. She arrived on the *Queen Elizabeth II*, had a stash of several kilos of near pure cocaine, and we checked the roster and discovered she had made the trip three times a year for several years. When we arrested her, she was haughty as hell. She acted like a haughty queen. You'd have thought we were her servants, the way she swept by us and looked down her pretty nose at us. We assured her we weren't joking.

"When we got her downtown she started singing more than she'd ever belted a number out on stage. She put together connections we had been looking for for a dozen years. Because of her, we were able to come down on several big busts in the D.C. area and several up north of Boston. She knew *everybody* in the business on the West Coast, and because of her cooperation, putting us on to some gentlemen who were into hundreds of kilos a month, we erased everything about her. As far as we were concerned, we never even talked with her," the anonymous agent stated.

When questioned by Delaware Republican Senator William V. Roth Jr.'s Permanent Subcommittee on Investigations of the Senate Committee on Governmental Affairs, convicted smuggler Harold Oldham said that he had seen entertainers trafficking during his career in the underworld. "While I was in Morocco, I met a rock star with a major rock group. Through my contact with him I came into constant contact with many of the major rock and pop groups in the United States and Great Britain. My association with these groups led me to the formation of Startrans, a company I set up for the purpose of renting luxury buses to these groups while they were on tour. Startrans was a legitimate U.S. company and business, though it had been capitalized by significant amounts of narcotics money which had been laundered through the Caymans.

"I can regretfully state that the use of drugs was pervasive throughout many major music groups during the period I was associated with them—1974–77. Cocaine and other drugs were everywhere, used by everyone from musicians to their equipment handlers. During this period I attended numerous parties in Hollywood and on the road. Most people associate wet bars with most normal parties. At these parties, trays of cocaine were as common as wet bars. Rent-a-cops were hired as bouncers but served as insurance against drug raids.

"Several of the groups had physicians traveling with them who would liberally distribute pills—controlled substances— to anyone in the troupe who wished them. It became a common procedure on the chartered flights taken by these groups for the physicians to set up shop. As soon as the plane took off, members of the troupe would literally line up at his shop for pills.

"I might add that heroin, though not as prevalent, was readily available from hangers-on within the entourage, and several of the major musicians were heavy addicts."

An agent in New York and another in Seattle complained that they could not watch "the highbrow entertainment people the way we should." In New York, an agent who asked to be identified as J.D. Kelly—an alias he had used while operating undercover in the Broadway theater circuit, watching the movement of hashish, cocaine, and heroin—said, "The ballet and opera companies come and go to and from foreign destinations almost at will. We give them a free passage, more or less. Once we had a very strong informant's word that as much as twenty kilos were coming in with an opera company from Italy, and it took a demand from Washington before we were allowed to move in with Customs and make the arrest. Then we were told to make the arrest discreetly, not to embarrass the managers or the stars of the show, to allow them to plead before a state court, and not to push it through federal court. We started to raise hell about this, seeing that they were going to get by with simply a slap on the wrist and that they would probably be doing it again in a month or two, but we were told by Customs authorities to keep quiet. They said this was happening all the time: they were told to keep silent about opera, ballet, or the symphonies. Can you imagine how much coke or heroin a musician in an orchestra would be able to smuggle if he or she were given total freedom to do so? Have you ever looked at those cases? Like the tuba? Or a bass drum? It's ludicrous, but it happens. We've caught only a very few, but we have knowledge that hundreds of kilos a month are entering this country."

In Seattle, another agent repeated a similar story. "If we make cases on these people who are the top society entertainers, we are asking for trouble. We back away from them. We don't want that kind of hassle. There are too many punks doing the same thing. We know that the big people in Washington with the clout don't give a rat's ass about the punks. But they'd jump us in a minute if we searched through a silk-stocking opera star's valise." The agent, who said he had been criticized previously for speaking out against some of the policies dictated by Washington bureaucrats, asked that he remain anonymous during several interviews.

Tennessee investigators in Nashville said they had never had a problem with superiors telling them not to watch country music stars. For more than two weeks in 1982, Special Investigator Lofton Brown and three men working with him kept surveillance on several headline singers, including self-styled "outlaw" Waylon Jennings. "We had information from an informant who had been reliable in the past that cocaine and amphetamines were being smuggled up from Florida and other sections of the country to these musicians, which included some of the most notorious names in the recording and television business in this town. Some of them try to get away with any personal illegal act like taking drugs, drinking too much, and driving crazily, and generally raising hell like spoiled youngsters. It becomes a kind of game with a lot of these stars in Nashville to see what they can get away with. Many times we just turn the other way and say, 'To heck with it. If it's only hurting them, let 'em have their fun.' But when it gets down to hard drugs, that's something else. We don't go out of our way to try and catch them, but we try not to let them get away with smuggling and dealing either."

As a result of the surveillance by Brown and his group, several musicians were arrested at the Nashville airport. But only a very small amount of the controlled substance was found. The arrests made the headlines as did the subsequent release.

A Nashville city policeman who had spent twenty-two years on the force said, "Arrests like that just make fools out of law enforcement. It gives the offender a slight spanking, like a naughty child, and it allows the others in the entertainment community to see that nothing of substance will happen if they smuggle drugs in and out of Nashville. If you go to a music party here—either on Music Row or out at one of the mansions up on Old Hickory Lake or down in Brentwood— you'll always be able to find coke or marijuana. These people have plenty of money, and people with plenty of money will always have anything illegal they want; I'm not saying they smuggle it into the area; they might. I am saying they have the wherewithal to get what they want. And I am not going to waste my time and the taxpayers' money trailing along behind a rhinestone- and fringe-coated cowboy in a silver Cadillac. In the long run, I don't think it's worth it."

In Washington, D.C., the celebrity mark for law enforcement was the politician. "We have to be careful in Washington because the Congress approves our budget. They want to see us cracking down on movie stars and rock musicians, but it is another thing indeed if we start snooping around in the back

rooms of Congress looking for some representative who has
made a number of trips lately to Paris or to Brazil," said a
DEA agent who had worked undercover at the National Press
Club as well as in the exclusive politico hangouts on Capital
Hill.

"U.S. politicians are generally privileged persons. When they
fly in from a foreign country they usually land at Andrews
Air Force Base and no Customs agents rush up to open their
bags. They certainly do not go through an X-ray machine to
make sure there is no contraband inside.

"During recent years we have worked very quietly in and
around Congress. Some have imported drugs from foreign
countries—coke from France, marijuana from South America,
even hashish from North Africa—but most of it has been for
their own use.

"Several years ago we found a congressman who was bringing cocaine into this country on a regular basis, selling some
of it to big-shot friends in Georgetown, where most of the
parties have it wide open on the table like it was some kind
of hors d'oeuvre or like another kind of drink. We slipped in,
actually caught him coming off the base back into this country, and put the strong arm on him before he got back to his
office. We were under strict orders to keep everything very
quiet. We took the coke and let him know that we could have
arrested him on the spot and caused him embarrassment and
a big scandal. We knew it wasn't a really big thing—not like
kilo after kilo—but it was enough; he would probably have
gotten his wrist slapped and he might have gotten defeated at
the polls, but we didn't think that was our business," the agent
said.

Asked what was his business, the agent said, "Higher-ups
in the department dealt with the congressman. I doubt seriously if he ever transported dope into the country again."

However, according to the agent, the congressman was caught
up in the ABSCAM scandals, was convicted, resigned his office, and later served time in federal prison.

"We are worried about politicians and the military," said another DEA agent who kept his trained eyes peeled on incoming military transport planes on several bases in the United States. "After the Vietnamese war, we had horrendous problems with servicemen bringing opium, heroin, and cocaine back into this country. We had several incidents of enlisted men bringing entire duffel bags filled with high-priced pure-grade narcotics into the United States. I'm sure some got by. We caught some. We court-martialed some.

"In the turmoil of returning from battle, we also found that some officers discovered there was a way to enrich themselves quickly. We discovered several high-ranking officers—lieutenant colonels and colonels—with trunks packed full of pure cocaine. This was 1971, 1972, in Seattle, Washington, and the street value even then was well over several million dollars. These men were allowed to step out of the Army and the Air Force gracefully. I imagine they are sitting back on some nice beach now drawing their pensions. How do you deal with these men? As common crooks?"

Chapter Five
The Florida Phenomenon

They called him the Baron of Baron River. He lived within five miles of Everglades City on the southwest coast of Florida, east of the Ten Thousand Islands. His name during the six years he lived in the cypress mansion built high on stilts overlooking moss-bearded trees of the swampland was Lowell T. Everett. A man of about forty years of age, a casual but stylish dresser, he carried himself like a member of royalty through the tiny towns of the canal country.

Even local police seemed to marvel at Lowell Everett, because he defied the odds of the federal government's massive buildup of narcotics patrolmen throughout the big boot of central and southern Florida in the early 1980s. "After President Reagan pinpointed Florida as the primary state for smuggling soon after he took office, there were more DEA, Customs, and other narcotics cops from Jacksonville to Key West and from Pensacola to Flamingo than there were smugglers. And that was a first," said Ralph Chatom, a retired lieutenant with the Tampa Police Department. "In the 1970s, Florida became a haven for drug smugglers. Everybody and his brother was in the business. If you had a fishing boat or a little airplane, you had the potential. Down this way, the top dog was the Baron of Baron River. I know that he had at least five different aliases. He was somebody different if he was in South America or the Caribbean Islands. And he had other false identities for dealing with people in Texas and New York. He had driver's licenses from at least a half dozen different states and birth certificates to match. He was really a clever and cruel operator. He was the most cold-blooded smuggler I've ever run across. I know he killed at least three investigators down around Shark Point just outside Ponce de Leon Bay between here and Key Largo. The investigators were on his trail. They had been getting into his boat operations and were at that time following a Hatteras he had had specially equipped for long and fast runs. It was ruled that the boat in which the investigators were riding exploded because of engine trouble, but a guy who was working for Lowell Everett later told me that Everett's henchmen— some of the real toughies who were deckhands on merchant ships before they got into real money with the smugglers— stopped the investigators, held them at gunpoint, worked on the engines, tied the policemen up, set them afloat, and blew up the boat. I *know* this guy wasn't lying to me. He was a good man before he got into debt to Everett, who also ran some gambling deals around Tampa, St. Pete, and even over in the Cuban quarters in Miami before he went into smuggling full time."

Florida, with its 8,426 miles of shore—much of which is desolate and perfect for the landing and unloading of sixty-foot fishing boats or forty-eight-foot cabin cruisers or thirty-five-foot sailing yachts like the ones owned by Lowell Everett—was targeted by the Reagan administration as the number one law enforcement state. After the notorius Black Tuna case of the 1970s, when at least 100,000 pounds of marijuana were seized from big mother ships arriving within the waters of the United States from South America, President Reagan appointed Vice President George Bush to chair the South Florida Task Force. Named coordinator of the task force was Charles F. Rinkevich, who had been with the Law Enforcement Assistance Administration in Philadelphia and, later, regional administrator in Atlanta.

Not only did Florida have the shoreline, it had hundreds of operational airports and abandoned airstrips, and because the

boot literally jutted out into the ocean, its geographical prox-
imity to source countries made it an avenue of narcotics traffic.

According to Rinkevich, between 70 and 80 percent of all
marijuana and cocaine and a large percentage of Quaaludes
illegally entering the United States traveled through Florida
on their way to other parts of America.

"The intense competition between smugglers, and rising
crime in general, had created a particularly sinister aspect to
south Florida's crime problem: the proliferation of illegal automatic weapons. These machine guns appear to be the weapon
of choice for gang warfare and drug-related assassinations. The
procurement of illegal firearms for use by the criminal element, and the exportation of firearms to foreign countries is
another dimension of this lucrative business," Rinkevich told
the Permanent Subcommittee on Investigations in October of
1982.

"Principally as a result of the smuggling of drugs, there had
been an influx of staggering amounts of criminally obtained
U.S. currency into south Florida, which resulted in Miami
becoming a major center for the laundering of billions of ill-
gotten narco bucks through its expensive, legitimate, domestic, and international banking community," Rinkevich said.

"In short, epidemic drug smuggling, laundering of illegal
megabucks, use of illegal automatic firearms, and illegal immigration had created a crime crisis in south Florida that seriously threatened the safety and quality of life of all of its
citizens—rights guaranteed to them by the Constitution.

"On January 28, 1982, President Reagan noted that in regard
to the south Florida situation, the federal government had a
special responsibility to fill in temporarily and do what it
could to reduce these problems. He established a federal task
force comprised of the very highest officials in his administration and chaired by Vice President Bush. This task force
includes the Attorney General, the secretaries of State, Defense, Transportation, Treasury, and Health and Human Services, as well as presidential counselor Edwin Meese. The task

force is not intended to supersede the responsibilities of state and local law enforcement, but rather to assist and coordinate federal efforts in order that together we can restore civility, safety, and calm to south Florida.

"On February 16, 1982, Vice President Bush reported on the plans and initial decisions taken by the task force in a speech before the Miami Citizens Against Crime. Incidentally, the MCAC was very instrumental in focusing the administration's attention on the south Florida crime situation and remains a successful example of an informed citizenry aroused in righteous indignation to address a serious community problem.

"The major objectives of the task force were to significantly reduce the influx of illegal drugs coming into the United States through Florida by greatly increasing air, sea, and land interdiction efforts and arresting and convicting smugglers apprehended during these activities. A concentrated effort is also being made to reduce the availability of illegal automatic weapons through intensified enforcement of federal machine gun laws.

"Further, insofar as there is a nexus between illegal aliens and violent crime, we are concentrating some of our efforts on locating and removing these illegal aliens from the streets of south Florida through various initiatives planned and executed with the Immigration Naturalization Service and its border patrol. Incidentally, we know that people in the business of smuggling drugs are also in the business of smuggling weapons or aliens and our efforts to interdict one impact on the other two.

"We also clearly recognized that the level of criminal activity in south Florida had almost overwhelmed the ability of the state, local, and federal criminal justice systems to deal with it. Thus, in order to realistically address our major mission, early on the task force addressed a whole subset of systematic problems which included insufficient manpower in many federal enforcement and criminal justice efforts, insuf-

ficient federal courtrooms, insufficient jail space, and insufficient offshore antismuggling surveillance, both air and sea,"
he stated.

When Rinkevich took control of the South Florida Task
Force on March 2, 1982, he brought into operation new DEA
agents, new FBI agents, new Customs personnel, new border
patrol officers, new assistant U.S. attorneys, and new judges.
Charged with the responsibility of coordinating all cross-agency
efforts, Rinkevich sought new ways to go about old-fashioned
law keeping. During the following months he put into effect
the program outlined to him by Vice President Bush.

From Key West to Jacksonville, seventeen groups of officers
were put into six locations. Their foremost mission was to
intensify air and sea drug patrolling efforts. They conducted
short-term follow-up investigations and developed their own
intelligence sources through infiltration investigations. These
smaller exterior groups freed the DEA district office in Miami
to concentrate on long-term major drug investigations which
had been hampered by the strength of the illegal activities in
the field.

The new task force worked with Coast Guardsmen assigned
to patrol the waters. More equipment necessary to bolster
efforts was purchased. More efficiency was demanded. At the
time the task force was formed, only two out-of-district cutters were patrolling the waters surrounding south Florida at
any one time. Six new Falcon jet long-distance search aircrafts
were added to the fleet. Two high-speed 210-foot cutters were
brought in from New England and Virginia. Three new surface
effect ships were moved to south Florida, where Captain John
W. Kime, chief of operations for the Seventh District of the
Coast Guard in Miami, said, "These very versatile vessels
enabled us to have much more flexibility down in the choke
points."

The choke points Captain Kime spoke of were first in the
Yucatán Channel. The cutters were assigned to the area with
helicopters aboard to patrol the most heavily used drug routes.

New offshore patrol boats were put in the waters just off the Florida coast, where they also used juiced-up Cigarette boats confiscated from drug traffickers. The Cigarette boats have capabilities of up to 90 miles per hour for distances up to 150 miles, when alternate fuel tanks have been attached and the twin 400- to 450-horsepower engines have been opened fully. "These babies are the only things that keep up with the smugglers," said Patrolman Edward Smith. "When you see them cutting across the nighttime water, you know they're flying. Then, when we rev up these engines—which were the best for rum running back in the 1920s, when this entire area was filled with these boats bringing illegal rum from Cuba, Jamaica, and other islands into the United States—they don't know what's after them. We really can cut down on them with this equipment. Before, they had the boat because we didn't have the money to purchase them. Now, since we've been using the newest helicopters available to us, we have stopped some of them and have seized maybe a half dozen."

New AWAC-type aircraft, like the U.S. Navy E2-C equipped with radar, usually used to track enemy missiles and jets, were put into irregular patterns crisscrossing the state attempting to detect unauthorized airplanes. When it was first put into action in Florida, the E2-C helped to seize forty-three aircraft in the first ninety days.

The Army loaned Customs a fleet of Bell Cobra helicopters, which swoop down like forest-green giant birds over landing areas, some armed with thirty-million candlepower spotlights that will brighten a landing area at midnight. Faster than anything the Customs agents had previously, the Cobras assured them of quick arrivals on the scene after planes had been spotted and were off-loading. The gun-toting adventuresome pilots paint tiny marijuana leaves under the cockpit for each interception and arrest. With the code name Bat, the helicopter team, initiated in April of 1982—with the loan of twelve single side bank radios from the Navy to permit them to launch special operations that were not possible without such so-

phisticated equipment—operated with great success in seizures and arrests.

Added to their fleet in 1983 was the Army's new Blackhawk
helicopter, which allowed them to carry a large number of
law enforcement personnel for a faster and quieter arrival on
the scene of the crime.

"There are at least 7,500 smuggling flights a year along the
southern border of the United States," according to Robert
Asack, the commander of Customs air operations from Home-
stead Air Force Base near Miami. "The majority come into
Florida. At any one time, there are a thousand aircraft involved
in it. Removing an aircraft doesn't slow them down. On average, it takes an organization six weeks to get another aircraft.
They can buy one, lease one, hire one, or steal one. No problem.

"But if we remove the pilots, that slows them. We reckon
there is a hard core of 2,000 pilots involved. Eating into that
has a big effect. They need good pilots, instrument-rated guys;
they can't just go out and get a cheapo out of flying school.

"It's a tough game, loaded with ifs for the pilot: If the plane
holds together; if he isn't ripped off before takeoff; if the load
doesn't shift; if the headwinds aren't too bad; if the Cubans
don't intercept; if he lands okay. Now, we can chuck in 'if he
gets caught,' " Asack told *Sunday Times of London* reporter
Brian Moynahan.

One of Lowell T. Everett's Cessnas was spotted by an AWAC
plane as it penetrated the ADIZ (Air Defense Identification
Zone) on the southwestern coastline of Florida early in May
of 1982. The small plane stayed low over the tops of the trees.
But the larger plane kept it sighted while radioing the Customs
team, which immediately began moving in.

While the killer Cobras, as they are known by doper flyers,
sped low across the Everglades, the Cessna bolted north with
a wide-open throttle. And every move it made was recorded
on the AWAC's radar screen and reported to the helicopter
team.

Somehow realizing that he was being stalked, although it was highly unlikely that the doper could have seen or heard the AWAC, the Cessna headed due north in a straight line.

Ahead of the Cobras maneuvered a fast-engined tracker plane, which had been seized in an earlier raid in the Fort Lauderdale area. With the Customs pilots spotting their target, they stayed behind him and soon knew that he had seen them.

Without taking so much as a second glance at an airstrip east of Port Charlotte, the doper pilot dropped down. Almost the instant his tires hit the cracked runway, the doors of the Cessna flung open. He skidded to a halt, twisted sideways, and both pilot and copilot ran for it, leaving their plane behind.

The tracker came in. The Cobras were minutes behind it. The copilot was captured little more than a mile away. He had turned his foot when he jumped from the plane. The pilot managed to escape.

On board the Cessna the officers found in excess of 200 pounds of cocaine and that much more Quaaludes. The copilot said they had picked up the sacks in Jamaica after they had been dropped there by another pilot flying up from Colombia. Much later, when prosecuting attorneys promised to recommend a light sentence, he said that he had been hired by Lowell T. Everett.

Everett was the top boss of a Mom and Pop smuggling operation that yielded him personally about $10 million annually. He appeared to be more careful than the average smuggler. He dealt with very few people on any given run. Unlike a huge empire-style smuggling ring like The Company (which will be described in the second half of this book), Everett kept his game relatively simple. He owned a fleet of small planes and boats that were scattered at various locations along the Gulf coast. He did not deal with large DC-type aircraft. He mixed his marketable goods from hashish, cocaine, and Quaaludes. He never ran a deal more frequently than every three months. He made sure that each person he used was of the highest quality for the particular role he or she would play.

Each deal was planned down to the tiniest detail by Everett and each deal was different from the one before.

Perhaps it was this bit of individualism that baffled the DEA and Customs agents more than any other. Several times they attempted to infiltrate his organization. Every time they found themselves waiting for hours at some out-of-the-way bar or restaurant and Everett never showed.

When he hired his pilots, it was for one trip. That was all. He paid well and paid promptly. But he didn't want the pilot to develop a routine that would be traceable. "He was unique among the smugglers," stated a Miami agent. "Most of them get into trouble by failing to pay somebody or paying somebody else too much while forgetting to pay somebody else enough. There is a lot of jealousy in the smuggling business. And where there's jealousy, we are able to work in through the cracks in the veneer. If people are jealous enough, they talk. Many times it is a woman who has been jilted. Sometimes it's a woman who has been given a lot of cash and diamonds and jewelry or a car by a smuggler. She gets too possessive. He drops her and goes with somebody else. She gets mad. To get even with him, she comes to us. Everett never had that kind of problem. Or it never manifested itself with us. He kept his cards very close to his chest."

One month Everett had a deal going in Jamaica, like the Cessna that was intercepted by the AWAC plane. At another time one of his fast Cigarette boats would leave Everglades City, go out into the Gulf, meet a mother ship from Venezuela, and bring in a load of marijuana. Three months later, after he had sold the goods and made his profit and paid his people, Everett would have a trio of good-looking young women in New York hired to travel through Europe. He paid first-class airfare round trip from New York to Frankfurt. The girls would travel through Germany, Austria, Italy, and into Spain. They would sail across the Strait of Gibraltar to Morocco where they would pick up high-grade cocaine from the source he had already dealt with. Less than a week later the girls would fly home from Madrid with the cocaine strapped around their bodies. The girls, whom DEA agents call mules, were met in New York by Everett. He took the goods. He wined them, dined them, and paid them handsomely in cash. And he never saw them again. To the young women, he was a businessman from Minnesota named Howes; he talked with a flat nasal accent; and the only address they knew was the Waldorf-Astoria.

On another occasion, Everett used an even more unique method of trafficking. He made his deal in Surinam with a merchant from Paramaribo who sent four young Indio women, dressed in loose clothing, on a ship bound for Miami. The women had swallowed balloons filled with cocaine. After they arrived at the port in Miami, Everett took them to a nearby motel where they were fed laxative until they extruded the valuable contraband.

Unless by some unusual method such as the use of swallowers, Everett never allowed drugs to be brought directly from South America into the United States. Many times his plane would bring the goods from Colombia to Jamaica, where he owned a beachside home near Port Antonio with an adequate strip carved into the jungle less than a mile away. The pilot would be paid and sent on his way. Approximately one week later another pilot, usually with a copilot, was hired to bring the plane into the United States. This cost Everett much more money. But his pilots were always fresh. They were always alert. And one pilot never knew much about his operation. Certainly they never knew his true identity.

"It was nothing for Everett to sit on 100 pounds of coke for a week, two weeks, or even several months in Jamaica or down in the Leeward Islands. In fact, we suspected once that he personally brought dope out of Venezuela, island-hopping slowly from Trinidad, up through the Windwards and Leewards, staying at a resort hotel in San Juan for a week, going on to the Dominican Republic, over into Haiti, and renting a small plane out of Port-au-Prince to the Bahamas," said the agent. "But did he ever get in a hurry? Never. It took him nearly three months to get back into the States. When he landed in West Palm Beach, a pilot from New Jersey was waiting with a Lear. As Everett walked away, he was clean as a Chinese laundry. The coke was already headed north to be cut down and distributed."

When the South Florida Task Force, responding to the pleadings of help from local law enforcement agencies, moved into Everglades City in early 1983 with infiltrators wearing hip mod clothing, gold chains, expensive watches, and flashing handfuls of hundreds, Everett was far ahead of the posse. Unlike the locals who had not seen undercover cops operating within drug circles, Everett knew the moment he witnessed Willie and Barbara Santos riding into town in their fancy black van, dressed in designer clothing, gold jewelry hanging around their necks, being much more ostentatious than the country scene called for, although there were others who dressed and acted the same way. The thing was: Everett knew the others. They had gotten rich quickly in the drug business. He didn't know the Santos couple but suspected they were bad news.

Everglades City and the surrounding flatlands in the backwater bayous with its thick forest growth and eerie pirate cove atmosphere had been perfect for a hideout. Everett liked the quietness of the place, although he knew it was becoming dangerous when so many local people got involved in drug smuggling. He knew that his days in this paradise were numbered.

"About two years ago things started changing around here," said Mayor Herman Askren in the rustic but comfortable Everglades Rod and Gun Club looking out over the dark and quiet Baron River with its sunset sounds of hidden birds and mysterious animals in the distant swamp. As mayor of the town of little more than 500, Askren, his wavy gray hair fluffy above bright eyes and white mustache, came to this town nearly twenty years before. He talked about how the sleepy little village became a "cesspool of criminal activity" during the late 1970s and early 1980s. "We had to do something about it. The young people looked around and saw their fathers half starving as fishermen, making a little money off the tourists who come down in the winter, but otherwise not making enough to make ends meet. Then they saw the newcomers, the guys with the fast boats and the Cadillacs and the gold hanging around their necks. These new young people with their beards and shaggy hair didn't do much work but made all the money. I hated it when I saw our young people getting into that lifestyle. It was really stupid the way they flaunted their sudden wealth," Askren, a retired owner of a sandblasting company, said.

When too many of the newly rich started making their homes in and around Everglades City, Lowell Everett started looking for a way out. A Tampa contact said Everett put his house on the market "in one of those national publications that sell half-million-dollar homes, like *Town and Country*."

By spring of 1983, after Willie Santos visited his house and looked it over, Everett had sold most of his Cigarette boats in harbors from Clearwater to Naples. At least two of his faster boats were sent to Jamaica, where he put them in dock at Port Antonio and Ocho Rios. He kept only two of his airplanes and liquidated the rest. "He got cash for everything from the dopers who needed good, fast merchandise from an inside source," said the Tampa source.

When the DEA, Customs, and other members of the task force raided Everglades City in July of 1983, Everett had vanished. He left few tracks. His Tampa real estate person said he had "gone south" but claimed not to know if he was in Jamaica or Brazil.

Following the series of raids that yielded more than 450,000 pounds of marijuana, more than 100 pounds of cocaine, some thirty-five defendants, seizures of thirty-nine boats, three airplanes, and twenty-one motor vehicles, Deputy Sheriff Charlie Sanders, who with six other deputies represent the local law in Everglades City, told *The Washington Post*, "I've been here eighteen years and I know everybody. I know their sons. I've seen a lot of friends go because of pot. I've arrested a lot of friends. But I will tell you this: these people would do anything in the world for you down here. They have been courteous to me for years. The trouble is they just don't believe smuggling pot is immoral. And the money is so good, they have to do it. One fellow gets a new car, some gold chains, and he's not working very hard, and his friend comes back from fourteen hours pulling stone crab pots and he gets the idea that he doesn't have to work hard either."

Sanders told Washington reporter Christian Williams, "I could have been a rich man. They've come to me, yes they have. They've come to me several times, but I have set them straight, and they respect me for it. The truth of it is, they don't even need to bribe me. We have six officers working a seven-day week. Anyhow you make up that work schedule, we'll be uncovered a lot of the time. Or all they have to do is wait for a wreck on the highway. That's where my men will be, and there won't be anybody to bother them."

The men of the task force readily admitted the same thing. The United States government was spending hundreds of millions of dollars. Hundreds of thousands of pounds of marijuana, thousands of pounds of cocaine, and huge sacks filled with Quaaludes were being confiscated; hundreds of people were being captured and sent to prison; and more than a million dollars' worth of planes, cars, trucks, and boats were being seized. Still, many of the big boys like Lowell Everett were escaping onto the seas or into the air. They continued to operate from somewhere. The massive need of America's affluent society was continuing to be supplied even after so many were being caught. "With all of the people and the equipment we have guarding the shoreline of Florida, we know that we still lose a certain percentage because we cannot cover every inch every moment of every day," said a Miami task force leader. "The word spread that we were here. Some have to give us a try anyway. Some know that we cannot catch everyone. And others have gone over us and around us and land daily or nightly in Georgia, South Carolina, North Carolina, Alabama, Tennessee, Mississippi, Louisiana, Texas, or Arkansas. I named nine states where we know that at least one plane every night lands somewhere within each state. We obviously generate a great need, we obviously have a great deal of money for which to pay for the drugs, and when the money and the need is present, somebody will take the chance."

Chapter Six
Yesterday

In the beginning, the United States didn't recognize narcotics as dangerous. Like other countries throughout history, opium and other drugs were viewed as medicine. And, in fact, opium-refined morphine was praised by the medical community in the early 1800s as a drug that could halt all addiction. During the Civil War nearly half a million men were administered morphine after having been wounded. Following the war, addiction became known as the Soldier's Disease. By 1900, it was conservatively estimated, at least 50,000 over-the-counter medicines were on sale in pharmacies and through mail order houses containing doses of addictive or toxic agents. Dr. Agnew's Catarrh Powder, advertised as a cure for the common cold, was laced with ten grams of pure cocaine in every ounce. That Adamson's Botanic Cough Balsam contained heroin did not chase away purchasers; they were told the drug was not addictive. Morphine sulphate, chloroform, and cannabis indica were all found in the popular Kohler's One-Night Cough Cure, and heroin was mixed with chloroform in Dr. Brutus Shiloh's Cure for Consumption. The poisonous opiate laudanum sold through the Sears, Roebuck catalogue for eighteen cents for a two-ounce bottle and two dollars for a one-and-a-half-pint bottle.

The United States never prohibited by law the sale, growth, distribution, or trafficking of narcotics until 1914, primarily because physicians lobbied loudly that federal regulation of doctors trying to cure the sick and maimed would be unconstitutional. Even when President Woodrow Wilson finally signed the Harrison Act on December 17, 1914, laying the foundation for federal drug enforcement for the first two-thirds of the twentieth century, it was little more than a revenue measure providing for registration and taxation of manufacturers and distributors of opium, morphine, heroin, and coca products.

The enforcement of this ambiguous law was put in the hands of the Treasury Department under the Bureau of Internal Revenue's Miscellaneous Division. The same division that hired 162 narcotic agents on March 1, 1915, watched out after the regulatory practices of oleomargarine, adulterated butter, filled cheese, mixed flour, cotton futures, and playing cards. By the end of the year, agents arrested a number of physicians and druggists who had been indiscriminate in supplying addicts; they had seized a total of forty-four pounds of opium and had won 106 convictions against 25 acquittals with ten years in prison as the maximum sentence. In the following year, the case against Dr. Jin Fuey Moy, a Pittsburgh physician charged with prescribing one-sixteenth of an ounce of morphine sulphate for an addict, reached the U.S. Supreme Court. The case had been dismissed in district court where it had been found that any regulation of medicine was a power reserved to the states. Government attorneys appealed, arguing that the law was intended to fulfill international treaty obligations, but Justice Oliver Wendell Holmes wrote in the majority opinion that nowhere in the Harrison Act was there a mention of such obligations. Many addicts who had been convicted under Section Eight, which stated that it was unlawful for anyone to possess drugs without registering them with the Division (although it also provided no instrument by which addicts could register) were immediately released from prison following the high court's decision.

Although the spokesmen for the Bureau of Internal Revenue stated at the time that the war against smugglers was being won, in retrospect it appeared that the court's decision had more or less cut off effective enforcement. Only 5.5 pounds of opium and not one ounce of morphine were seized during 1917. As was the situation until modern times, the narcotics agent's attitude was that he was given the short end of law enforcement while the Federal Bureau of Investigation and other agencies took front row seats at press conferences and budget time. That year agents were paid a starting salary of $1,500 a year with per diem of $3 a day. Collectors and deputy collectors drew a bounty on taxes collected; in order to receive the highest salary of $4,000, a collector had to tally $1 million in collections for the year. Because the agents were given no advance funds with which to operate undercover, they had to work from hand to mouth or case to case. An agent assigned to Texas that year wrote to the Deputy Commissioner of Internal Revenue from Dallas: "Court just closed here. I got thirteen convictions, one for moonshining and the balance for narcotics violations. I expect to leave here this week for Fort Worth, which has the reputation for being a real dope town. My only experience there so far was the loss of fifteen good dollars two months ago buying an eighth ounce of morphine. I got the morphine and the man all right but not the fifteen, as unfortunately the Revenue Agent here did not have the funds to reimburse me." Another agent in Washington, D.C. was forced to slip $900 cash from Treasury Department funds to use as a flash roll to buy from the Mayor of Chinatown, who sold him twenty cans of opium for $45 each. As soon as the bust was completed the agent had to scurry back to the office and replace the funds before the vaults were closed at 5 P.M. Shortly thereafter the agent unwrapped the dope, which was wrapped in California newspapers, and discovered the cache was part of an old Customs seizure off the West Coast. In the aftermath, he reported, "In the Purveying Depot of the Public Health Service, located on the first floor of this building, there is stored a large stock of opium and narcotics turned over to the service by the Internal Revenue Bureau, which has no more protection than a wire grill or screenwork in the

windows, and if the peddlers and addicts knew of its existence
and accessibility they would break into the building and cart
it all away within forty-eight hours."

Like the Civil War, World War I brought about the Soldier's
Disease again in the form of drug addiction. But following the
war, the states ratified the Eighteenth Amendment outlawing
the country's number one enemy, alcoholic beverages, and the
Bureau of Internal Revenue was given the added duty of en-
forcing its regulations. In March of 1919 the Supreme Court
heard another drug case very similar to the *U.S. v. Jin Fuey
Moy*. In this case a physician was charged with prescribing
morphine to an addict patient with no intention of curing the
illness. This time the high court upheld the constitutionality
of the Harrison Act, giving enforcement a stronger tool; but
the overriding problem for the Bureau was controlling illegal
whiskey activities in the nation. Armed with 170 agents in
thirteen district offices, the Narcotics Division operated under
the leadership of Levi G. Nutt, a former pharmacist who in
1920 worked with a budget of little more than $500,000, or
twice what it had been the previous year. With the law backing
them, the Division counted 1,583 convictions in 1921 and
only 119 acquittals; and 1,417 pounds of opium, 373 of morphine, 32 of heroin, and 286 of cocaine were seized by agents.

That year, however, the first agent was killed in the act of
duty. Near El Paso, Chief Agent Stafford E. Beckett and Agent
Charles Wood crept up to a rural ranch house. As they approached, a shot rang out from the house. During a two-hour
gun battle, Wood attempted to crawl back to cover. A bullet
lodged in his back, killing him. When the assailants were
captured and tried in state court because killing an agent was
not against federal law at that time, they were found innocent.

As the following case pointed out, few local communities
had sympathy for the lawmen who were attempting to stop
the trafficking of narcotics. In 1922, Agent Joseph W. Floyd
led three others to a residence in downtown Houston where
they were to search for narcotics and whiskey. Riding the

running board of a car as it swerved into the front yard, Floyd caught a shot and died an hour later. After gunfire was exchanged, the remaining agents took control, arrested five, one of whom was prosecuted under the Harrison Act and given one year and a day in prison. No one was charged with Floyd's murder.

On May 26, 1922, the United States took the first step toward putting its finger on the pulse of international drug trafficking when Congress passed the Narcotic Drug Import and Export Act. With the creation of the Federal Narcotics Control Board, consisting of the secretaries of State, Commerce, and Treasury, it proposed to prohibit the importation of opium for any reason other than medical use, and the exportation of opiates to any nation without adequate licensing control. When amended two years later, the act also outlawed the manufacture of heroin in this country.

This strong-minded chairman of the House Committee on Foreign Affairs, Representative Steven G. Porter, insisted that the way to halt the steady flow of narcotics into the United States was to stop it at the source.

Leading the U.S. delegation to the Second International Opium Convention in Geneva in 1924, Porter grew impatient with attempting to deal with opium-producing nations. He stated to the press during the long and grueling hours of negotiations that he wanted a strong law or no law. Finally, after more than two months of attempting to deal with France, Turkey, Germany, and other countries attending the conference, Porter walked out in protest. In his absence, however, three months after the convention had begun, the other countries gave in to the absent negotiator's wishes and signed the second international agreement. The agreement provided such innovations as the adoption of an international record-keeping and licensing system, import and export regulations, a statistical reporting method and bureau, and a supervisory Permanent Central Board that would work independently within the League of Nations.

Porter never signed the agreement because it did not include the American principles he fought for. He was on a ship sailing home when he received a wire stating that the conference had agreed only in part to his proposals and had disagreed with his two basic concepts: that if the purpose of the first convention at The Hague was to be achieved, it must be recognized that the use of opium products for anything other than scientific purposes was not legitimate; and that to prevent the illegal abuse of the products, it was necessary to control production of raw opium to ensure that no surplus would be available for nonscientific purposes.

However, Porter did not give up his constant preaching for a narcotics law with real teeth in it, a comprehensive program to assist with the cure of addiction, and a separate bureau to enforce narcotics laws. "A billion dollars a year!" he shouted in a speech in the late 1920s, making the very sound of it ring like a box full of gold coins. "When you count its part in hospital, prison and asylum upkeep, trials in court, loss of earning capacity, maintenance of 'narcotics squads,' and destruction of property through robberies and holdups, drug addiction certainly costs the United States one billion dollars per annum."

While Porter's persistence in Washington made headlines, so did a scandal within the narcotics bureau in New York. A federal grand jury found "wholesale padding of records of the local federal narcotics office." And in what *The Nation* magazine called "the startling charge" and "unsavory exposure," the grand jury reported "evidence of gross dereliction and incompetence" on the part of agents assigned to New York. It also stated that there was proof that "at least one of the agents is a user of drugs." When the *New York Post* and *The New York Times* reported that a female agent was not only an addict but was known to have peddled drugs in Broadway nightclubs and to well-known personalities in the theatrical world, the three officials responsible for the leaks were transferred to Chicago, Kansas City, and Honolulu, but there was no investigation. Several months later, Deputy Narcotics Commissioner Levi Nutt's son, Rolland, and his son-in-law, L. P. Mattingly, were accused of doing business with drug trafficker Arnold Rothstein in Manhattan. Not only were Rolland Nutt and Mattingly discharged, but Levi Nutt was transferred to another department.

Harry J. Anslinger, who had served as chief of the Division of Foreign Control for the Treasury Department, was named to take Levi Nutt's place. For several years, Anslinger had coordinated narcotics intelligence between Treasury and the Department of State. In 1930, after Congress established the Federal Bureau of Narcotics, President Herbert Hoover appointed Anslinger Commissioner of Narcotics. A handsome, smartly dressed, soft-spoken bureaucratic leader, Anslinger worked diligently in Congress and received the power to place his agents in all U.S. ports of entry to harness the flow of narcotics. He told his people that the primary goal was to find the sources of supply and stop them, and he believed, he said, that most of these sources were outside the United States. During his more than thirty years as commissioner under four presidents he made an all-out effort to put into effect the international agreements the U.S. negotiators had proposed years earlier. He reached personal agreements with heads of more than twenty narcotics offices in foreign countries with whom he would exchange intelligence information. With such cooperation, seizures jumped dramatically from 3,440 ounces of morphine in 1929 to 26,492 in 1930. With British and French agencies forwarding information to Anslinger's people, narcotic agents in New York intercepted the *Ile de France* as it arrived and seized 51 pounds of heroin and 104.5 pounds of morphine. In another case, when agents received a reliable lead from Antwerp authorities, they boarded the steamship *Innoko* at the harbor in Hoboken, New Jersey and found 214 pounds of morphine.

With such facts being uncovered, including sterling silver syringes and diamond-studded pipes used by celebrities, the newspapers and radio commentators had a field day, to the delight of the law enforcement officials. However, when in the early 1930s a fear of what the press called "The Killer Drug: Marijuana" spread through the Southwest, the FBN was mixed in its reaction. First, the Bureau noted in its annual report, that the publicity "tends to magnify the extent of the problem and lends color to the inference that there is an alarming spread of the improper use of the drug, whereas the actual increase in such use may not be inordinately large." A year later, the Bureau wrote, "A disturbing development in quite a number of states is found in the apparently increasing use of marijuana by the younger element in the larger cities." At that time the illegal cigarettes could be purchased for fifteen cents each, three for fifty cents, and a small handful-sized sack for five dollars—thus the term "nickel bag."

One of the most interesting outlaws of the "terrible thirties" was a woman named Ignacia Jasso Gonzales, otherwise known as La Nacha, the queen of the border dope traffic. Hiding in the Sierra Madre mountains outside Guadalajara, she ran opium-derivative drugs across the border into California, Arizona, New Mexico, and Texas. A heavy-set, plain-looking woman of Aztec extraction, she worked dozens of Indians in the mountain fields where she cultivated and harvested raw opium from the poppies. In makeshift laboratories in the middle of the jungle environment, she and helpers from Guadalajara refined the opium into morphine and she supervised each step of the elaborate operation. She had large garages built next to the laboratories where she brought the latest models of U.S. automobiles. Mechanics built false gasoline tanks that fit under the trunks. Sacks of morphine were packed into the tanks which could be detached and unloaded when they reached their destination.

In an operation that took months to fabricate, a small bank of undercover FBN (Federal Bureau of Narcotics) agents posed as renegade druggists selling narcotics to Indians. They sold themselves so convincingly to Ignacia Jasso Gonzales that she took them on a guided tour of her fields, laboratories, and the garages. On their return to the states, the agents filed charges against Señora Gonzales and thirteen of her compatriots, several of whom were convicted when they were caught north of the border, but Mexico never granted extradition of La Nacha.

With the fighting in Europe closing down the Mediterranean traffic and the combat in the South Pacific halting traffic from Asia, the Federal Bureau of Narcotics concentrated primarily on gangland personalities during World War II. Louis "Lepke" Buchalter and his two partners traveled around the world six times, on each trip picking up pure heroin in Singapore, Hong Kong, or Turkey and always unloading in the United States, where their distribution connection was Lucky Luciano.

Luciano had first come to the attention of narcotics law enforcement officials in 1914 when he was arrested in New York for possessing heroin. He was sentenced to a year in Sing Sing, served six months, and arrived back on the streets of Manhattan as a lieutenant to a well-known Mafia boss. In 1924 Luciano was arrested for selling heroin, was questioned by federal agents, and was released because he had "cooperated." Before the scandal involving the son and son-in-law of the top official with the federal narcotics law enforcement agency surfaced, Luciano was arrested and charged with the murder of Arnold Rothstein, who had been accused of fixing the 1919 World Series. But after Luciano's name was connected with the high officials in government, the murder charges were dropped. He became the boss of syndicate activities in New York, distributed Lepke Buchalter's drugs, and was arrested and convicted in 1938. Seven years later he was paroled and deported to Italy where, until his death in 1962, law enforcement authorities believed he was the number one drug trafficker in the world.

As for Buchalter, he and thirty-one others were indicted for conspiracy to violate federal narcotics laws. After being sentenced to twelve years, Buchalter became a fugitive. A codefendant in the case was killed in upstate New York. While the investigation continued, several other bodies of persons in the case were discovered. Through famous radio commentator Walter Winchell, who among other newsmen had termed the Mafia's enforcement arm "Murder, Inc.," communication was established with Lepke Buchalter. The famed newscaster persuaded Buchalter to give himself up.

After he was in custody, a murder charge was brought by New York Attorney General Thomas E. Dewey against Buchalter, who became the first and only high-ranking member of the Mafia ever to be legally executed in the United States.

In retrospect, a 1939 report from FBN Agent Anthony Piazza appears prophetic, pointing out prosecutorial problems that took another four decades to alleviate. He wrote that "the Italian underworld is a well-organized and fully controlled syndicate with sectional bosses in absolute control of their immediate districts. These bosses control every racket within their jurisdiction. These bosses are also directly and indirectly concerned with the narcotics traffic. In order to secure a successful prosecution against the underworld bosses, it is essential to secure evidence against the major narcotic violators first, then develop the affiliations and the ties connecting them with the underworld bosses as coconspirators. Prior to the war, the bulk of narcotics smuggled into Brooklyn was handled by the Lepke mob, which dealt in 50- and 100-kilo lots. At the same time, however, individual Italian dealers were smuggling in heroin in 2- and 3-kilo lots. This latter group is now considered to be controlling narcotics." It was estimated by others that Lepke Buchalter's group had smuggled at least $10 million of heroin into the United States. After his execution and other mob connections were locked up, the heroin supply on the streets of New York and other major cities in the United States was reduced to a dribble.

During the war most opium derivatives went to meet the needs of the wounded in combat. Even a substitute pain-killer called Demerol was developed. However, after the war, the production was still high but the legitimate market low. For the first time in fifteen years the illegal importation of cocaine in 1947 showed a significant increase.

Although drug trafficking was growing, especially in metropolitan areas, the manpower of the FBN was about one-fourth the size it had been before the war. Its budget was about the same as it had been for years: less than $2 million a year. The FBN field force was no larger than the police departments of Hoboken, New Jersey, Cambridge, Massachusetts, or Sacramento, California, although it had been responsible for the arrest of about 10 percent of the inmates in federal penitentiaries.

In 1952, responding to a public that expressed shock over young people's attraction to drugs, the FBN published "Living Death: The Truth About Drug Addiction," showing that the first step to addiction was the first puff from a marijuana cigarette. Overstated, it was ridiculed by the sophisticated street juveniles of the cities, but FBN personnel could readily point to statistics showing sharp increases in addiction among the young and a lowering of the average age of drug offenders.

Unlike other federal law enforcement agencies, the Bureau of Narcotics worked closer and closer to organized crime. FBN agents knew that the syndicate or Mafia was synonymous with drug trafficking, particularly in the big city areas. And one of the most important busts of the decade was that of Mafia hit man Joseph Valachi who, in return for special consideration, told about some of the narcotics activity in and around New York City.

While serving a term in the Atlanta Federal Prison, his cell mate, Don Vito Genovese, one of the most powerful bosses in the New York Families, bestowed upon Valachi the ceremonial kiss of death because sources had told him Valachi had talked. Afraid for his life, Valachi beat another inmate to death with an iron pipe. With the promise of around-the-clock security, Valachi began telling of Cosa Nostra's smuggling. But the FBI, which had turned its back on organized crime because Director J. Edgar Hoover did not believe the Mafia

existed as a big-time operation, took over the questioning of
Valachi, who afterwards always denied that he personally dealt
in narcotics extensively. He told his biographer, Peter Maas,
that the Cosa Nostra feared the dogged harassment of the
Bureau of Narcotics. Maas wrote in *The Valachi Papers*, "Valachi's complaint against the bureau was that it did not play
fair, and it is doubtless true that, quite aside from him, some
of the bureau's tactics from time to time may have been ques-
tionable. A good deal of this is because no other agency had
dealt with the Cosa Nostra at such close quarters, known its
nature so well, or seen so much that it often could do so little
about."

In 1963, the year Valachi testified before the Subcommittee
on Organized Crime and Narcotics, a "special employee" of
the FBN was killed during a raid. When the man's widow sued,
the court ruled that she was entitled to compensation. As a
result, the term "informant" entered the drug enforcement
vocabulary.

One agent who hated the Mafia as much as any one individual was Sicilian-born Charles Siragusa, who worked the
neighborhoods of New York undercover during the early forties. Because the Mafia had killed his grandfather when he
was a child, Siragusa worked doggedly to put an end to the
organization's stranglehold on American crime and especially
narcotics. An adventuresome and wily lawman, Siragusa was
an Office of Strategic Services agent in Italy during World War
II, when he met Vito Genovese for the first time. The Mafia
boss was in jail in Italy awaiting deportation back to the United
States after having run a black market dope racket with a
laboratory where heroin was manufactured legally during the
war. After the war, when the Mafia and other money hungry
gangsters began utilizing the extra supply of narcotics, Siragusa was assigned by FBN Commissioner Anslinger to travel
back and forth between the United States and Italy as a go-
between in a concentrated attempt to stop the drug flow. And
after the 1950 and 1951 meetings of the Commission on Nar-

cotics Drugs of the United Nations, when many foreign countries agreed to cooperate, Anslinger named Siragusa as the permanent chief of the foreign office. He set up operations in the U.S. Embassy in Rome with branch offices in France, Lebanon, Turkey, Malaysia, Thailand, Hong Kong, and Mexico with fourteen agents around the world.

In January of 1959, Siragusa and other FBN agents cheered Fidel Castro's takeover of Cuba because, he wrote in his autobiography, "Here at last was our chance to chase the diehard corps of international dope peddlers from Cuba, an operating base less than 100 miles from our shores." Siragusa became an intermediary with the higher-ups in the new Cuban government, carried with him to Havana a list of known mobsters who had been living in Cuba, and asked that these figures be extradited to the United States. They included Meyer Lansky, who had been a close friend of Lucky Luciano and who had operated casino gambling and cocaine trafficking from Cuba; Santos Trafficante, a Tampa, Florida, boss of the Mafia who had escaped from the United States to avoid service of a subpoena in connection with the shooting death of Albert Anastasia, who had been fingered as a chief executioner of Murder, Inc.; and Giuseppe Catalanotte, aka Cock-Eyed Joe, a Detroit Mafia boss who had been one of the first to recognize the financial profits of cocaine. According to Siragusa, Cuba was the prime terminal for cocaine traffic. "In the first years after World War II," he wrote, "cocaine, otherwise known as 'coke' or 'snow,' had been practically unheard of in the New York and Chicago underworlds. But in 1948, while I was still working out of our New York office, narcotics agents began seizing sizable quantities of the illicit drug. Increasingly large amounts were being sold by dope pushers, especially in the Puerto Rican section of upper Manhattan." He added, "Cocaine went for a price; and because the price was right, everyone wanted to get into the act—smugglers, dope addicts, and gangsters. Even a Peruvian politician smuggled cocaine under protection of his diplomatic passport, aboard a Navy vessel. And all the while the traffic between the United States and Cuba was building up."

According to Siragusa, Castro lent a deaf ear to his proposals, more cocaine than ever began slipping through Cuba and into the United States, and none of the known gangsters was deported.

At the end of Siragusa's eight years as a foreign agent for the FBN, he and his team had seized almost five tons of heroin, opium, morphine base, hashish, and cocaine. And they had arrested 750 persons.

Despite gargantuan efforts from agents like Siragusa, the flow of illegal drugs from foreign countries was far from stopped. As a matter of fact, the flow not only increased but young people, protesting an unpopular war in Vietnam and shaking their fists in the faces of parents and other adult authority figures, learned to make new narcotics by combining chemicals in the simplest of laboratory facilities. So-called mind-expanding or hallucinogenic drugs, such as LSD and PCP, became popular. Long-haired teenagers stood on big city street corners like Haight-Ashbury in San Francisco and openly smoked marijuana, which they called grass or pot. Rock festivals provided open-air symposiums where thousands joined in pot-smoking rituals. Disgusted by the happenings, President Richard Nixon pushed for revision of the laws to cure what he called "the drug menace that is rising like a sickness in our land." With Attorney General John Mitchell mapping the plans, the Comprehensive Drug Abuse Prevention and Control Act was passed in 1970, replacing old legislation that had been the law for more than half a century. The enforcement provisions, known as the Controlled Substance Act, no longer were based on the tax collecting arm of government but on the authority of Congress to regulate interstate commerce. Among its inclusions to strengthen law enforcement was the power to break and enter dwellings at any time during the day or night under certain conditions. This no-knock provision was hotly debated and became the subject of contro-

versy after April of 1973 when agents of the Office of Drug
Abuse Law Enforcement broke into homes in Collinsville and
Edwardsville, Illinois. The occupants, who later claimed to be
victims of the overreactions of the narcotics agents whom they
said were armed and dressed as hippies, were given front page
headlines across the nation. The White House, which had been
taking a publicity beating because of the mounting discontent
over the Watergate burglary and a possible cover-up from the
highest office in the country, saw the incidents as a way to
shift the attention of the press. The men in the know—John
Ehrlichman and Egil Krogh and Ronald Ziegler—knew *The
Washington Post, The Los Angeles Times*, CBS, and other
news organizations they considered liberal would jump on the
Collinsville happening with all their journalistic power. And
they did. One couple posed for reporters and cameras on their
front porch. The pathetic-looking woman claimed that she
was held at gunpoint while dressed only in a thin and revealing
nightgown. Another couple told a heartrending story about
how these federal agents from St. Louis kept the husband of
a woman crippled from a back injury from going to her aid
after she fell to the floor. They said the agents pointed a rifle
at the couple's son when he attempted to telephone for help;
then the agents searched the house and found nothing incriminating.

The agents involved in what was termed "a tragic fiasco"
by White House sources were told to keep quiet, issue no
statements, make no comments, while the so-called victims
were continuously interviewed by the press. Dick Cavett flew
the families to New York, interviewed them on nationwide
television, and *Time* and *Newsweek* carried stories and
photos.

In the White House, G. Gordon Liddy and Howard Hunt
suggested through Charles Colson that Nixon capitalize on
the situation. Now was the time to move, the espionage and
sabotage experts said, to create the kind of clandestine drug
enforcement organization they had always dreamed of: an in-

dependent super agency with ultimate authority in stopping the ever increasing danger of drug smuggling and distribution.

The President declared an "all-out global war on the drug menace" and asked Congress to consolidate all antidrug forces. Other politicians, including U.S. Senator Charles H. Percy of Illinois, who held public hearings of his Permanent Subcommittee on Investigations with the "victims" testifying about their terrible treatment from the agents, got into the picture.

It was stated time and again in editorials that a new type of law enforcement group was needed to handle the gigantic drug problem facing the nation, and each time Collinsville was used as the prime reason. Pointing to the evidence and insisting that he had come up with the right tool, Nixon approved the formation of the Drug Enforcement Administration (DEA) on July 1, 1973.

The superagency Nixon had longed for as an investigative tool, whose strength he could use for domestic surveillance, was at last in existence. The DEA would have given him such an organization with undercover authority for wiretaps, no-knock warrants, several thousand well-trained agents from Customs, FBI, CIA, IRS, and other agencies, as well as a small separate branch to work directly under the orders of White House executives Ehrlichman and Krogh. But both of these palace guards fell with Watergate, and Nixon flew westward after resigning.

Before their fall, they put into operation a prosecution of the drug agents who had entered the houses in Collinsville and Edwardsville in southwestern Illinois. "We entered those houses because the people were known drug suspects, we had information on them longer than your arm, and we were doing our jobs," recalled one of the eleven agents who were finally indicted by a federal grand jury in Alton, Illinois, after lawyers from the Civil Rights Division of the Justice Department were sent to the Midwest with specific orders to indict and convict the agents involved.

The government attorneys paraded witness after witness

before two grand juries that reported there was not enough evidence to indict. When the third grand jury was impaneled, the U.S. attorneys went to prison to find witnesses to testify against the agents. Men who had been sent to prison because of evidence collected by the agents who were being charged were allowed to tell the jurors what they thought of the cops. But the jurors had no knowledge that the witnesses were actually convicts.

When St. Louis agent in charge, Ed Irvin, sent word back to Washington that his agents were being railroaded by government people, he was suspended for thirty days, demoted, and transferred to Chicago.

When the indictment came down against all eleven agents, U.S. Attorney Donald McKay refused to sign it and stated that it should have been brought against the "victims." But the specially appointed government lawyers continued with their case.

During the trial in Alton in March and April of 1974, U.S. District Judge Omer Poos, an elderly magistrate, continually called the defendants the prosecution and the prosecution the defense. All defendants were exonerated by the jury which stated that, in their estimation, the prosecution's witnesses should have been on trial rather than the police. The jurors apologized to the agents for having to endure the hardship of such a trial.

In the years after the trial, the agents who were tried and found innocent proved themselves time and again to be proud carriers of their DEA badges. Ed Irvin, the agent in charge, who had been moved to Chicago because he tried to defend his men, was brought back to St. Louis and became the leader of Operation Gateway that arrested and convicted more than 150 persons in one of the largest drug-smuggling organizations ever to be busted in the United States. By his side during the entire investigation, as intelligence analyst, keeping track of the complex maneuverings throughout the Midwest and

Southeast, was one of the eleven, Dennis Moriarty.

Both Irvin and Moriarty played significant roles in the breakup of this major gang of smugglers. For his part, Irvin was presented the highest award the DEA offers for duty performed by an officer. And Moriarty, who continued to work on cases involving The Company—which consumed the energy of all of the police in Operation Gateway—was told by the Justice Department that the government could not and would not pay for his and the other agents' legal expenses, although they were found innocent of all charges.

The DEA endured. For nearly a decade the huge bureaucratic agency fought the drug wars side by side with state and local police. In 1981, after President Ronald Reagan spoke out against "the worst enemy of the United States: the uncontrolled trafficking of illegal drugs," Attorney General William French Smith made a move he said would help in the enforcement. He gave the Federal Bureau of Investigation and the DEA "concurrent jurisdiction" in federal drug cases, and sources high up in the DEA said that "feathers were ruffled by the decision to divide the authority and the responsibility." It appeared to some that President Reagan and Attorney General Smith were turning back the clock. During the ten years of its existence, the DEA had fought the dope wars with vigor and single-mindedness.

For the public, FBI Director William H. Webster, to whom the DEA was ordered to report, stated, "I consider drug trafficking to be the most serious problem facing law enforcement in the United States. No other area of law enforcement calls for a more concerted effort at all levels than our efforts to rid this nation of the scourge of narcotics and drug abuse." It was Webster's contention that his 7,800 agents stationed at 500 locations throughout the United States would add considerably to the DEA's efforts. "The FBI and DEA must lock arms in a true alliance and step out together to lead in the efforts to solve this country's most difficult and important crime problem. Because effective law enforcement is the twin brother of national security, we cannot, we must not, and we will not fail," he added.

His rhetoric, however, did not stand up under scrutiny. When Justice Department personnel out in the field, assistants to U.S. Attorneys, Assistant Attorneys, Generals, and other prosecutors, were questioned, they said that DEA, Customs, and Internal Revenue agents, working with FBI agents, seldom were able to work together because of conflicting regulations handed down by the bureaucratic leaders within the various departments. Assistant U.S. Attorney Jay Ethington for the northern district of Texas told the Senate Subcommittee on Investigations that cooperation was needed among agencies. "The way it works now is the Drug Enforcement Administration would disclose to an Internal Revenue Service agent information in my office regarding a narcotics trafficker. That information would go up through the channels, back down through the channels, and two years later that same IRS agent would come in to me and say, 'I have this case.' We had already heard about it two years ago. It is the same information. It just has to go through the channels and back down again. It is unworkable. By that time, the narcotics trafficker is in the penitentiary, his assets have been disposed of, and the case is over with." According to Ethington, an IRS agent has been sitting on one side of his desk and a DEA agent on the other, "and they are both working on the same trafficker or violator. If the IRS agent is to tell me anything about the case, the DEA agent must leave the room because IRS cannot disclose to the DEA agent. In the execution of a search warrant in this case in the lawyer's office, an IRS agent was present and gathered information, evidence, documents, in the law office. Simultaneously, a DEA agent was going through the same file cabinet. The IRS agent could not tell the DEA agent what he found."

Because of this untenable situation, which in Ethington's words put the DEA agent in the predicament where he "doesn't know whether to come to the office with wingtips on and look like an FBI agent or wear his cowboy boots and try to work undercover," the Reagan administration made the change to place DEA under the FBI. However, according to some of the agents themselves, the situation has worsened instead of becoming better. "Things have become more complicated than before," said a DEA agent in Denver, Colorado. "We are now DEA-FBI agents. We have more money. We have the tie-in with the Organized Crime Information System, but it was always available to us if we wanted to ask the FBI for it. Now we just have another bureaucracy as our umbrella cover between us and the Justice Department, we have to go through so many more people, and way up on top there must be somebody who can make decisions. We—the people who fight to try to keep the streets and the schoolyards and the neighborhoods clean of drugs—have always been the stepchildren of law enforcement. We have always had to beg for whatever handouts they wanted to hand down to us. It's true on the state side, it's true on the federal side, and I'm told it's true with the international guys. There is one truth: it costs money to clean up a drug source; it can't be done for peanuts."

Today, more than ever before in history, because there are more people with more money and a more sophisticated system of communication and transportation, drugs are accessible to the average citizen. Not long ago, only the very rich traveled on transcontinental flights. Today millions of tourists on tight budgets whiz back and forth across the seas on multi-engined jets. It was easier to spot the organized crime figure as late as the 1960s. Today the man down the street who owns an import-export antique store or jewelry salon or travel agency can come into contact with drug dealers in foreign countries, and getting into the business is a very real possibility and temptation for him.

BOOK TWO:

THE COMPANY: OPERATION GATEWAY

ORGANIZATION CHART
THE COMPANY

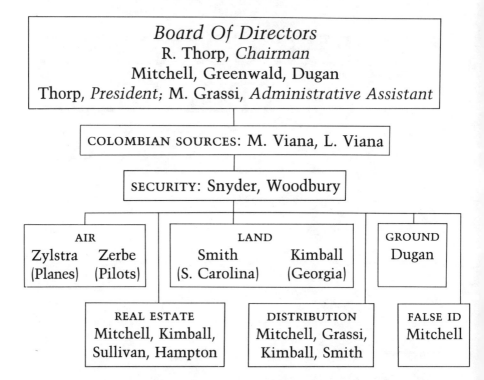

Board Of Directors
R. Thorp, *Chairman*
Mitchell, Greenwald, Dugan
Thorp, *President*; M. Grassi, *Administrative Assistant*

COLOMBIAN SOURCES: M. Viana, L. Viana

SECURITY: Snyder, Woodbury

AIR		LAND		GROUND
Zylstra	Zerbe	Smith	Kimball	Dugan
(Planes)	(Pilots)	(S. Carolina)	(Georgia)	

REAL ESTATE	DISTRIBUTION	FALSE ID
Mitchell, Kimball, Sullivan, Hampton	Mitchell, Grassi, Kimball, Smith	Mitchell

In the organization chart DEA Intelligence Analyst Dennis Moriarty drew to show the extent of involvement of the 200-plus members of The Company, these managers had many others listed beneath them for various duties.

Chapter One
The Beginning

Alton is a quiet, lazy town of about 40,000 nestled high on a bluff overlooking a wide expanse of the Mississippi River in the industrial valley of southwest Illinois. At first glance it appears an unlikely birthplace for the largest drug-smuggling operation ever to be broken by the investigative powers of the Drug Enforcement Administration and the prosecutorial arm of the U.S. Department of Justice.

As you walk down the sidewalk above Front Street that parallels the contour of the river's banks, you look down at the barge making its way slowly through the locks. Passing the ancient home of the *Alton Telegraph* and several antique shops in old street-front buildings, the visitor wets his whistle in a place that succinctly reads COLD BEVERAGES in patriotic red, white, and blue above the double doorway. Inside the typical dark and seedy bar, which still smells of last night's brew and yesterday's cigarettes, a scantily clad hard-faced barmaid draws a glass of draught Bud. When asked about some of the men who were from this area and who got rich from smuggling ton after ton of marijuana from South America, she says, "Yeah, I knew 'em." And just as a pony-sized Harley-Davidson squeals loudly as it speeds onto the street outside, she adds, straight-faced, "They were wild, man."

It was not far from here: down the hill to the tallest, most imposing structure in town, the huge Peavy Flour Mill, and then north on Piasa Street, to an unassuming tudor front with a small wooden sign reading simply TONY'S. That was where it all started.

Tony's spaghetti house was where, in March of 1976, a quartet of Illinois natives sat down and planned the beginnings of an organization which would come to be called The Company. The founders of The Company talked positively about a great economic future for their business venture.

Already the leader of the group and a seasoned drug trafficker was twenty-nine-year-old, baby-faced, hazel-eyed, slight Richard Dial Thorp, a veteran of Vietnam and a native of nearby Wood River. Rick knew the area and he knew the people, and with a great deal of thought he sought them out and arranged the clandestine meeting around a table in the restaurant. Thorp knew that the area was well suited to be the capital of a drug empire because of its basic rural setting both in Illinois and Missouri and because it was relatively close to heavily populated urban areas such as St. Louis, Chicago, and Indianapolis. Also, the interstate highways from east to west crossed near here, providing a gateway between the country's two major regions.

At the time of the first meeting at Tony's, Thorp, who had first dealt in dope in the jungles of South Vietnam where he served as a helicopter gunner, expressed his dream of making billions of dollars through the business of smuggling cannibis from South America into the United States. He had already lined his pockets with what he termed "chicken feed." Since November 20, 1975, he had been listed as a fugitive by federal authorities when he failed to show up for trial in Georgia on charges of conspiracy to dispense marijuana. Since then he had continued to operate openly, living under various aliases. He had become dedicated to the proposition of "doing it big and doing it right," he told the men who were destined to become his partners.

Looking at them with his powerful eyes that at first appeared almost feminine with their narrow almond shape, Thorp said, "I have connections in South America. I have worked on this plan for a long while. I've gotten in with someone who can furnish us with all of the marijuana we can transport and sell. These people are number one producers. I know them to be good people. I've checked 'em out, and I will continue to make sure they are our people. We have to always be on top of security. If we cannot trust our own people, it will be impossible to deal with them; and we have to make sure that they know we are checking up on them all the time."

The others nodded. One suggested that they use polygraph tests periodically, the way many major companies legitimately check out their employees for security purposes.

Thorp liked the idea.

He continued, "I have also made connections with people who will be able to furnish us—for a price and for a piece of the action—big airplanes capable of flying from here to South America, pick up a load of number one grade grass, and return to a given point. It will take thoughtful brain power, much expertise, and strong leadership. But I think we will be able to carry out everything. We all look like top leadership to me."

With Rick was one of his best friends from days at East Alton-Wood River High School. James Dugan, a former teammate, now crippled, had wrestled and played football with Thorp in high school where a friend remembered them as "good, decent, middle-class kids, full of energy, well liked by almost everybody, and generally the kind of guys you would expect to succeed. They had good heads, intelligent without being bookish, and they were very patriotically oriented. When they went off to the service, they really meant it. They were all for fighting in Vietnam." A once handsome brown-haired and mustachioed young man who now wore a constant pained expression because of his multiple injuries in Vietnam, Jim Dugan in his own way was as bright as Rick, the leader. Dugan was a hero after returning home a paraplegic following a land mine explosion that ripped off his legs, hammered his eardrums to partial destruction, and injured much of his internal anatomy only twenty days before his twentieth birthday. He said later he didn't feel like a hero. When Dugan returned, he worked long hours at rehabilitation, became a tough and hardened vet who honed his upper body muscles and displayed pride in being able to perform feats such as climbing up and down stairs on his hands, using his arms as legs. Dugan, despite his being in a wheelchair, worked with returning soldiers at the Alton Veterans Service Center. "At first he put a lot of energy into his work, but it is very time-consuming and often the rewards just aren't there on a day-to-day basis. His patience was short, he expected much and received little, and he turned sour when his projects did not work out right," the friend continued.

When he was twenty-five, Dugan decided to use his hero's status in an attempt to catapult himself into politics. He ran for mayor of East Alton, a highly industrialized town of about 7,000, but he quickly discovered it took more than heavy war injuries to become a successful vote getter. Dugan was defeated soundly at the polls.

After he went to Texas to visit a high school sweetheart, Dugan enrolled in an air control traffic managing course, became a security dispatcher at Houston's Intercontinental Airport, and then married the girl friend in 1970.

Rick Thorp outlined the program he had in mind for The Company, telling them: "Dugan is my main man. Every company must have a strong organization, and Dugan will be the number two man in charge. He's exactly what we need." However, as they were to discover in the next few months, Thorp changed his number two man but kept Dugan in top management.

Not only was Dugan an air control traffic manager and a skilled electronics man, he was tough inside and out. He had a strength that belied his crippled body and showed through in his personality. Dugan would be their radioman, their communications expert, in charge of bringing airplanes to their destinations and off-loading the goods from planes to trucks, Thorp said.

The third member of the group and the oldest, forty-five-year-old James Anderson Mitchell, a handsome supervisor of sales with the Olin Corporation of East Alton, listened intently as Thorp gave a detailed outline of his duties with The Company. "You'll be one of the top board members with the rest of us, Jimmy," he said. "And your talents will be necessary for the success of our operation."

Mitchell ran his long fingers through his brown wavy hair and then fingered the edges of his neatly trimmed mustache while he listened.

Thorp said that Mitchell's duties would entail the providing of real estate and distribution centers for The Company. He would purchase rural airports in areas where planes could land without drawing suspicion from neighbors and/or law enforcement.

Because he was more mature than the others and had an established reputation in the community, Thorp stated, Mitchell would be perfect as The Company's warehouser, controller, and general marketing expert. Besides, he had experience with Olin, where he had worked since 1953 and where he was paid a decent 1976 salary of $20,000 a year. Thorp suggested he remain on the Olin payroll for a while to avoid suspicion.

The six-foot two-inch Mitchell, who considered himself a swinger, was ready to make some big money. According to Don Matteson, narcotics analyst for the Illinois Department of Criminal Investigation, Mitchell "was paid well, but he also began to incur other expenses about the time he got involved with The Company. He had begun wandering away from home. He liked the young girls, which was why he got into trouble with his wife and was divorced. And when you start associating with the kind of young people Mitchell was, you tend to pick up their habits."

Matteson continued, "Mitchell was growing marijuana himself, not at his Brighton farm but at a place near Foster, Illinois. The money was good, but he found out that growing it was a lot of hard work and there was no insurance that somebody wouldn't rip him off."

Mitchell's answer, "Count me in," was a solid agreement to being in the top leadership of The Company. He was ready to get started making big-time loot.

When Rick Thorp got around to Wilbur Lee Smith, he too was eager. He wanted to get his hands on the big bucks Thorp had been describing.

Smith had been a truck driver most of his thirty-eight years. He knew trucks and transportation backwards and forwards. He knew the highways, he knew drivers, and he knew how to deliver a load from point A to point B. And he also knew how to buy a truck for the best price, where to go to find the best deals, and how to avoid suspicion in purchasing trucks and trailers. It was as simple as that.

Smith was an uncomplicated individual, an Illinois native like the others, a rough-hewn buccaneer with shaggy longish brown hair and steel-blue eyes and a slightly off-center mustache. Like Mitchell, he liked a good time with the ladies, was partial to late-night parties, and had never made enough money to enjoy himself the way he would have liked.

Within the next several weeks the quartet met at Tony's two more times. They talked about their venture, ate well, and appeared satisfied with the way things were going.

By the end of March, Mitchell reported having traveled to Kansas City, where he had used a fictitious name in approaching a businessman with the offer to purchase an airport near Monett, Missouri. Mitchell offered $135,000 for Friend Air Park, and the owner said he would need $35,000 down payment. Mitchell opened his briefcase, gave the man $20,000 in five-dollar, ten-dollar, fifty-dollar, and one-hundred-dollar bills. Mitchell, who refused to tell the man where he lived but offered a telephone number in the Illinois area, said that he would bring the other $15,000 on his next trip to Kansas City.

Thorp agreed that it was a job well done. More money would be furnished.

Two weeks later, Mitchell returned to Kansas City with $15,000 in cash and agreed to pay $25,000 every six months until the mortgage was paid off.

In the meantime, Smith began buying and making deals to lease trucks, Dugan oversaw the outfitting of a super-grade command van in which he had the most powerful and up-to-date electronics equipment installed, and Thorp's group spread across the country in search of pilots, planes, and information.

Because he had been in the business before, Thorp was familiar with the problems involved in rounding up the necessary people, making sure they were the *right* kind of people for this work, and keeping them straight once they had been hired.

"If they want to leave after one job, let's make sure they leave," Dugan put in during one of the initial meetings.

The others glanced at him. His face was completely open. "I mean, they should be paid and told, 'Go!' We shouldn't deal with 'em if they want to leave. That's it. Scram. And if they don't do the job properly, the same thing. We don't want any screw-ups in this thing."

The others agreed.

According to members of The Company, Rick Thorp, whom they also knew as Lee McDade, knew exactly what he was doing. During the following months, Thorp kept The Company on hold. Elsewhere, however, Thorp was still doing business. He brought The Company along slowly. "Money came in like you wouldn't believe, only not in the quantity that it poured in later. He was still bringing in boats on the west coast of Florida and up in the Florida panhandle and even north of Brownsville, Texas, and we were distributing the drugs through the Alton, St. Louis, Indianapolis, Chicago quadrangle. We did not yet have New York and Washington the way we did later, and just a little of the stuff drifted in down around Houston and Dallas. We were doing so well that every two or three days our pilots, Ed Goldberg, Jack Goldman, Ted Powell, and Ted's girl friend, Kayelynne Ryan, flew money to the Bahamas. On several trips Powell and Kaye flew together to Bimini and George Town on Cayman. It was not until November that we started in real heavy on the big plane trips, and before that Billy Greenwald and Michael Grassi got involved very high up in the organization. They came in right under Thorp with Grassi taking second place in the overall structure," recalled an early participant.

Rick Thorp had known Michael John Grassi for a long time. He was lean, hard, and tough. A clothes horse with thick, longish brown hair, olive complexion, and big blue eyes that attracted the women, Grassi was also known for his brains. He was a confidence man of the old school, knew how to live on his wits, and needed a job in the underworld because he had been in trouble with the law for several years.

On January 2, 1975, he and several cohorts, all officers in Interstate Syndications Inc., were charged with land fraud by the U.S. Securities Exchange Commission. In April of 1977, he and three associates were indicted in federal court in Tampa, Florida, for interstate transportation of obscene materials. Finally, on June 16, 1978, while he was deeply involved in illegal activities of The Company, he was found guilty on eleven counts of conspiracy to transport obscene material across state lines. When he started with The Company Grassi was out on an appeal bond and later won the case in appellate court.

"Mike Grassi was the best talker in The Company," said a fellow member. "His words were mesmerizing. He was a born salesman, somebody who was a natural leader, and after you got to know him you would follow him blindly into a burning building if he asked you to."

Even the DEA agents who ultimately arrested Grassi liked him. "When we began interrogation sessions, going over the various activities of The Company during all the years it operated successfully, we knew that Michael Grassi was a high calibre individual who could succeed in anything he really wanted to do," said DEA Intelligence Analyst Dennis R. Moriarty, who questioned Grassi for hours during the final

phases of Operation Gateway, the DEA's name for the ultimate overall investigation of The Company. "When you listened to Grassi, you thought what a shame it was that he had
not used his talents and energy and fantastic personality on
something legitimate. If he had, he would have been a millionaire—probably many times over," Moriarty said.

Another member of The Company agreed with the assess-
ments but added, "He could talk with a platinum tongue. He
was great if you didn't look past his words. But Mike's one
big weakness was that he didn't know the truth from lying.
He'd rather lie than tell the truth. He was always the biggest,
the best, the finest, had the most, could do anything, and had
done everything. If you pushed him for the truth about the
money situation in The Company, he'd lie. I don't think he
ever once really told us the truth about how much money we
had, or how many trips successfully came into this country;
he kept a tight hold on the money, and he would never open
up.

"He was for sure a romantic guy. The women'd go straight
for him. We'd be in a bar in Atlanta without our women, and
he'd look around over his shoulder and pick out the best-
looking girl in the joint, and I guess he'd wink or something,
because the girl would come straight over. He had those big,
dark-blue, romantic eyes; even my wife and daughters have
told me he was the sexiest man they have ever seen."

He was the new man Rick Thorp tapped to be his second
in command—bookkeeper, accountant, treasurer, administrative assistant, and/or executive vice president. He knew the
elements of power, and he put them to work for The Company,
wheeling and dealing, making sure everyone was paid adequate sums for the jobs they performed and generally keeping
the personnel happy. According to most of those who worked
with him, he did his job professionally. A pilot, later serving
time in a federal prison in Florida, said, "Mike Grassi would
have made a great manager of a large airport like Atlanta
International or O'Hare. He had the kind of mind that could

switch from one to another of a dozen or more problems, still keeping track of what went before, and he always dealt with people fairly. As to the charge that he was a liar, I'd say he tended to exaggerate in his personal life. But we're talking about over a drink in a dark bar. He could fight harder, stay up later, add a longer column of figures, and he'd pat you on the back and make you believe you could do it too. That's just plain leadership ability, whether you're in a smuggling deal or running General Motors."

Several years later, Mike Grassi assessed his role with The Company as being "the business manager for a major narcotics operation known as The Company. As such, I kept books and records and shared in the profits of most of its marijuana smuggling operations.

"When I first began with The Company, I sold marijuana on a consignment basis. In 1976, I sold several hundred pounds, and in 1977 I sold between 6,000 and 8,000 pounds. I tried to net approximately $15 per pound and could sell approximately 1,000 pounds in a week which netted me approximately $15,000 a week profit, clear. My customers were friends or mature people whom I knew and trusted and went to school with. I usually transported marijuana in the trunk of cars or in small trucks.

"The president [Thorp] and I structured The Company along corporate lines. I handled much of the money for The Company, helped coordinate its logistics on many of the trips and basically handled all of The Company's financial records. I shared in the profits of many of the thirty-seven loads with which I was involved and otherwise made $15,000 a load. The board of directors consisted of the major decision-makers in The Company, though the president had the final say.

"Our Colombian connections handled all communications with the Colombian suppliers. Our staff people handled false identifications, electronic surveillance and countersurveillance equipment, money washing activities in the Caribbean, internal security and polygraph operations. We had crew chiefs who handled air operations, landing operations, land transportation, marijuana storage and distribution.

"Our employees were mostly family men and legitimate businessmen who held regular jobs.

"The Company had extensive assets which we either owned, leased, or used. We had a fleet of planes ranking from Cessnas to DC-7s. We used all types of trucks, vans, and automobiles to haul with in order to distribute the marijuana. Our truck fleet included fuel tanker trucks, semitractor trailers, and ten-ton box trucks.

"We had an extensive network of warehouses throughout the South and Midwest, most of which we leased. Most of our landing strips we also leased. We also surreptitiously used a small public airstrip on several occasions," Grassi said.

Another top man brought into The Company by Thorp near the beginning was Billy Greenwald, a twenty-two-year-old drug-smuggling whiz kid when The Company was formed. Out of his headquarters at his home in Stuart, Florida, a small town on the east coast north of Palm Beach, he had been known by insiders to operate a smuggling business for at least two years. Greenwald had had several boats which he captained or sent out with other people doing the pickups. When large mother ships brought huge loads in from South America, ran the eastern coastline from Miami to Jacksonville, moving slowly just outside the seven-mile U.S. jurisdiction, Greenwald and others ferried their smaller boats out, took loads, returned them to the shore, and sold directly to distributors from the northern metropolitan areas.

"It was definite that Greenwald was already a wealthy young man when he made connections with The Company," recalled an early Company associate. "Shortly after the organization was formed in Alton, Billy Greenwald came aboard, and everybody knew that he was a member of the board of directors. He put money up for some of the first loads, and through his connections with Marvin Zylstra in Fort Lauderdale, he put

Rick through to people in Colombia. It was fairly well known throughout The Company that by 1976 Greenwald wanted out of the baby-load boat business and into something more profitable."

Greenwald had lost more than one boatload of marijuana to pirates who lay in wait in the darkness of the small islands of the upper Bahamas. When his people went out and sought the mother ship, the pirates, who started their activities in the early 1970s when drug smuggling became the biggest business in the state of Florida, would wait until the boat was loaded. Then the pirates slipped in silently, overran the smugglers, shot, knifed, or drowned everyone on board, and usually stole the boat and the cache. They were ruthless, deadly, and totally without regard for human life. In these otherwise smooth, calm, beautiful waters off south Florida, they made what had seemingly been a nonviolent crime—drug smuggling—a heavy risk, a very violent, blood and guts type of criminal activity. By 1975, all smugglers in these waters carried knives and guns.

A young man who had worked the waters for what was termed square mackerel, Greenwald was well aware of the dangers by 1976. "I knew Billy Greenwald in those days," said another young man who had been arrested by DEA agents before the pirates got to him. "We were all the same out there on the water. Once one of our boats came on one of his back this side of Great Abaco, and before we knew it, two of our guys had fired into the dark at the Greenwald boat. We didn't know it was his boat. Our guys thought it was a pirate boat. That was how spooked we were. They shot in the dark, and they actually hit a man over there, wounding him in the shoulder. Everybody was dead silent for a few minutes, then this frantic call went out over the radio, and we picked it up, and we realized it was from the boat we had fired on. We answered them, pulled up alongside, and we were all very relieved to know we were just two smuggling boats out there running dark, trying to stay away from the feds from the shore and from the pirates in the islands. Damn! When I think back on it I wonder how any of us made it through all of it.

"Once early in the morning I was called by a buddy down to Fort Lauderdale. We had to go to a funeral home to identify a friend whom we knew also ran dope. He'd been doing it for three years at the time. We had talked about the pirates over beer, knowing they were an unknown entity out there in the night, like ghosts or something. When they pulled out that stainless steel drawer and we looked down on his face, seeing it smashed like it was a pecan smashed in a vice, I got sick. Man, it was awful! I stopped going out for several weeks after that, but I did go back to it, and then I got caught.

"I was never *that* close to Billy Greenwald, but I know the death rate and the loss rate out in the water had to take its toll on him just like it did all of the rest of us. I know that sometime in about 1976 he went with the big outfit they called The Company."

One of the first things the board of directors of The Company solidified after the organizational meetings at Tony's was the tightest possible security. Everybody in the group was required to pass a polygraph test administered by an expert. Thorp found Robert Jackson Snyder, a South Carolina native who lived in Lexington, Kentucky. A man with a reputable national reputation, Snyder had worked with a number of investigatory groups, including state attorney generals and district attorneys, and had been one of several lie detector examiners hired by the select subcommittee of the U.S. House of Representatives investigating the assassinations of President John Kennedy, Senator Robert Kennedy, and Dr. Martin Luther King, Jr.

Snyder not only tested most of the members of The Company but also their girl friends, always warning that if they talked about what they saw and heard concerning the organization, something terrible might happen to them.

After the security end was taken care of, Thorp flew to Florida to talk with a number of pilots. He had worked with some of them and names of others were given to him by his friend Marvin Zylstra in Fort Lauderdale.

Among the first to be hired were Edward James Goldberg, a native of New Jersey, Theodore Bruce Powell, who had moved south from Illinois, his girl friend, Kayelynne Ryan, and Jack A. Goldman, who lived in Miramar, Florida. All of the pilots were familiar with the Bahamas and the Caribbean.

A number of preliminary trips were made into the islands by the pilots. But marijuana was brought into the United States only in small quantities via airplane and by the mother ship method until late in 1976.

In November of 1976, after The Company had worked successfully on smaller loads for seven months and after a more or less novice pilot called Quaalude Bill made several unsuccessful attempts to bring marijuana back from Colombia, Goldberg made three quick trips into the Caribbean. On each, he returned the same day he left. In mid-November, he was sent to Colombia for the first of four big loads.

The ground crew was set up by Dugan at the Friend Air Park near Monett. Dugan also arranged for an alternate landing area at a rural strip near the Lake of the Ozarks. If law enforcement showed up at Friend, Dugan planned to send the approaching airplane to the secondary strip.

"Dugan was an electronics genius," said one of the first ground crew members. "He had developed an extra sense while he was in Vietnam. He knew the airwaves, radio frequencies, radar, and then he had this way of listening to things that were not really there. He like looked out into space at nothing in particular; you didn't see it, but he knew what it was.

"Dugan was also a taskmaster, and he started with a heavy hand on the very first load. He was very military. He took no bullshit. 'If you don't want to do it right, we don't need you,' was the way he looked at the entire organization; and he had that attitude about everybody from Rick down to me.

"Two nights before the first big shipment came in, we were staying at a motel near Springfield, and everybody was a little antsy. Dugan, with earphones on at a radio he had set up inside his room, said, 'Everything's going to be all right. I feel it in the air. We're getting good vibes back from South America. Everything's going just right down there.'

"On the next night he called us all in. I was one of the off-loaders. There were four of us, and there was a truck driver. He had us all stand around his bed while he pulled himself up and out of the wheelchair, perched on top of two pillows, and leaned over and took a toy truck out of a paper sack. He put it on the edge of the bed, heading toward the middle, then he took out a toy airplane, which he said represented the Lodestar that would be coming in later. He circled the middle of the bed, which he said was Friend Air Park, and then he let it land about two feet in front of the truck.

" 'At this point, you move!' Dugan barked. He looked up at the truck driver. 'Don't drive too fast or too slow. Just go about your business steady.'

" 'You,' he said, and he looked at us, 'will be in the truck and ready to go. As soon as the truck is here,' he stopped it next to the side of the plane, 'you guys will be moving. The quicker we unload, vacuum out the inside of the plane, and it takes off, the better off we are. As soon as the plane takes off and the goods are moved out by truck, we're home free.' "

Late that night, Dugan was at the controls in the fancy silver command van, bringing the plane in. He also guided the off-loading of twenty bales, each with Colombian written across the burlap wrapper, amounting to 1,100 pounds. It went as quickly and smoothly as the ground crew director had planned it on his motel bed.

The next two pilots who took planes to South America aborted their missions before picking up marijuana in Colombia. One made a quick pass over the field on the northeastern Guajira Peninsula that pointed like a sore thumb toward Puerto Rico across the Caribbean. Below he saw another airplane waiting and thought that it was DEA. He pulled up, headed toward Nicaragua, and radioed Dugan that he would wait another day before trying the trip again. On the following day he bought fuel in Managua that caused his plane to sputter and lose altitude over the blue-green water. This time he traveled past Colombia and landed on Trinidad where he refueled again and headed home. The next pilot panicked when two chase planes followed him into the airstrip on Guajira. He took on fuel, flew north, and didn't stop until he reached Tampa.

Thorp knew he had to find a super pilot. He scouted the east coast before his old friend and business acquaintance, Marvin Zylstra, owner and operator of Custom Air Limited in Florida, suggested Earl Richard Zerbe, who he said was "the best pilot I've seen on four continents and half the world."

Chapter Two
Super Pilot

Earl Richard Zerbe was sitting on ready. He never made much money, but he was a world-class pilot. He got his training flying crop dusters in Arkansas. He was one of that unique breed of daredevils who got up with the dawn, mounted a single-engine plane as if it were a wild bronco, and rode that creature until it was tamed. He knew the feeling of dropping low over a cotton or soybean field, hanging tough for hundreds of feet while unloading chemicals onto the fields, then teasing death by pulling back on the stick just in time to clear electrical wires or treetops.

"He knew airplanes like the back of his hand—even better," said Tom Kimball (see Foreword), who later worked with Zerbe. "He became a part of the plane. He and the plane operated together as one. I'd fly with him anywhere in the world as long as I knew he was at the wheel." Others expressed similar admiration for the man who in 1976 was flying freight for a company near Detroit, Michigan.

The five-foot nine-inch pilot had that gleam in his blue eyes common only to men who have seen death staring at them only seconds away. He also had a left leg that had been amputated nine inches below the knee; it happened in 1965 while he was parachuting from a biplane. He liked the old planes as well as the new and had sought to master them. While he was jumping from the plane, his foot caught in a cable. Luckily, he lived. And less than ten days after the foot was amputated he was flying again.

At the time Rick Thorp started searching for the best possible pilot for The Company, Zerbe was flying freight as he had been for a number of years. "We'd work our tails off for months, especially during the heavy season before Christmas; then around Christmas time every year they'd lay us off and we'd all be unemployed for several months. We went and stood in the unemployment lines just like anybody else," he remembered.

Through the years he kept in touch with Marvin Zylstra, with whom he had first flown near Pontiac, Michigan, in the late 1960s. "I called Marvin and said, 'Looks like I am going to get laid off again. Is there anything down there I can do?' " Zylstra was operating Custom Air Limited, an airplane sales company, in Fort Lauderdale. "I told him, 'I'm interested in making money,' and he said, 'A little money or a lot of money?' and I said, 'I want to make as much money as I can,' and he said, 'Well, if I come across anything I will call you back,' and later he did call me and said there were some people he thought I would like to meet," Zerbe said.

Zylstra sent him a ticket; he flew south and met with Billy Greenwald and Rick Thorp in Florida. They told him they were in the marijuana smuggling business, had brought some loads into the country, said they had an airplane, and asked if he could fly it. Zerbe assured them he could indeed fly the plane but was not sure he wanted to do something illegal.

Thorp threw out a figure: $15,000 for the first trip, more after that, when they saw he could do what they hired him to do.

Zerbe didn't immediately jump at the job, but said he would think about it and said he wanted to make sure the airplanes he would be piloting were in the best of shape. "I didn't want to fly junk all the way across the ocean to some foreign country and try to bring it back," he said.

"They said they would contact me, but asked if I would

take a polygraph test before going home and waiting for them, and I said, 'I'll be happy to,' " he remembered.

Zerbe stopped in Atlanta, went to a hotel, met with Bob Snyder, who administered the test, after which he "showed me the nature of the business and told me the consequences of what would happen if I talked about them after I was hired. He said he knew I had a family, and he made it plain to me that if they couldn't get me, they would get somebody. I fig- ured somebody means daughters, sons, mothers, brothers, or whatever. And, quite frankly, I believed him."

He flew home and waited. In about two weeks Ed Goldberg called and asked if Zerbe could meet him in Kansas City to look at an airplane.

Zerbe met the pilot from Fort Lauderdale. They took off from Kansas City and made two circles around the small air- port near Monett, Missouri, which Goldberg said would be the primary landing area for Zerbe's first trip.

During the flight over Oklahoma and Texas, Zerbe was able to determine quickly what repairs the plane—a medium-sized four-engine World War II style bomber converted by Lear for civilian use—needed to put it in top-notch shape.

"I never saw Richard Zerbe when he was not an absolute perfectionist when it came to planes," recalled Tom Kimball. "He might have risked his life dozens of times, but it wasn't in a bad plane. If he could, he would have it working perfectly before he left the ground. And, if it didn't work perfectly, he knew how to compensate for the sorry state some of the planes might have been in when he got them. He always insisted on the best mechanics and the best parts we could find."

They put down in Dallas where they left the plane for re- pairs. Zerbe received some money and was told to go home and wait again.

About one week later he received a second call from Ed Goldberg, this time telling him to meet in Dallas.

The repaired airplane checked out under Zerbe's minute inspection and the two flew it to Montgomery, Alabama, where

Goldberg again said there would be a delay.

"I was ready to go," Zerbe said. "The airplane was gassed. I wanted to get this thing on the road. But we let the airplane sit in Montgomery for another two weeks. Then we met back in Montgomery where Ed had all the book work, the approach plates and necessary navigational equipment, and we took off for the small clandestine strip in Colombia.

"We flew down to Colombia," he continued. "And we started looking for the strip that Ed said he knew right where it was. We flew by the strip, and I said, 'Is that it over there?' and he said, 'No, that's not it.'

"This was my first time in a foreign country like that doing what I was doing, so I didn't know what the procedure was.

"We flew probably fifteen to twenty miles south of the strip before he said, 'We've gone too far.' We turned around and came back right to the strip we went by the first time. He said, 'There was a fence across the strip,' and he added that they should be there to meet us with gas and with the marijuana and so forth, so we flew down the strip and there was no fence, but you could see where one started and one ended. So now we were flying around in a foreign country, made a pass at the strip, and we turned and landed.

"When we landed on the strip, there was nobody there. We didn't have enough gas to go anywhere. We had come all the way from Montgomery, probably 1,600 miles, and we didn't have enough gas to go anywhere."

They got out of the plane and walked up to a hacienda-type house where a Colombian stepped out looking surprised.

"Where is everybody?" they asked.

Zerbe spoke no Spanish and Goldberg very little.

The Colombian "indicated that he would get the people we were looking for," Zerbe said. "So we just sat down and waited, and this was some time in the afternoon.

"Well, darkness came and we still hadn't seen anybody of substance, hadn't seen any product or any gasoline or anything. And I am sitting there saying, 'You know, is this like it is all the time?' and he is going, 'I don't know, you know.' "

Goldberg had been on several trips to the Guajira Peninsula in northeast Colombia before. He had made at least one successful trip, bringing a load back to Monett, and one that had been aborted because of mechanical problems on the plane he was piloting.

"After dark, the fellow shows up in a Jeep," according to Zerbe. "He was completely drunk, and with him was a fine-looking little lady. He was the man that was supposed to load us and have petrol for us and everything was going to be all right, he said, no problems.

"Well, about three or four hours later, we still didn't have product or gas or anything like that. And they said they were going somewhere to find out what was going on, what was happening, and when we would receive what we were down there for.

"Before they left, we heard people in the jungle-type foliage cocking their guns, and I said, 'Wait a minute.'

"Then the army came out of the weeds. The man who was our contact talked to the commander of the army, and they chatted back and forth, and everybody seemed happy after that. The army left, and he again said he was going to leave but that he would leave a policeman behind to keep anybody from bothering us, that everything would be okay, no problem.

"It's about twelve o'clock at night and we don't have anywhere to sleep, so we decide we will sleep in the airplane.

"We were laying back up in the plane trying to sleep when all of a sudden the door opened and a fellow with a flashlight came in with a gun and said we were under arrest.

"I said, 'We have our policeman. What's the problem?' and they pulled us out of the airplane and put us on the ground. They were what they call F-2 down there, like our CIA, underground government troops. They were from Santa Marta, a little town right on the coast of Colombia.

"Well, they held us until almost daylight, and they put us in a Jeep, and at that time another vehicle came in and they started yelling and dispersing their people with guns and so forth to intercept the vehicle that was coming down the runway. I thought: 'We're going to have a gun fight right here,' but we didn't. It was somebody else coming.

"All of them just talked for a while, then they put us back into the Jeep and started heading for Santa Marta.

"Outside a little town we passed another Jeep, and both stopped and started talking to each other, and in the other Jeep was the head man and his lady friend again. I had heard her called Maria or Mary back at the landing strip.

"Well, they both stopped and started talking for about ten or fifteen minutes, yelling back and forth. Then each got in their Jeep and started to take off.

"I said, 'Wait a minute, Mary,' and Mary looked and said, 'Oh, the gringos,' and they got out and talked for another ten minutes.

"We got in the other Jeep with the head man and the lady. He took us back into the little town we had just come out of and hid us for a day. We were put up in hammocks in some little store and told that the pot would be there that night.

"Well, about eleven o'clock that night the product did finally show up and the gas did show up. We were supposed to pick up 4,000 pounds, but in actuality we got 2,300 pounds. It was loaded onto the Learstar through the back of the cabin, forty-six fifty-pound bales.

"We were in the center of the runway, halfway down, and I started the airplane up after we gassed and loaded and taxied back to the end. We turned around to take off, really not knowing what the situation was. We had picked up so much dust off the strip that I had to hold there for two or three minutes to let the dust settle.

"We were still not wanting anybody to see us, but we were making a lot of noise. We put down the landing lights and saw that we were still in a bank of dust. I knew that there were vehicles approximately halfway down the end of the runway. I didn't know whether they were off to the side or coming up the runway or what, so I felt I had to wait until the dust settled so I could get a view of the runway.

"I turned the lights back on and as far as the lights could see there was no more dust.

"We ran the engines up and proceeded on our takeoff. Shortly thereafter, we went right back into the dust cloud," he said.

At that point, Zerbe hit the Jato for a power-assisted takeoff, which he said, pushed them "like a rocket under the belly of the airplane, giving us another 600 horsepower thrust."

"So I hit it, and as I hit it, we gained air speed. And just as we lifted off I noticed that we passed a couple of trucks on the left-hand side. But we were then airborne and on our way."

The airstrip from which they soared was cut from the jungles on the western banks of the hills of the Guajira Peninsula. The Guajira is a very arid, dusty, and almost flat peninsula, ideal for constructing large airstrips. However, the hills seemed to rise in front of Zerbe from the inlet between Santa Marta and Barranquilla, and as he began to reach altitude, Zerbe looked down to see the darkening waters of the Caribbean spread out below.

He aimed due north toward the western side of Haiti, flew for several hours over the sea, cut between Haiti and Jamaica, circled northwestward around the eastern tip of Cuba, and headed directly for Great Inagua. He then followed the chain of islands to Florida.

About 100 miles off the Florida coast he let the plane down to low water, within 300 feet, to avoid Norad and air traffic control radar. The Norad or Air Defense Identification Zone was broken, according to Zerbe, when he dropped his speed to about 180 miles an hour until he made it into the interior. Using this basic evasion-type technique, he continued over Lake Okeechobee and then climbed back up to altitude as he came close to Okeechobee Airport to make the air traffic control personnel believe he had just left the airport in that area.

Zerbe then cut north across Montgomery, Birmingham, Memphis, and Fayetteville. At Fayetteville, he took an OMNI heading (to tell what direction under instrument flying he needed to travel in order to reach his destination) he had created because they could not contact towers for a heading, using it as an approach to airports in case of weather, low ceilings, and low visibility. "In this case, we made up our own [OMNI setting]. We came in and hit Fayetteville, and from Fayetteville we went up to Monett," he said.

The off-loaders worked quickly, efficiently, and within an hour the vacuumed airplane had taken off for an airport where it would remain until the next trip south. Zerbe was taken to Springfield from which he flew commercially to Michigan.

He waited nervously for his money. He had heard that many people who worked for smuggling organizations got ripped off after they did their jobs. He had been told he would receive his money as soon as the marijuana sold on the streets. Thorp had personally told him he had nothing to worry about. But he did worry. He knew he was completely in the hands of other people, and that was not a good feeling for a super pilot.

About two weeks later he was told to come to St. Louis and get his money. He left on the next flight out.

In a hotel near the Lambert International Airport Thorp gave him a small briefcase filled with $30,000. "It was more money than I had ever seen before," he said, and within a month he made another successful trip south.

During 1977 he flew nine missions to the jungles, returning to various locations, including Darlington, South Carolina, and Fitzgerald, Georgia, picked out by the president and board of directors of The Company. He put money in a number of banks. For the first time in his life he spent thousands of dollars on himself. He gave his girl friend presents. He drove a new car. And he invested in a business in Michigan.

In the middle of February in 1978, Zerbe made what he called his first "fiasco" of a trip.

"We had flown down to the Guajira, thinking that we were going in to a strip that I thought was the wrong strip. We went down and the loaders weren't there. Nobody was on the radio.

We shot an approach to the strip. And, in fact, we touched down and then took off again. Seeing nobody, we knew that something was mixed up. We climbed back up to altitude.

"When we had gotten to altitude we made contact with Manny Viana, the Cuban guy who was our man in Colombia, and he told us he was at the strip where we were the last time," Zerbe said.

Viana was a Cuban married to a Colombian woman whose family furnished most of the marijuana bought by The Company in South America.

"I knew the strip where Manny and the others were. I had been in there before with a DC-4, and I didn't think it was adequate for the DC-7 we were now in, but we were getting low on gas. That's where everything was. And I thought: 'Well, we get in there, we can't get out. We won't put on a full load,' " he continued.

They landed and put on what Zerbe considered to be about 18,000 pounds of gas. When they taxied out toward the end of the sloping runway, "the wind on our nose, the nose wheel sank through the runway at about halfway point on the gravel-type homemade runway.

"The airplane that we were in grossed out 145,000 pounds, so we were quite heavy. [It is a] very poor airplane to be using for that type of thing.

"It was late afternoon, and there we sat with our nose punched through the runway almost all the way up to the gear doors, and the propellers picked up just a little bit of dirt on numbers two and three, and at that time we thought our plane was all through."

The main front wheels on the airplane had sunk into the outer surface of the runway.

"We got out and looked at it. The runway was very narrow, and the gear of the big airplane is twenty-eight feet wide, so instead of being on the runway, we were off both edges with the main gear, which, while sinking into the runway, put an excessive weight on the nose gear to the arm of the airplane.

Consequently, we went through the runway and that was the reason for our trouble.

"We came to a decision that we were going to be there for a while. We had to make the decision whether or not to burn the airplane and just walk away from it or whether we should get it back on its feet, so to speak, and see if we could salvage the trip.

"We thought possibly that we still had good engines, and examining the nose gear and so forth, we found nothing broken or bent. So we spent the rest of the night taking the gas out of the airplane and putting it back into the gas truck so that we could lighten the airplane.

"We put all the marijuana that was in the airplane in the back part. We threw everybody that was there loading in the back of the airplane. Then we got two trucks that were used to bring the product out to the airport hooked on to the tail of the airplane.

"With the trucks pulling in one direction and all of our people in the back to make the weight concentrated there, we were able to pull the tail back down and hold it there until we filled in underneath the nose gear.

"When we got it filled and the nose gear back up, we examined the gear and everything that we could with a flashlight and determined that the airplane was then properly air worthy. And we decided we should try and save the trip.

"We also decided to unload the product from the airplane, move it over to another strip on the Guajira—the first strip where I thought we should go in the very beginning—and send the trucks, the gas trucks, and all the rest over there. We would have just enough gas on board to go maybe an hour and a half or two hours. That would lighten the airplane as much as we could so that once we did get it started and got it to the end of the runway, then all it would be was a matter of cranking up and getting off the ground.

"We did just that. We started the airplane up, taxied it out to the end of the runway, and thought we would wait until morning to give the trucks and gas and so forth a chance to get from the runway we were on to another one that was located approximately fifty miles away.

"We stayed in the airplane and tried to get some sleep until daylight. Very shortly before daybreak, we were buzzed by a Cessna 310. On the second pass, I felt like we were having our picture taken. I knew it was either a DEA airplane or a Colombian government airplane.

"We started the engines up and proceeded to get out. I believe the DEA records will show that was the time several Colombians shot at the 310 flying over."

A DEA agent assigned to Bogotá, Robert James Bancroft, who had previously spent two-and-one-half years in Santiago, Chile, worked primarily as an intelligence gatherer. On that day in February, he recalled, "I was flying with one of our DEA aircraft. I was in the copilot seat. It was a Cessna 310, twin engine, and we were flying the Guajira area of northern Colombia, and had checked out several airstrips. In fact, at this time we were photographing for information purposes every airstrip that we had located.

"We were flying approximately fifteen miles inland from the coast over some trees. We were fairly low. I would imagine we were flying at probably 100 feet altitude. And we kind of surprised ourselves because all of a sudden right underneath us was a DC-7, a rather large four-engine aircraft, in the process of loading marijuana."

He shot photos of the plane he thought was being loaded, making several passes over the top, seeing that the registered number on the side began with N, which denoted that it was a United States aircraft.

Zerbe remembered: "After we were buzzed twice by the Cessna, we saw another Aero Commander join it at high altitude. So we cranked our airplane up and took off with only our crew members aboard.

"We turned north and headed over the ocean like we were going to the United States with the other airplanes in pursuit.

We continued on our course probably thirty or forty minutes, knowing full well that the smaller airplanes would not be able to keep up.

"Then we made a right turn and flew up the coast another fifteen or twenty minutes and made another right turn and came back in. Needless to say, we were running very low on fuel.

"When we got back to the Guajira we landed on the first pass. We sat there the rest of the day, waiting for the product, the gasoline and so forth to arrive.

"It was like an earlier time. The people came around and wondered what we were doing, asked what our business was, said we should vamoose and get off. We had a crew of three and none of us could speak Spanish.

"We tried the best we could. We said, 'No petrol.' They understand petrol or gasoline. They harassed us for about three or four hours, injecting that they would be happier if we left.

"But there was nowhere to go. We couldn't leave.

"When our people finally did arrive, everybody seemed quite happy. They knew everybody. And, well, everything was okay.

"We gassed, loaded the airplane back up again, with 24,000 pounds, and we burned off an hour and a half—or about 800 gallons—on our little sauntering out over the ocean and back in and so forth.

"They asked me if I wanted to wait for more gas. They thought they had some coming. But night was coming up on us. I didn't know if we had anybody waiting back at the destination at Darlington or not. We didn't have a weather report or winds aloft report or anything. It was just either get it on the road or forget about it. They thought we had gas coming, but there is no guarantee down there that you have anything coming. I decided not to wait for the gas.

"We took off and headed for the States. We came in as previously and headed up the coast to Darlington.

"There was no way to check the weather other than get a report on the low bands and in the general area. At that time it looked good and we continued up toward Darlington.

"Upon reching Darlington, however, there was a heavy fog condition there. We shot an OMNI approach, using our distance-measuring equipment that told us how far we were away from the station. We couldn't see the airport and we knew we were getting into a low gas state. We went on and shot another approach but still couldn't see the airport.

"I decided we would go to the alternate. We headed south, and very shortly I knew we didn't have enough fuel to get there. I had a group of people on board and 24,000 pounds of pot. I knew I didn't really want to land into a large airport. I decided to go into a small airport at Thomson, Georgia, where I had been earlier that year. It was lit all night and I knew it was 5,000 feet in length."

They landed easily, abandoned the DC-7 and the load, stole a Cessna, which they flew to The Company's South Expressway Airport near Atlanta. The crew deplaned and Zerbe left it at Bear Creek Airport about eight miles away where a car and driver awaited him.

That experience was enough for Zerbe. By now he owned several airplanes, a business, had more than $100,000 stashed away in foreign bank accounts, and didn't have the stomach for another fiasco on the Guajira. "I had had enough of the business. I was going to retire and take what I had and try and live in peace the rest of my life," he said.

But Thorp and the board of directors set up another trip with a DC-7 they had brought in from Spain. The pilot who had flown it across the Atlantic was supposed to take it on to Colombia, but he backed out.

Thorp called and told Zerbe, "We have the airplane ready to go in Saint Maarten. We have the product in Colombia ready to go. We have things all set up back in Darlington. Would you please take the trip?"

Zerbe replied, "No, I really don't want to take the trip." Then, he said, "They made me an offer I couldn't refuse—told me if I took it they'd give me 15 percent of the profit, which could amount to between $50,000 and $100,000. And finally I said, 'Okay, I'll go ahead and do one more for you.' "

He traveled to Saint Maarten and waited around with Thorp for two weeks, lying in the sun and resting, before the trip got underway. Later, he recalled, "I just didn't like the idea of the trip. The karma wasn't right. The airplane was running good. The crew was working there. The product was waiting. The things were set up. And we had good weather reports. It was supposed to be an ideal situation. It just didn't feel right to me."

On Sunday, April 23, 1978, Zerbe took off from the Guliana Airport in Saint Maarten with three crew members aboard heading toward Colombia.

While the plane was en route to South America, The Company's ground crew began making preparations at Florence, South Carolina. Dugan, Wilbur Smith, Thorp, and several others moved into rooms at the Ramada Inn.

The same DEA agent who had photographed them earlier on the Guajira spotted them again. Robert Bancroft recalled, "I again was flying as copilot. This time we were in a Piper Navajo, one of our own aircraft, a twin-engine, and we were in the same area. We were working a joint venture with the Colombian Air Force, utilizing two helicopters and basically we were out trying to locate aircraft on the ground.

"We saw it land on a clandestine strip located very, very close to the coastline. I would say probably three miles inland.

"We happened to have been flying at approximately 5,000 feet. I happened to look down and saw the trail of dust going along the runway. At first we weren't sure what it was. We thought possibly it was a truck because we couldn't see anything.

"Then the pilot on board hit what are known as reverse thrusters. It's a braking system, and it just threw dust all over the place, and all at once we saw the aircraft sitting there. It was a DC-7.

"I got on the radio and spoke with the two helicopters in

Spanish, told them that we had just observed an aircraft land, and we gave them the aircraft's location.

"We climbed up to approximately 9,500 feet. We were worried that possibly the people on the ground would hear our motors. We circled for approximately thirty-five or forty minutes, waiting for the two helicopters with the Colombian troops to come into the area, which they subsequently did," Bancroft said.

Zerbe remembered: "We stopped, turned around, and had them start putting gas in the airplane, loading the airplane. I got out and inspected the runway and asked them if they would please fill in the tracks that we just landed in as I felt they would hinder us getting off again.

"We were on the ground approximately thirty or forty minutes with a tremendous amount of people down there working to fill in the runway, at which time I was in a Jeep talking with Manny [Viana] when somebody yelled, 'Helicopters!'

"Well, when you hear 'Helicopters!' down there, you don't waste any time. I ran toward the airplane, ran up the ladder, told the engineer, 'Let's get out of here.'

"I no sooner got in the left seat when a large helicopter of the Huey type that the Air Force uses set down in front of us, hovered, and let out approximately fifteen soldiers with automatic weapons.

"And at the same time, they let down another group in back of us. So with our people scattering like rabbits in all directions, and trucks going off and the helicopters in front and in back, and the men with the machine guns, we felt that it wouldn't be too advisable to start the airplane up.

"We sat in the airplane trying to decide what to do. And in the meantime, the people are yelling at us and pointing the guns at us, and the helicopter is coming up and pointing guns at us also.

"And I thought maybe we had better get out of the seats and go in the back and talk this over—which we did. We could hear the gunfire in the distance, and we didn't know at that time if they were shooting our people or if they were scaring our people or what the situation was.

"We sat in the airplane for approximately twenty-five, maybe thirty-five minutes—we didn't really time it—deciding what we were going to do. None of the crew members were armed, and we decided then, after thirty or so minutes, we might as well give up. There was nothing we could accomplish by sitting there. Besides that, we didn't know what they were doing on the outside, whether they would start shooting after a while. So we went up to the front end of the airplane and waved the flag and were subsequently captured by the Colombians."

Zerbe said that DEA agents "asked us our names, where we were from, where we were going, and explained to us what the situation was."

According to DEA reports of the event, Zerbe stated that he had flown the DC-7 from New Iberia, Louisiana, the day before, and was to return it to the same airport. The copilot, Ted Powell, refused to talk and told Zerbe, "Keep your big mouth shut!"

After searching the plane and the area, Zerbe recalled, the DEA agents "said it was rather grave. But I guess we kind of figured it out by then. And [they] told us that if we cooperated with them that nothing would happen.

"The Colombians were very professional in their manner of capture and generally considerate of our situation. They left us with the airplane and a contingent of the Colombian guard. They took pictures, got our names, addresses, passports, etc., and left us by the airplane. We were handcuffed and each crew member was put at a wheel, and they would come by us and talk to us, drink all our Coke and took all our ice and our water, and took some of our gear, put it on and were quite jovial.

"We were a little bit nervous thinking maybe that staying outside an airplane like that we could either be used for hostages or as incentive for our people to either come back and get us or do away with us at the time.

"We didn't know for sure what was going to happen. Later that night, I asked them if we could be put inside the airplane rather than be outside."

The Colombians released their handcuffs, ordered them inside the plane, tied them down with ropes, and kept them inside the plane for the rest of the night.

As a result of The Company plane landing, Agent Bancroft stated that the Colombian military found more than 705 tons of marijuana in trenches along the runway, ready to be loaded.

Zerbe remembered: "In the morning the helicopters came back and transferred us to Riohacha, where we had the ability to watch how that operation went. They had a small army base outside Riohacha, and if they had an airplane land on the Guajira, they simply called in from the DEA's airplane that was circling overhead, the soldiers ran, got on the helicopters, and dispatched to the area. This happened twice that day that we were in the compound waiting to be transported to where we didn't know at the time."

Later that afternoon they were placed in the jail at Riohacha on the Guajira Peninsula. On the following day, Zerbe said, "They came and got myself and one other member of the crew, and we were interrogated at the mayor's office.

"They had sent up a lawyer from Bogotá because nobody else in town could speak English. And he interrogated us and told us what we should say and how we should act and why we were there. And I thought it was quite obvious why we were there. But he said, 'Well, you are to tell them that you had airplane trouble.' And I said, 'Yes, sir, we sure did. We had a propeller getting bad on us, and we landed there.'

"And he said, 'Well, you weren't on the airplane when you were captured.' And I stated at the time, 'Well, we sure were. There were eighteen people out there that saw us get off the airplane.'

"He said, 'It makes no difference. You tell them that you were not on the airplane.' And I said, 'Well, okay. I will tell them whatever you tell me to tell them.' "

After the interview they were taken back to the jail. The authorities would interrogate the other two the next day, they said. But on the next day the English-speaking man came to them in the afternoon and said they would be leaving at midnight.

Zerbe said, "I asked him, 'Are we going out legal, with paperwork and everything.' He said, 'Don't worry, you are going to go out.'

"So I went back and explained to my people to be ready at midnight and not to say anything to anybody else, as I was told not to do, and we would be leaving there at approximately midnight.

"And they said, 'How are we going to be leaving here at midnight? Legal?' I said, 'You can form your own opinions on that.'

"There was a small TV set up in our cellblock there, and every night they would get it out and dust it off and turn it on, and we were on the news there, either a name or pictures of the airplane, so forth, etc., most of the entire week we were there.

"It seems there was a big political thing going on, and that they were saying, 'Gringo, Bogotá, Bogotá.' So we knew that possibly the next day we were going to Bogotá.

"Well, twelve o'clock rolled around and nothing happened. We thought the guards were acting a little bit strange, as they were throwing things down to us and they were pointing the rifles at us. The compound was such that it was one area that was enclosed. Another area was completely open. And there was an area here where the guards were on the roof. They could look down into the compound all the time, and they always had one or two guards up there.

"They treated us well, but we didn't know what was going on most of the time. So they pointed the rifles at us and grinned at us and generally made us feel a little uncomfortable.

"And [when] we found out we were going out at twelve o'clock, we were even more uncomfortable. We didn't know if we were going out for political reasons, they would shoot us on departure, or if in fact they were getting us out by our own people.

"As it turned out, about two o'clock, we hear someone rattle the bars, saying, 'Rapido, gringo, rapido!' And there were several people with guns at the door. They opened the door and said, 'Gringos only.' "

Back in the States, the word of the arrest had reached the leaders of The Company quickly. A hurried meeting was set up in Atlanta. "We sat around a plush room in the Peachtree Plaza, and Lee [Rick Thorp] told us that the Colombians had our people," remembered one of the principals. "He had been contacted by Manny, there was a way to break everything loose, if we could come up with about $200,000 in cash [a figure that would change from person to person as each recalled the incident]. Mike [Grassi] said there was no problem; he had the cash for insurance in case of such emergencies; no problem. But he said he wanted everybody to know where the money was going. Everybody nodded kind of sad-like and said, 'Send it south.' "

The men who came into the jail at Riohacha to fetch them, Zerbe said, "were wearing army uniforms. Again, I didn't know who they were or what they were. It was the first time we had ever seen them. But they dispatched us out of the jail, off the front porch and, going off the front porch, I stepped on one of the jail guards. It was dark as you can well imagine, as they had turned off the electrical system in the whole city of Riohacha."

A pickup truck was waiting outside "and we jumped in the back of the truck," Zerbe said, "and they stayed inside for just a little while and got our clothes that were there and our wallets, so forth, etc. They didn't at that time get our passports.

"They came, jumped in the truck, and about four gringos and four Colombians went racing down the highway in the middle of the night in this Ford Ranger.

"The roads down there are such that only the main roads are paved; the roads going say from Santa Marta, Riohacha, Barranquilla. All the other roads are dirt roads or like our paths back in fields and pastures here.

"We went right by the airport, so at that time I knew we weren't going to be flown out, which was my hope. The fellows handed us a jug of whiskey and handed us a joint and handed us a revolver, and said, 'Gringo, don't worry. Everything is going to be all right.'

"And at that time we knew that we were probably not going to be assassinated or were on our way somewhere else other than home."

The DEA agent who had been present at the arrest was told by Colombian government higher-ups that the four American smugglers had escaped from the Riohacha jail after two unidentified men posing as police officers broke into the jail, overpowered the guard, tied and gagged him, and left the country with the outlaws.

Zerbe and the others were actually carried south and west of Riohacha into a remote mountainous jungle. After traveling through thick jungle for what seemed like hours, they arrived in an opening with several large thatch-roofed huts without walls under which tens of thousands of pounds of marijuana were stored.

After more than two weeks at the jungle campsite, a young member of The Company, Jacques Thomas Delannoy, appeared one afternoon. The four captured Americans rushed to his side. Each clasped hands. Delannoy, a New Jersey pilot who had moved south to Decatur, Georgia, to work with the organization, said he had contacted Manny Viana and had delivered payoff money to him. The pilot assured them, "Don't worry. Everything is being taken care of. I'll be back in four or five days."

Zerbe remembered: "In four to five days, they loaded us in another truck and took us to another airport" where Delannoy met them with a small airplane and took them across the Caribbean to Tampa.

Following the "escape" from the jail in Riohacha, news articles appeared in the Bogotá press insinuating that the entire episode was an operation of the Central Intelligence Agency from the United States. A reporter in Bogotá subsequently stated, "There were strong indications at that time that the CIA was testing the political and military waters of Colombia just as they had in Argentina, Chile, Nicaragua, El Salvador, and other Latin American countries. According to our politicians, the U.S. authorities were working to infiltrate our system of government. The breakout at Riohacha was reported as it was told to the press by the officials in Bogotá."

During the following week, a source at Drug Enforcement Administration headquarters on I Street in Washington said a communiqué from the CIA informed: "Epidemic drug situation in Colombia must be cured. If no solution provided, we will eradicate."

A celebration was held in Florida with Company personnel expressing happiness at having their people home safely.

Zerbe was talked into making two more trips for The Company. Long after he finally quit smuggling, he was talked about by outlaws and lawmen as a true legend among the kings of smuggling.

Chapter Three
Downtime at Darlington

While The Company was having success after success, although it was losing a rare load now and then and suffered several arrests in 1978, Jim Dugan continued to worry about what he called "downtime syndrome."

Basically a military man, Dugan considered his best training not in school but in the U.S. Marine Corps where he was taught that nothing beat efficiency. "If we have minimum downtime, we will succeed in our operation," he told a number of ground crew members after operations proceeded in full swing.

Zerbe first brought a load into the small airfield at Darlington, South Carolina, early in 1977, and it became one of the two eastern mainstays Thorp had contracted as central staging areas. At Darlington Thorp's manager was Bryan O'Neal Sullivan, also known as Buddy or Reb, five-feet seven-inches tall, graying hair, a gray-splotched beard, and a tense, snappy personality. Before he was recruited into the drug smuggling business Sullivan had been a furniture merchandiser and later had gone bankrupt in an attempt to manufacture mobile homes in the mid-1970s.

Sullivan had been hired as a real estate hunter for The Company. "They decided that my function to earn money could be best used to locate real estate, as they described it, which I learned in their vernacular meant airstrips to land large airplanes," he explained. He found the Dovesville Airport near

Darlington and made a deal with George Gedra, the owner and manager of Gedra Air Service, to pay him $7,500 per airplane that The Company landed successfully.

Several years later the Internal Revenue Service was to discover that while Sullivan indicated on his American Express credit application that he earned a total of $25,000 per year, for 1978 alone his charges on the card were $26,968.89.

In January of 1978, Dugan led the fast downtime unloading at Darlington. He trailed behind the trucks that transported the load north to James Mitchell's warehouse in Batchtown, Illinois. Dugan weighed it out at 11,000 pounds and made sure every bale was tagged. Then Mitchell oversaw the distribution in the Chicago area.

In mid-February, members of The Company were notified that a new load was due in at Darlington. On the evening of St. Valentine's Day, the men prepared to meet the aircraft. From his command van, Dugan assisted in radio communication. The radar scanned the sky which had become thick with fog. And it was not long before Zerbe, the pilot, made the decision to turn back. This load became the one that was ultimately ditched at Thomson.

After Darlington, Dogpatch, near Fitzgerald, became the most active strip on the east coast for The Company. Grassi's South Expressway Airport was thought to be too close to the Atlanta action. After a plane had been off-loaded and vacuumed, it was usually taken to South Expressway for maintenance and storage until the next trip.

Under the direction of Thomas Riley Kimball, a tall, prematurely gray-haired engineer with a neatly trimmed mustache, Dogpatch, with a 5,000-foot runway, was set in the midst of the south Georgia piney woods. It was located in rural countryside with little traffic, and almost everybody in that part of the world knew Tom Kimball because his family had operated a dairy farm for generations. Kimball was familiar with aircraft and small airports, and had been recruited by his old friend, smooth-talking Mike Grassi, who told him, "This is the best and quickest way I know to make a million—and keep it."

Prior to their association in The Company, Kimball had worked with Grassi. "We had been in insurance together," he said. "We had lived through hard times down in Tampa during the recession of the early 1970s." They had been involved in Interstate Syndications Inc. in an attempt in 1973 to sell and develop real estate. The corporation through which both were charged with land fraud by the U.S. Securities and Exchange Commission was listed at Kimball's Roswell, Georgia, address.

In 1976, when Tom Kimball was selling insurance in Atlanta, he bumped into Grassi on a flight home on a Friday afternoon. "I was particularly worn out and discouraged after trying to sell a $500,000 policy to a man who had turned me down that morning. I had made a long trip, spent several days, and felt absolutely dejected. Not only had this customer been negative, the entire insurance business at the time was down. None of us seemed to be doing what we felt we should have been doing.

"I ran into Mike Grassi. He was riding first class. I was back in tourist. He had on a new tailored suit that looked great on him. I felt somewhat disheveled in my own suit. He was styled to perfection, not one hair out of place. He moved me up to first class with him, we had a drink, and he began telling me that he was doing great, had never been better, and business was booming. He didn't say what business.

"At the Atlanta airport we had another drink at one of those bars on the concourse. I started to make a telephone call to ask my wife to pick me up. Mike said, 'Hey, I'll give you a ride.' We went to the parking lot where we got into his new Mercedes-Benz. And on the way home we stopped by his new house, where he was living with his girl friend, and we had another drink, and he said, 'How would you like to have all this?' I kind of laughed sort of nervously and said, 'Yeah, it's real nice. It's real fine.' And he said, 'You can make $100,000 a year and then some. But there's a risk element. It's not exactly legal.'

"Well, I went home and didn't have to think about it very long. Things really didn't look very good for us then. We liked to live well, have good things, but now I was in debt, wasn't able to make enough to meet the deadlines on the payments, my wife was having to answer all the angry phone calls asking for their money, and none of this added up to happiness. To live the way we wanted to live took money. It was as simple as that.

"Several days later I called Mike and told him I wanted to meet with him, I wanted to talk with him about the situation he was in.

"We met, he told me about The Company, and I decided on the spot that it was something I wanted to do and that it was something I could do. I knew something about airplanes, about airstrips, and I knew I could learn whatever was needed to function successfully in The Company.

"That was the key to The Company. Mike Grassi never let you forget it: success. It was just like a huge corporation that was managed efficiently. All corporations need an idea man. The idea man in The Company was Rick Thorp. All need a hard-working, well-liked, motivational manager. The manager was Mike. And all need equally hard-working, efficient, no-nonsense, technically knowledgeable middle-management people. The technical managers were Jim Dugan, Jimmy Mitchell, Marvin Zylstra, Richard Zerbe, and, for a while, Billy Greenwald."

From February 1977 to February 1979, the DEA and the Justice Department became sure of at least thirty loads brought in at Dogpatch. It was estimated that each trip averaged about 24,000 pounds of marijuana.

While many members of The Company were doing their own thing within the operation, the top boss was always baby-faced Rick Thorp. At one time he purchased four airplanes: a Grumman G-1 for $550,000; two Cessna Titans for $260,000 each; and a reworked DC-6 for little more than $100,000.

Thorp moved continuously through the Bahamas, the West Indies, Mexico, Central and South America. "Much of the time using the name Lee McDade, Rick made many foreign contacts," remembered a former Company member. "He got along with people famously. He moved in and out of fast-moving circles. They accepted him. He had a lot of money, a lot of clout, he knew what was happening. He's the kind of guy who exudes confidence. He really is a natural leader. During this time, of course, he was making deals constantly, arranging for marijuana to be shipped back by boat but mostly by air. Rick really knew how to operate. When he was going full speed ahead there was nothing stopping him. He even had some really fantastic setup down in the islands where the planes would airdrop loads of marijuana to boats sitting and waiting; then the boats would transport the goods to shore. And once he even had helicopters coming out from Louisiana, meeting the boats on the tiny islands, and bringing the load inland. Nobody ever suspected the helicopters down there because there were so many of them going and coming from the oil derricks out in the Gulf."

Although the DEA was aware of the existence of The Company, the organization's efficiency in getting planes into the small airstrips, unloaded, and out again gave the law enforcement people headaches. As St. Louis DEA Chief Ed Irvin, who headed up Operation Gateway—a task force designed to stop The Company—told reporter Don Corrigan, "It's no big deal identifying a plane coming back from South America loaded with marijuana. You can take a look at some of them and figure out that they're carrying something. The big trick is to catch them while they're loaded, to catch the planes on the ground when they're unloading.

"What they [The Company] did was disguise the numbers, tape over them and paint over them. They would fly in, unload somewhere, and tear off the strips. They'd take off and land at an airport—five people get out—and you can't identify anything. Where's your case? It becomes a difficult matter for prosecution.

"The matter of just seizing the evidence isn't effective. You certainly can't brag about grabbing a ton of marijuana and no defendants. It was just a thorn in their side, because they'd turn around and go back for ten more tons. If you grab ten tons of marijuana and have no defendants, it's a real embarrassment," the veteran lawman stated.

While The Company was continuing its massive operation, the DEA was building its forces out of the second floor of an office building in the heart of Clayton in suburban St. Louis. Agents from Washington, Atlanta, Miami, Chicago, Houston, New Orleans, and from throughout the eastern half of the United States came and went from the offices. Each was briefed on the known and suspected activities of The Company.

State law enforcement agencies were also made aware of certain illegal operations by The Company across the eastern seaboard and into the Southeast and Midwest. "It was the largest operation I have ever seen," said Intelligence Analyst Dennis Moriarty. Investigators in Georgia, South Carolina, Tennessee, Alabama, Mississippi, Louisiana, Missouri, Illinois, Kentucky, Indiana, Maryland, New Jersey, and New York agreed. A supervisor with narcotics in New York City said, "We have a massive supply of drugs pouring into the city every day. There is no way we could stop it unless we had 100 times more manpower, 1,000 times more money, and the expertise those guys in St. Louis showed with their Operation Gateway. I have never seen a group of more dedicated policemen than the ones I saw working out there when they were moving to stop The Company. I've seen a lot of police departments operate, but they were tops. Sometimes those guys spent 80 to 100 hours a week going after one lead. They wouldn't stop. I wish I had two of them here, I'd let six guys go. I know we got some of The Company dope. We get dope from everywhere."

*   *   *

William Wade Hampton, Jr. of Columbia, South Carolina,
who had helped with a number of off-loadings at Darlington,
decided in the late summer of 1978 that his luck was running
out and that he no longer had the stomach for the smuggling
business. A direct descendant of Confederate General and South
Carolina Governor Wade Hampton of the late nineteenth century, Hampton had been instrumental in purchasing cars, trucks,
and other vehicles as well as renting the Brantley County
Airport in Nahunta, Georgia, for $25,000 down and $16,000
per quarter. That summer, Hampton and another Company
member, Harrison Stephens, purchased a 150-gallon tank
mounted on skids and they manned the Brantley County Airport as the alternate for a load that went into Fitzgerald. Afterward, the two men traveled to Atlanta and met in the Colony
Square Hotel with Rick Thorp, who paid Hampton $2,700 and
Stephens $1,000, although both did the same work.

Not long afterward, Stephens was told that Thorp had paid
Hampton a total of $20,000 this year for his work with The
Company. Stephens had not received that much. Knowing
that he should have been paid the same amount, because, in
his estimation, he had done basically the same thing Hampton
had done, Stephens began to keep his ears perked for any vital
information.

In August, Stephens was asked to join Bryan Sullivan, Mike
Grassi, and Rick Thorp at the Sly Fox Lounge in Atlanta. With
Stephens present, Thorp said he had discovered that Wade
Hampton had talked with George Gedra about using Gedra
Air Service at Darlington for future smuggling runs that had
nothing to do with The Company.

In the dark lounge, Thorp sat back and stared coal-eyed into
Stephens's face. "I *know* that you and Hampton gave Gedra
$10,000 good-faith money," he said. "And I *know* that you
promised him $25,000 per load for stuff some other gang will
be bringing in," he added.

Stephens attempted to speak, but Thorp was on a rampage.
"While you worked with us, we brought in 110,000 pounds,

but during the same time we lost 55,000 pounds. It doesn't add up to profit."

Stephens shook his head.

"What's wrong?" Thorp demanded.

"I haven't seen where we've lost that much," he said. "I know I haven't been paid for 110,000 pounds."

"Because we *lost* 55,000 pounds." Thorp got red-faced and loud. "It doesn't add up to profit, don't you see?"

"I just think I want out, if it's not profitable. That's why I got in this business to start with."

"Look, we've paid you $52,500 already," Thorp said.

Stephens again shook his head. "Not that much," he said.

"How much?" Thorp asked angrily.

"Not as much as you've paid Hampton," Stephens said.

"What the hell, you guys been comparing salaries? You ought to be more loyal. You and Hampton shouldn't be out to screw the people who've helped you. You ought to think about that, you really should. It's not very healthy to go around trying to screw the people who've done everything they could to help you."

Stephens went back to South Carolina. Bryan Sullivan visited him and offered him $2,000 to stay with The Company, he told DEA agents at a later date. He said he turned down the money but later took $3,000 in cash that was owed to him by Sullivan.

Throughout this time, DEA agents and local law enforcement officers in Missouri and Illinois continued to watch James Anderson Mitchell's warehouses. Company drivers were arrested in Lincoln, Illinois, Newnan, Georgia, Hamilton County, Florida, Fulton, Mississippi, and other places. Each time, considerable amounts of marijuana and valuable vehicles were confiscated.

Regardless of the rough times they were having, The Company was still making money and its members were living high on the hog. On Friday, November 10, a bonanza birthday party was planned for the president and chairman of the board in Fort Lauderdale.

"Every lease plan Lear jet on the eastern seaboard was hired with private pilots, bringing people in from all over. Big shots from New York, the guys from Alton and St. Louis and Chicago, and some connections in Louisville, Cincinnati, Cleveland, and Detroit were there. People were dressed to a T with anything and everything and nothing on. Gorgeous gals with see-through evening gowns, little wisps of things, and others with long evening gowns cut low but covered with mink stoles, everything like that," recalled a member. "Everybody threw in some money, assessed by Mike according to how much they had made during the year from The Company. But no expense was spared."

Limos with chauffeurs met the jets at three different airports in and around Fort Lauderdale and took them to the plush private country club rented especially for the occasion. Food was catered, with large tables filled with imported caviar, smoked salmon, a steamboat round of roast beef, piles of ham and turkey, and all the trimmings. Half a dozen bars were set up around the floor of the ballroom. The finest champagne and Rothschild wine were served.

There was all the coke anyone could ask for, although the men sneaked off to the bathroom, like high-schoolers slipping off for a drag on a Lucky, to toke a line. One of the pilots, his head reeling with the enjoyment of everything fine, walked limber-legged from the basement locker room where a shapely young blonde was straightening her gown. He said to one of his buddies, "You can get a piece of anything around this place for a sniff of coke," and he laughed crazily.

At midnight everyone toasted Rick Thorp, who had gotten semiangry several times during the evening when people began snapping photos. He didn't want pictures made, he said, "for obvious reasons," and he had the cameras and film destroyed.

The 300-plus guests sang "Happy Birthday" and "For He's

A Jolly Good Fellow." While the singing continued, Thorp was presented with his gift—a replica of a German Duesenburg car made especially for the movie, *Gable and Lombard.* While Rick fit himself behind the wheel and grinned from ear to ear, the crowd pushed tightly around the shining car and "oohed" and "aahed."

At three o'clock in the morning much of the festivities continued, although some of the guests and the guest of honor had already said their good-byes.

A few days after the party, Thorp, Grassi, and the other directors decided that, with the absence of Hampton and Stephens in the Darlington area, they needed to beef up power contacts in South Carolina.

They sent William Russell Jackson, a trusted member of their South Carolina ground crew, to visit thirty-seven-year-old, slightly built, quick-witted John Ray Etheridge, a well-respected attorney in Darlington.

Jackson began his conversation by telling Etheridge that the group of businessmen of which he was a member wanted to employ the lawyer's services to act as a go-between with local authorities. He said they would pay top dollar, they had made a great deal of money, and they planned to make much, much more.

After Etheridge showed interest, Jackson told the attorney that his group, called The Company, had been smuggling marijuana into the Darlington area and transporting it throughout the United States.

"We want your help to get in with the sheriff," Etheridge said Jackson told him. "We have a lot of money." Jackson opened a briefcase and showed what he said was $10,000 in cash. "If you can buy us protection, we'll pay you $10,000 cash and a bonus. All we want is protection from being arrested up there. We've been operating for some time, and we feel now that we need some more insurance."

They made an appointment, and two days later the two traveled to nearby Florence, where Jackson introduced Etheridge to Bryan Sullivan, who gave him more information concerning the operation.

The following day, Etheridge, a former Darlington County Democratic Party chairman, approached the sheriff and said he wanted to discuss a matter with him. They were old Democratic Party political buddies, had been friends most of Etheridge's life, and it was not unusual for them to talk about matters of personal and professional interest. Besides, the sheriff knew that Etheridge was in tight with President Jimmy Carter, was a strongly rumored possible nominee for a U.S. District judgeship, and was presently considering running for the Democratic nomination for the House seat in Congress if Sixth District Representative John W. Jenrette, Jr. chose to run for the U. S. Senate instead; in short, Etheridge was certainly a man Sheriff A. J. O'Tuel would listen to. They went for a ride in the sheriff's car and Etheridge explained to O'Tuel that The Company would be bringing marijuana into Darlington but that all of it would be shipped out to other parts of the country. O'Tuel listened. Etheridge said that this group was very rich and would be willing to pay for protection. When Etheridge finished, O'Tuel said he would act as a lookout and would give protection—as long as the marijuana would be distributed elsewhere. Etheridge assured him it would.

After Etheridge reported his conversation to Sullivan, it was arranged for Etheridge to take a polygraph test at the Howard Johnson Motel in Florence. Bob Snyder examined Etheridge and said afterward that he had passed.

Five days later, Sullivan and Jackson told Etheridge they wanted him to talk with William "Billy" Mozingo, an investigator for the South Carolina Law Enforcement Divison (SLED), from whom they also needed protection. They gave Etheridge the authority to pay Mozingo $5,000 for small loads and $10,000 for large loads.

Etheridge talked with Mozingo, who accepted $500 as a down payment for his services. Later, Mozingo told a jury that at the initial meeting Etheridge told him the sheriff was "not in the big money like you and I. He's nickel and diming it." At that point, Mozingo, who had been attempting to infiltrate the group, made his first entrance into the operation of The Company.

On the next day, Mozingo accompanied Etheridge to the Howard Johnson Motel, where Sullivan gave Mozingo an extra $250 in cash.

"We've almost got everything worked out," Sullivan told them. "We're the biggest in the country. Right now, we stretch all the way from Darlington to California. You can't get much bigger than that." Then he asked Mozingo if he could find somebody on the inside of the Florence police department to cooperate with them, and if he couldn't do that, perhaps somebody with SLED at Georgetown, South Carolina. Mozingo said he would try.

In the second week of December the group met a number of times. On various occasions, Sullivan gave Etheridge money to pass on to Sheriff O'Tuel, $5,000 to give to Mozingo to guard Gedra's Air Service, and finally said he would pay Mozingo $50,000 to bribe two Georgetown police officers for protection of a future boat smuggling deal. He said a large boat would be able to enter Winyah Bay, make its way up the inland waterway, and unload hundreds of tons of marijuana at a rural location just north of Georgetown if the officers would cooperate.

Sitting around a room in the Holiday Inn in Florence, Sullivan, Jackson, and other members of The Company bragged about having the most sophisticated electronic equipment available to detect police activity during a smuggling operation. Jackson, who owned a large tobacco warehousing company, said he had been allowing The Company to use his business equipment.

During the week before Christmas, everyone became particularly nervous, short of temper, and floor-walking anxious
because a plane was due in from South America. On the night
of December 23, Sullivan said the DC-7 would not be arriving
because "the Orkin man" (The Company's expert in discovering electronic bugging devices) had found a bug on the plane.
Sullivan gave Mozingo $5,000 and Etheridge $1,000. After
talking about the bust in Louisiana, which he said was "bad
for us and cost at least $750,000 in forfeited bonds," Sullivan
assured Mozingo that he would be taken care of by The Company if he was ever arrested.

Three days after Christmas, Sullivan told Mozingo the deal
was on. He added that "J.D. [Dugan] will be there with Gedra,
and we've got to have minimum downtime. That's forty minutes to off-load 20,000 pounds."

On New Year's Eve they talked again, and Sullivan said,
"It'll be here in the next few days."

Two days later at Darlington, Gedra told the undercover
agent that something had gone wrong. He said people in The
Company believed another group, much smaller, was smuggling marijuana through the airport using a Cessna 310, and
The Company didn't want to get caught in the heat caused
by another, smaller outfit.

On the next day in Florence, Sullivan told Mozingo, "Things
have been going badly. We lost a DC-7 down in Colombia
with more than 650 tons on board."

"Lost?" Mozingo asked.

"The army down there got the plane and the grass," Sullivan
said. "They were operating under the instructions of the
DEA or the CIA, we don't know which, but it cost us," he
added.

After a trial run on Thursday, January 4, 1979, which took
them to Gedra's Air Service on the edge of Darlington's Dovesville Airport, Sullivan paid Mozingo and Etheridge another
$5,000. He said they had been spending a lot of time with the
group and nothing had happened yet, but they shouldn't worry.

A week later, Mozingo and Etheridge sat around a table in a dark lounge with Sullivan and three of his cohorts. Sullivan said the weather was too bad in the Darlington area to bring in a DC-6 but that they might fly a Cessna Titan instead. Sullivan said the boss of The Company was a smart thirty-one-year-old "who has been taking care of a lot of people for several years." He said Mozingo and Etheridge should not worry about anything, because they had all made a lot of money. He talked about the bust in Louisiana again and about losing an airplane and a load in Thomson, Georgia, and about the arrest in South America, but he added, "We've always come out on top." And at the moment, he said, The Company had at least $75 million in cash reserves being held in secret bank accounts and another $2 million set aside for bonds and legal fees.

On Tuesday, January 16, Sullivan told them that two Cessna Titans would be arriving early the next morning. He then went over the plans in detail.

Mozingo drove to his assigned position near Gedra's Air Service at dusk. He saw that others also arrived, checking in at Gedra's and moving out to their locations. Everyone had a job to do when the airplane landed. Jim Dugan assigned inside men and outside men for chores within the airplane and on the exterior of the plane. In his room at the Holiday Inn in Florence, Dugan had pulled himself onto the bed with his powerful arms. With the same tenacity he had demonstrated at the first meeting in Missouri, he placed his staging game on the spread, using toy cars, vans, airplanes, and tanker trucks to explain each assignment. And, afterward, he gave each of the crew detailed assignment sheets written in abbreviated code, noting that Dave GM1 would be located at a certain place and Steve GM2 would be at another and Leroy Tank would travel to a given spot, et cetera.

When the plane came in after midnight, the crew converged upon the Titan piloted by former astronaut trainee Arnold Gene Sims and copiloted by Lawrence Phillip Lamovec, who was on his first trip and who had been promised by Marvin Zylstra that he would receive $15,000 for each trip and a minimum of $100,000 per month.

Sullivan drove his car to the plane to pick up the pilots but Lamovec stayed while the crew began refueling, unloading, vacuuming, and checking for any other mechanical problem.

Nearby, Dugan listened for any problem from his command van in which he had a radio scanner, automatic computerlike cards with frequencies of every sheriff's department and some police departments.

After Sullivan picked up Sims, the pilot asked, "Where is Lamovec going?" and Sullivan said, "I have no idea. I don't know where he's going, probably down to Atlanta," and Sims replied, "Well, he doesn't have any charts."

Sullivan remembered, "I proceeded to circle the airport, which is about a fifteen-mile circle, and to come back around to go into the airport so Mr. Sims could give Lamovec these charts to Atlanta or wherever he was going. And as I came back up on the outskirts of the airport, there were several law enforcement officers blocking various roads around there. And they stopped us on down the road and we were arrested there and taken back up to the airport."

In the meantime, officers closed in on George Gedra, the owner, who had opened the facilities for the group and who had turned on the runway lights and was on the telephone in his office. By the time the police entered, Gedra had hung up and was hiding under his desk. The telephone rang and undercover agent Mozingo answered. A male who identified himself as Lee asked for Dugan. Mozingo told him, "Dugan's tied up, can I give him a message?" The voice said, "It's very important that I talk with him. It's about the second load." Mozingo asked, "What about the second load?" Lee left a telephone number and hung up. The number Mozingo wrote on his pad was for the telephone at South Expressway Airport.

Another group of SLED and DEA authorities surrounded Dugan's command van where he was listening to police frequencies. However, in this case, the local, state, and federal officers had changed frequencies during the operation.

A number of other workers were arrested at the airplane, and the officials seized 1,380 pounds of marijuana. A total of fifteen arrests were made on the spot. All fifteen were indicted and tried, although Sullivan skipped on a $50,000 bond.

Etheridge pleaded guilty and cooperated with the state. Under heavy guard, he agreed to testify against the smugglers with whom he had been working.

Because he cooperated with the prosecution, according to Circuit Judge Paul Moore, Etheridge was sentenced to only one year in prison on the charge of bribery and conspiracy to possess marijuana. Others were sentenced up to five years each in state penitentiary. All were also wanted on federal charges.

Darlington was the real beginning of the end for The Company. It marked the first heavy fall the group had suffered. But it was a shot in the arm for the law enforcement people who had been tailing them for more than a year. "We knew that they would become desperate after Darlington and it was only a matter of time before we had the entire group. We kept working, watching, waiting, knowing that soon they would trip up and turn the tables on the heart of their organization," said one of the 100-plus agents who dogged the case.

Not only were The Company's personnel arrested and sentenced to prison, but the organization spent a great deal of money on bonds and even more on attorneys. "When our people wanted to fight their cases we paid for it all the way to the Supreme Court, if they wanted to take it that far," said Mike Grassi. "In my opinion, the only people who make money in the smuggling business are the attorneys," he added.

Also at Darlington, law enforcement officials confiscated more than $800,000 worth of vehicles and equipment. In front of Gedra's old World War II hangar sat the brown command van with oversized tires and raised suspension rigged with hand controls so that a man without legs could operate it. The van was filled with sophisticated electronic equipment: three radio scanners, portable generators, two-way radios, and walkie-talkies. A twin-engine Cessna Titan II equipped with extra gasoline tanks was valued at about $300,000. And as a result of information gathered at the scene of the Darlington raid, the Cessna's duplicate at the South Expressway Airport near Atlanta was seized. Other trucks and automobiles were also impounded after the Darlington arrests.

In December, Sheriff O'Tuel, who had been indicted on five counts of bribery, was tried by a local jury. Etheridge admitted making a deal with authorities and working as an undercover agent for SLED in the investigation following the raid. He said that on five different occasions he paid O'Tuel money. The first payment, when they drove around in the sheriff's car, he said, was $500. The other payoffs, he said, occurred in the sheriff's office. Six tapes of conversations between O'Tuel and Etheridge were introduced by the prosecution. At one point in the trial, Etheridge said that O'Tuel's drinking problem was the main reason he felt comfortable approaching him and offering him a bribe. A seventh tape, which was made by State Law Enforcement Division agents, was demanded by the defense. On the final tape, in response to Etheridge's questions, O'Tuel denied any knowledge of payoffs. "I don't know anything about any money . . . I don't know nothing . . . I have nothing to hide, and you know that, Johnny," he said. When cross-examined by the defense, Etheridge said he had lied when he told an undercover agent for SLED that other politicians were involved with The Company. During his final argument, defense attorney John Charles Lindsay, a Democratic state senator, called Etheridge's testimony "tilted, stilted, and forked-tongued." It took the jury thirty-five minutes to find O'Tuel innocent of all five counts of accepting bribes.

About six months later, after he spent about three weeks in a psychiatric institute for alcoholism treatment, O'Tuel was arrested for driving under the influence after he lost control of his Darlington County patrol car while driving north on New Market Road at about 8:45 P.M. The car ran off the

left side of the country road north of Hartsville, South Carolina, hit a culvert, ran back onto the road but with a badly
damaged left front wheel. O'Tuel was found by a highway
patrolman who arrested him for DUI. He was ordered hospi-
talized by the court for further alcoholism treatment, after
which O'Tuel did not offer his name for reelection.

Chapter Four

The Final Squeeze

The DEA's Operation Gateway was moving with renewed strength and vitality. "We figured we had them by the balls after we had gotten into them in South Carolina, and it made our people work even harder than they had before," said an agent who was in the middle of the action from the crowded offices in St. Louis to the fields of southern Georgia. "It was nothing to work eighty hours a week during that time. When we stayed up night after night after night for something like three months watching Mitchell's warehouse down in Potosi we'd grab an hour of sleep now and then. But for the most part, we were alert, staying on top of it, watching every little twig of every tree when a breeze would sweep by.

"Down in Potosi we were stuck out there in a little beat-up shack that we rented in the middle of the field. There was no heat. Hell, you couldn't even light a fire in the stove because the place might burn to the ground or the stove might fall over. We got some portable heaters brought in there, but always one side of your body was freezing. We were definitely under physical and mental stress and strain, but we stayed with it. It was like tiger hunts you read about in India where the hunters stay on the trail for months at a time. We had a tiger by the tail, and we were damned if we were going to let it go before we had it captured," the agent added.

Following the Darlington arrests a number of members of The Company were arrested while transporting marijuana from the Potosi or Chigger Ridge Ranch to St. Louis, East Louis, Chicago, and other destinations. Each time bonds were set and made, the defendant was allowed to go free and trial was scheduled for a later date. The Company furnished bond money and legal fees, and usually the attorneys asked for as many continuances as possible.

"At one time we considered that there were at least 100,000 pounds of marijuana in Mitchell's warehouse, where he kept six ten-ton trucks and a fuel tanker truck," said the agent. "We watched him so closely that only one or two truckloads got away from us after January of 1979. We established, through our continuing efforts and continuing contacts within the organization (something that was developing literally every day), a way in which we could continue our surveillance and pick off a truck here and a truck there selectively. By February 12, we figured that there were only 12,000 pounds left inside the warehouse, and we got at least 4,000 pounds of that."

According to a secret report of the DEA, "The area surrounding the Mitchell warehouse is a 'closed community,' and getting the proper position for adequate observation was difficult. A piece of ground was rented and the surveillance vehicle was brought in. However, to minimize the comings and goings, officers and agents from the St. Louis County police, St. Louis Police Department, Illinois state investigators, Washington County Sheriff's Department, DEA and other agents volunteered to spend three days on 'point.' As a result, they were able to maintain [twenty-four-hour] surveillance of the warehouse for the next seventy-nine days without being detected."

A number of future defendants were spotted and recorded coming and going from the warehouse in transport vehicles, according to the reports.

Rick Thorp, using the name Jason Bennett, hired a charter jet at Lambert International Airport in St. Louis, flew to Atlanta, then to Miami, and back to Atlanta, paying for it with $4,100 in one-hundred-dollar bills.

At a big meeting at the Omni International Hotel in Atlanta, Thorp called together the Darlington fourteen (not counting Etheridge, who had already announced that he would give testimony for the prosecution).

"This was an emergency meeting," stated Tom Kimball. "Rick talked up a storm to everybody, telling them that we had to be more careful from now on, that we could trust no one we didn't know for sure and then we couldn't trust them until they had taken a polygraph. He said we were on the verge of making a lot more money than we had ever made before, that there were really riches up ahead if we'd just keep calm.

"Rick walked up and down the floor and said, 'You have got to hire ground crews that you are familiar with, pay them, and to hell with it. That's that.' He said we had gotten into a lot of trouble, especially up in Darlington, by getting involved with people who drank a lot and had girl friends they talked with too much and generally let too much information out into the community.

"Somebody said, 'We don't have the Titans now that they've been confiscated'—one in Darlington and another at Mike's South Expressway. And somebody else said, 'We'll have to dig the DC-4s out of the mothballs.' Everybody kind of laughed, but we knew that was what it would take to get things kicking again. And somebody mentioned the business up in Illinois, around East St. Louis, of the cops getting on everybody's ass and arresting them and taking their trucks and confiscating the marijuana. It was really getting to look bad and we knew it, but we didn't want to really think it. We wanted to believe Rick."

During the next few days Kimball and other members of The Company flew to St. Louis, visited the Potosi warehouse, moved around the area in a pattern that the DEA said showed "definite criminal activity." Several loads were picked up, taken into Illinois, where the transporters were arrested and charged.

"It was a nervous time for us," Tom Kimball recalled. "We

were trying to put things together for a new trip with a super load of marijuana from South America. We also were trying to rid ourselves of excess cash, get cashier's checks that could be spent or deposited, and selling the rest of the marijuana in Jim Mitchell's warehouse.

"This kind of helter-skelter runaround operation continued for quite a few days with guys getting caught right and left. We didn't know where the DEA was, but we knew they were out there somewhere, watching us. It's a weird feeling. When some of the guys got arrested in Lincoln, Illinois, we were afraid some of our biggest distributors out there were going to be put down. But The Company put up the bonds and paid the fines. I think it ran $50,000 in one case and more than that in another. We also lost the marijuana and the trucks they were driving."

About this time in South Carolina, a Company ground crew director, Jay Woodbury of Charleston, who had escaped being arrested with the others at Darlington, approached John Ray Etheridge, pulled a gun, and held it to the lawyer's head. He uttered words of intimidation and laughed menacingly. Two weeks later, Etheridge told federal investigators that William Russell Jackson said The Company was willing to pay $100,000 "hush money" if Etheridge would refuse to testify. Etheridge's wife said she saw and heard her husband being threatened with his life if he continued to cooperate with the prosecution.

After Bob Snyder was sent to federal prison, The Company's hierarchy decided it was time to find a new polygraph man. Jay Woodbury called an operator in Savannah, Georgia, and told him, "I've talked The Company into using you. We need you bad. The Company's willing to pay $500 per test. Drop whatever you're doing now. Everything must be confidential. You will answer only to me. You will not ask any of the people their names or anything else like that. We are missing something like $1 million every two or three months because of the opposition, and we're going out of our minds. And you've got to do the tests in Illinois. We've got to have you." The polygraph man, who immediately after the conversation contacted the Georgia Bureau of Investigation and the DEA, said, "I'm not licensed in Illinois. You'll have to get somebody else." Woodbury said, "Where are you licensed in the Midwest?" And the lie detector expert said, "In Missouri. I can do it there because there's no licensing required." Woodbury said he would have to check back with his people and added, "You are not to inquire who the bosses are. As far as you're concerned, I'm your boss. You work only for me. Is that understood? I am the key man for liaison." The expert said he understood.

On the following day, Woodbury called back. "It's okay," he said. "The top man in the organization says, 'Fine.' We can test in Missouri. Meet us this afternoon at the Savannah airport and we'll have a jet waiting for you."

Thorp, traveling as Jason Bennett, and Woodbury picked up the polygraph man the next day. They flew in a Lear jet to St. Louis, during which the expert told Thorp, "You don't have to worry about me. I've worked for the FBI, the CIA, a number of police departments," after which Woodbury said, "Don't say things like that. Jason and the others don't want to hear that. They get nervous when you say things like that."

In St. Louis a number of Company personnel were tested.

When the polygraph man was returned to Savannah several days later he was paid $5,000 in cash for his services.

The DEA kept busy with constant surveillance, following the lie detector expert while he gave other tests, doing telephone toll analysis of various known members who had either been arrested in several different locations, or had been fingered as suspects, or had been seen coming and going from the warehouses in Missouri and Illinois.

At about 3 P.M. on the afternoon of Friday, March 30, Granville Leroy Bryant and his brother William Frank Bryant drove two ten-ton trucks out of Mitchell's Potosi warehouse and headed north. Agents followed them to St. Louis, where they pulled into Skelly's Service Station. They parked and walked inside. They did not leave until late at night, when they drove through East St. Louis, down through southern Illinois, into Kentucky and Tennessee. The agent following recalled, "That was one of the longest tail jobs I've ever been on. I'd stop now and then and call Ed Irvin and say, 'Hey, I'm in Kentucky,' and he'd say, 'Stay with 'em.' And every time we'd get into a new state, I'd radio the state police and let them know what was happening. By late Saturday morning, when we were pulling into Georgia, we had a convoy of policemen going down the interstate behind those trucks. There were more policemen than bad guys."

The team of law enforcement personnel watched as the trucks parked near the Edgemont Hotel near Atlanta. The drivers got a room and waited. The policemen stayed with it. "As far as we could tell, they were waiting for a message from someone about where to go from here," said the DEA agent who had started the trek south. "They did not come out of their room for two days. When they wanted something to eat or drink, they'd send out for it. That was pretty monotonous, but that's police work," he added.

"As far as we could tell, we did something to throw them off," the agent remembered. "After two days, William Frank Bryant got a taxi, went to the airport, boarded an Eastern flight, rode first class to Fort Myers, Florida, where agent Robin Cushing followed him to his mother's house. A day later, Granville Leroy did the same.

"In Atlanta, some of the driver guys with The Company moved the trucks around the city, taking them to a truck stop, parking them, letting them sit, going first this way and then that, and we never lost them. I guess they were going about crazy, thinking they'd never lose us. We spotted a lot of new guys, found some locations of their hiding places, and made some good notes which we knew we could use later," the agent said.

During the same month, Jim Dugan made arrangements to meet with a detective in Riverview, Illinois. Dugan made two passes in his silver-gray van before he stopped, searched the officer for a bug, and then said, "I've got to have my case taken care of."

The detective played along while Dugan said, "I know damn well I'm in a lot of trouble. My fingerprints were found on the trunk of a car and on marijuana found inside. They've got my M-16 and my digital scales. I really do need that stuff back."

After the policeman said he didn't know what he could do, Dugan added, "If you can help me, I'll make sure you get $1,500 for helping us. You will be on the inside. We've got more money than you've ever seen before. You play along with us, and there'll be a lot of money coming to you for what you can do."

"What's that?" the detective said.

"You could furnish us with certain information we need from time to time," Dugan said.

The officer shrugged uncertainly.

"You join us and you'll get rich. But first you'll have to take a polygraph test. We require all of our people to take a polygraph," he said.

As soon as he returned to his home base in Missouri, the detective reported the incident.

The new lie detector expert was whizzed to St. Louis to polygraph a member of The Company who had been arrested and later freed on bond, Terry Capstick, and another man that Jim Dugan was very anxious to have tested. In the motel the polygraph man was given a list of questions to ask: "Are you working as a police officer? Did you agree with the police officer to reveal J.D.'s secrets to him? Did you make a deal with the police officer to bust J.D.? Have you revealed any of The Company's secrets to the police?"

After Capstick failed the test, the polygraph man informed Woodbury and added that he would not test the policeman under the circumstances.

Dugan lifted himself up from his wheelchair, his hefty muscles bulging and his shoulders stiffening. "Dammit! He's got to be tested!" Dugan shouted. The detective had already shown Dugan a doctored dummy copy of a printout on Dugan which he said he had obtained from his friends in the DEA, which he hoped would prove to Dugan that he was an inside man.

The polygraph man shook his head. "I will not test him," he said. "There're probably cops all over this place."

"We'll go to another hotel," Dugan suggested.

"No," he said.

"You've *got* to," Dugan said. "He has the gun and the scales in his trunk, and I have to get them. He's also got the marijuana, but I don't give a damn about the marijuana. I do want my M-16 and the digital scales."

But he could not convince the polygraph man, who left immediately and returned to Savannah. He informed the DEA that he had been hired by The Company and gave his statement.

Also in April, members of The Company drove to a 10,000-square-foot warehouse on 2.17 acres in Conley, Georgia, southeast of Atlanta. One of three men in a 450 SEL Mercedes offered to buy the warehouse from the manager of a local realty company. When told it wasn't for sale, the man said he would pay $100,000. The manager said, "No, I really mean it. It isn't for sale. But I'll lease it to you for $1,100 a month." The Company man said, "You've got a deal. It'll be perfect with this high fence around and the locks on the gates for a truck repair business."

A few days later Mitchell called a real estate manager in the Potosi area and said he wanted to sell his warehouse there.

"I'm planning on moving my operation down to Georgia."

In early May, agents followed the last three trucks from Potosi south to Georgia. The trucks pulled in to the warehouse in Conley, the steel gate was opened, and the trucks were parked inside.

As at Potosi, a round-the-clock surveillance was set up with Georgia Bureau of Investigation and DEA agents to keep a constant watch on the Conley warehouse. According to incident documentation of the law enforcement agencies, "A series of events almost identical to a series of events at Mitchell's warehouse and elsewhere took place over the next few days. Knowing that, plus all that happened before in this investigation, the GBI and DEA were totally convinced that this warehouse was being used for The Company purposes and that there was marijuana inside and this was definitely a Company operation, particularly in view of Mitchell's statement . . . that he was moving his operation to Georgia and the fact that all the players were Company members. No other conclusion could be reached."

During the next few weeks, Tom Kimball recalled, members of The Company were "even more paranoid than we had been before. The tenseness in the air tightened around us. We were trying desperately to get something new started. We had changed locations and were putting on a new front."

A load containing 15,000 pounds of top-grade marijuana had landed at an abandoned World War II airstrip near Demopolis, Alabama. The strip, like many scattered across the Southeast, had been used for touch-and-go drills by naval training pilots from Pensacola, Florida, in the 1940s. Parallel to the Black Warrior River, it was located close to the Gulf States Paper Plant from which twenty-four-hour-a-day production noise drowned out the roar of the DC-6 that landed early on Saturday morning, May 26. The strip had previously been used in January and March of the same year. By the time the lawmen started watching the Conley warehouse, the trucks had already delivered the shipment from Demopolis.

On the Wednesday night following the delivery, Mike Grassi and Rick Thorp visited the warehouse. At 9:15 P.M., they drove out of the compound in a new blue Dodge van, with a third occupant, Richard William Larson.

Officers led by Georgia Bureau of Investigation's David Hallman stopped them and asked who they were. Grassi, who was driving, said he was Michael P. Hastings. Thorp said he was Warren Vincent Mason. Richard William Larson, who had operated with Grassi in Atlanta, identified himself as Carl Richard Martin. All showed Michigan driver's licenses the police knew were phony. The police arrested them. A small sack of cocaine was found next to Grassi, and in the back of the van searchers discovered a bale sheet listing a total of 15,000 pounds, and in Grassi's pocket were two notebooks listing prices of marijuana.

A few minutes later, when Granville Leroy Bryant and two others drove away from the warehouse, GBI Agent Mike Eason stopped and arrested them. All of them used false driver's licenses.

Later that night in Chamblee, after the 15,000 pounds of pot corresponding to the bale sheet were found inside the warehouse, Tom Kimball and others were arrested.

All of the defendants were arraigned in state court and awaited trial in Conley.

In August, under directions of James Mitchell, Ronald Ray and Steve Carriker (whose brother Joseph had taken possession of the sixty-eight-foot, eighty-three-ton boat called *Maria Jane*, which had been purchased by Mitchell) arrived in Benwick, Louisiana, near Morgan City. They made plans to take the boat out and rendezvous with a mother ship. Carriker said he would fly over them in a twin-engine Titan as they entered the Gulf of Mexico from the Atchafalaya Bay. He would make contact with them and guide them to the mother ship over the shortwave radio. Preparing to go out, the group talked about their "unfortunate situation at the Conley, Georgia, warehouse," where they had attempted to hide the marijuana under sacks of Vidalia onions, hoping the pungent odor of the vegetable would keep any law enforcement officer or tracking dog away. Ronald Ray bragged about being in on many big deals with The Company and added that the group would be moving into cocaine smuggling later in the year.

Early the next morning, the men took the *Maria Jane* out into the inland water and started slowly toward the Gulf. Before the boat reached the Gulf, however, a major leak developed in the black and white fishing boat's hull, and the trip had to be cancelled.

In Conley, Georgia, the defendants arrested in and around or connected to the warehouse hired attorneys to fight their cases. Mike Grassi's attorney, John Carpenter, who also was hired by several other defendants, met a fellow Atlanta area attorney, Lynch Friedman, on Sunday night, September 9, in a restaurant. They had not seen each other in several years.

Carpenter explained to Friedman that he was representing several of the persons arrested at the warehouse. The case had received certain notoriety in the past few months with newspaper articles and television stories. Friedman said he had heard about it and that he knew the district attorney down in Clayton County.

"Well," Carpenter said, "I want to do everything I can for my clients in this case."

Friedman appeared agreeable when asked if he might be able to help with the DA. "We need all the help we can get in this one," Carpenter said.

"I know him, and I'll be glad to put in a word for you," Friedman said to his old friend.

Carpenter indicated that "there was sufficient money to make a payoff if necessary and that he would get in touch with Friedman at a later date," according to investigators' records.

"If you can help us out with this, I know we can get up

$50,000 each for you and the DA," Carpenter said.

On the following Monday morning, Friedman repeated the conversation to the district attorney and to investigators with the Georgia Bureau of Investigation.

On Tuesday, attorney Carpenter telephoned Friedman and asked, "How are things going with the situation down there?"

Friedman said, "Everything looks okay. I think it can be done."

They made a date to meet at an Atlanta nightclub Wednesday night.

During the day Wednesday a videotape camera was set up behind a two-way mirror in the nightclub. Friedman was fitted with a body transmitter to make tape recordings of their conversation.

Shortly before he was to meet Carpenter, Friedman entered the club behind the district attorney who was accompanied by a female GBI agent.

When Carpenter joined Friedman, the latter twisted his head in the direction of the DA and his lady friend, a date which Friedman said he had arranged, and Carpenter appeared to appreciate this detail.

The two lawyers made small talk, and when Friedman mentioned the bribe, Carpenter wrote notes on cocktail napkins and passed them to Friedman.

"As I told you, we want this one," Carpenter said. He wrote the figure $100,000 on a napkin. "Mike and the others—all ten of them—want out on this one. It's ridiculous."

When Friedman reached for the napkin, Carpenter crumpled it into his fist. His expression stiffened. He looked around the room uneasily and glanced toward the DA. "If you're setting me up, it'll be the last time," Carpenter said.

"I'm not setting you up," Friedman assured him.

"If you are," he mumbled, *"you'll* be fixed." He looked around the room again.

"Well, are we going to make the deal?" Friedman asked.

"Not now. Not now," Carpenter said nervously. "I want to check something out first. Then I'll be back with you." He pushed his chair back. "I'll be in touch with you."

On Thursday, Carpenter, accompanied by Mike Grassi's father, Michael Grassi, Sr., went to Friedman's office. "We want to do business with you," Carpenter told the attorney. "Let's go to lunch."

At a nearby restaurant, Carpenter pulled out a notepad after he cased the place enough to become half comfortable. "We want to make sure you have confidence in us," Carpenter said. "This will be yours up front," he said. He wrote the figure $10,000 on the pad.

Friedman nodded.

Not being as cautious, the older Grassi said, "I want you to know that I've got friends."

Friedman did not reply to the statement.

Grassi Sr. added, "I've got some good friends up in New Jersey. I've done some business with the family of Sam De Calvalcanti, Sam the Plumber, and we know each other personally. And I've got some friends in New York," he said and mentioned several names of mob figures from the eastern coast. "If they know my boy's in trouble, they'll want to help. You know?"

Friedman nodded.

Carpenter went back to his notes. "You've got your up-front figure. When the case is out of the way, you'll get . . ." And he wrote $100,000 on the pad. "We need either a nol prosse [all charges dropped], or they can grant a motion to suppress all of the evidence. When that's done, everything'll be yours."

They chatted around the case without making straight questions or answers.

Finally, Carpenter said, "Maybe not too long from now you can take a little test for us."

"Test?"

"Yeah, we'll talk about that." He stood, ripped the paper

into shreds, put the pad into his pocket, strode to the restroom, and flushed the scrap paper down the commode.

During the next few days the two attorneys talked several times and arranged to meet at the nightclub on Wednesday night, September 19, where Carpenter balled his fist and punctuated his words with emphasis on the point that his client's father, Michael Grassi, Sr., was "mob connected," and added that Friedman should not forget it for one moment. "If you try to set us up, he'll chop you up, bones and all," Carpenter warned.

Friedman insisted that he was "on the up-and-up'" and would never try to set up anyone.

The two agreed to meet on Thursday night at the Rue DeParee Restaurant.

Throughout Thursday morning, GBI agents scurried around the Rue DeParee. The investigators had become well aware by now that Carpenter would rather write incriminating words or monetary notations than to speak them. He was a man who apparently knew the limits to which he could talk and after that only jotted down communication that might be used against him. During the morning, GBI agents prepared a table within the Rue Deparee, lining the top with writing paper and gingerly placing over it a layer of carbon paper. Over the carbon, they placed another sheet of regular paper. All of this was cut to fit the dimensions of the table. And on top of all of their preparations they replaced the tablecloth. Then the electronics experts anchored the videotape camera behind a two-way mirror and wired Friedman again with a transmitter. Agents were dressed as waiters and busboys; several female agents sat at tables with their male counterparts; and the electronics experts listened through earphones.

Friedman arrived first and went straight to the table that had been prepared for the meeting.

When Carpenter arrived, they shook hands and sat.

As before, they had a short talk. Then Carpenter said, "I've got good news. This will be waiting for you." With his pen, he wrote on a napkin $10,000. "And when the fix is made, you'll get . . ." And he wrote $100,000 on the bottom of the same napkin.

"For the final figure, we need action now," Carpenter said. "We need the DA to go along with suppression of evidence. If we need to, we'll get the nolle pros later.

"Right now, I'll enter a motion for a speedy trial, like we want this thing to come up tomorrow. Then we'll just wait a while. Not too long. But a few days. Let the motion to suppress come up and go into play, and then all the defendants will be free.

"We've got to have 'em *all* out. And free. Mr. Grassi wants his son and all the others out. And I want them out," he added.

Friedman agreed that he would go along with the deal. But, he added, there had been a lot of talk and that was about all up to this point.

Carpenter reached into his pocket and pulled out 100 hundred-dollar bills. "This is yours, as soon as I get the final word," he said. He stood, wadding the paper on which he had been writing. "I'll be back in a minute," he said, and he walked to the restroom where he disposed of the napkins in the commode.

Two days later, prior to preliminary hearing in the Conley warehouse case, Friedman saw Carpenter with the defendants and Michael Grassi, Sr. in the hallway of the Clayton County Courthouse. According to Friedman, one said, "Did the stuff come in?" and another said, "Yes, it came in, and it's better than we thought it would be."

Carpenter pulled Friedman aside and said, "We think there's going to be a federal indictment in this case. We've heard there's going to be. Do you know anything?"

Friedman said he knew nothing about such an indictment.

"Before we pay, we've got to see what happens," Carpenter said.

*   *   *

In Darlington, South Carolina, a week later, Circuit Judge Paul Moore sentenced most of the fourteen Company members arrested earlier in the year to five years each for possession of 1,380 pounds of marijuana and added two-and-one-half years for limited conspiracy to run concurrent with the five-year sentence. The defendants regarded the sentences as a victory, because they would serve approximately one year each after which they would be released on probation. Bryan Sullivan, who had jumped bond prior to trial, was pronounced officially absent, and his $50,000 bond was forfeited. First-time pilot Lamovec was allowed to pay a $2,500 fine and go free. Two others were also found guilty only on the conspiracy charge and posted appeal bonds.

In October, Mike Grassi signed over a warranty deed to the South Expressway Airport to his attorney, John Carpenter, in return for the sum of $10 "and other good and valuable consideration." The deed was recorded in the Clayton County Courthouse, witnessed by Michael Grassi, Sr. and Mike's wife, Janet, and a notary public.

When the two attorneys met again on Thursday, November 15, Carpenter told Friedman, "The deal can still go." They made a lunch date for the next day at the Moulin Rouge Restaurant.

"We're taking a big chance on you with this thing," Carpenter said.

Friedman remained quiet and listened.

"For something this big, we have to check you out thoroughly," Carpenter said.

Friedman nodded in agreement and said that was perfectly all right with him.

Carpenter pointed to the hand-sized tape-recording machine he had put on the table when he first came into the room. "This is a new instrument," he said. "It's a voice stress analyzer. It's better than a lie detector machine that's strapped to your blood flow and nervous system. It can tell in an instant if someone is lying or telling the truth. But it won't work with all the noise inside the restaurant. Let's go outside."

In the parking lot, where hidden GBI agents were taking pictures with telephoto lenses from a nearby van, Carpenter put the microphone close to Friedman's mouth. "Answer the questions while I read the meter," Carpenter said.

Carpenter asked, "Are you working with the police?"

Friedman answered, "No, I'm not."

"Are you trying to set me up?"

"No."

"Are you a cop?"

"No."

"Have you talked to the cops about what we have talked about?"

"No."

"Are you a cop?" he repeated.

"No."

After more questions, Carpenter sighed and said, "You passed the test, and I'm glad. I wouldn't want anything to happen to you."

Two days later, Carpenter told Friedman the "best way we can do business is for you to fly into my airport [South Expressway], and we'll put everything into place."

Before he took off in his private plane from Fulton County Airport, Friedman was again wired by GBI agents. His personal plane was searched by the agents to make sure no bug or explosive had been planted.

After Friedman flew around for less than an hour, he landed at South Expressway, was met by Carpenter, and escorted into the airport building where he was introduced to Carpenter's wife. "How do you like this place I bought from Mike Grassi?" Carpenter asked.

Friedman said it was an outstanding small airport. "I bet they really made use of it in the business they're in," Friedman said.

Mr. Carpenter looked at him askance.

"I'd like to fly into this place with just one big load," Friedman commented.

Mrs. Carpenter turned to her husband and said, "I'm tired of all this. I want this to stop! No more of this!"

Friedman apologized and said he had thought Mike Grassi had been very successful in his dealings, after which Mrs. Carpenter said, "Oh, yes, they were. They flew three Titans a day full of marijuana into this place. Those Titans are capable, you know, of carrying a couple of tons of marijuana."

Friedman said he didn't know that.

Carpenter told Friedman to follow him and they walked to another part of the building. Carpenter opened an attaché case. He took out a fat envelope which he handed to Friedman. "You have $10,000 here," Carpenter said, while Friedman opened it and looked inside. "Whatever happens, it's yours," he said, and added that if the prosecutor would forget the case another $50,000 would be forthcoming. "If the charges are dismissed, there'll be another $100,000," he said.

"Maybe I should keep the extra $50,000 for myself," Friedman said.

Carpenter disagreed. He said to be sure and tell the district attorney "about it for the extra incentive."

Friedman said he would. He flew out, back to Fulton County, where the GBI stripped him of the recording apparatus and kept the $10,000 as evidence.

Within a few weeks, the Clayton County grand jury indicted Carpenter and Michael Grassi, Sr. Carpenter was ultimately convicted, his airport confiscated by the county authorities, and a jury could not decide either to convict or acquit the older Grassi.

The group of Company members arrested in and around the Conley warehouse were brought to trial. After the state presented its case, the defense attorney recommended that they enter guilty pleas and ask for mercy.

Rick Thorp sat at the defense table every day until the last one. He failed to appear on the day the lawyer made his rec-

208   FLYING HIGH

ommendation. On that morning he disappeared. "He never said one word to any of us about where he was going. He simply vanished," said one of the defendants.

Although the DEA and local agencies continued thorough investigations, it was not until late in 1980 that Marvin Jay Zylstra, the tall, slender brown-haired airplane broker from Fort Lauderdale, was arrested on a federal warrant. Also arrested was Ligia Viana, the slight Colombian brunette married to Manuel Viana. She was charged with her husband in a forty-five-count indictment, but he was believed to be out of the country. The forty-nine-year-old Zylstra was accused of murdering two men, one of them an undercover DEA agent, by sabotaging their airplane as well as being the recruiter of personnel and plane broker for The Company. Ligia was held on a $5-million bond and Zylstra on a $1-million bond.

U.S. Attorney Clifford J. Proud and U.S. Assistant Attorney General Gregory Bruce English, assigned as a special prosecutor, worked around the clock with DEA agents and other law enforcement officials, oftentimes wading through waist-deep piles of documented evidence in the large conference room of the St. Louis office. The indictments were put together with a tedious combined effort.

On Thursday afternoon, December 4, 1980, after he and a group of Company members had been watched for more than a week, James Anderson Mitchell was arrested along with Bryan O'Neal Sullivan in the Governor's House motel in Montgomery, Alabama. The DEA and Alabama Bureau of Investigation agents had zeroed in on the group which was believed to have been waiting for the arrival of a plane filled with drugs. However, the plane had developed mechanical problems in Oklahoma City. The agents decided that the plane would take much longer to make the trip than they had anticipated. To avoid any further difficulties, they would move in and make the arrest. At the time, Mitchell was believed by authorities to be the chairman of the board of The Company. It was later learned that he was the warehousing and marketing manager for the international organization. Authorities were correct in their belief that Sullivan was the real estate executive and an organizer for The Company.

Within a few months, some 150 members of The Company, including those already serving state time in Georgia and South Carolina and Illinois, were charged under various federal statutes. When attorneys for the individual defendants examined the evidence held by the team of prosecutors, they advised their clients to enter pleas of guilty. With such massive evidence against them, they said, there was no need to fight prosecution. Besides, most had been upstanding or at least average citizens before they became involved with The Company. If they cooperated with the government, perhaps they would receive leniency from the court at the time of sentencing.

Only one decided that it was best to fight and go to trial. That was Marvin Zylstra, known at various times as the Flying Dutchman and Starvin' Marvin. He told friends that he had had a vision in a dream that the jury would believe him and he would be found innocent of all charges.

Chapter Five

The Trial

Marvin Jay Zylstra was a romantic figure to some in the Fort Lauderdale area. The six-foot three-inch, 175-pound figure with the thick brown mustache that curled down over the corners of his mouth walked with a knowing swagger around the concrete skirts of Custom Air Limited. When Robert Andrews, the young man who worked for him, watched Zylstra fold his body into the cockpit of a plane, "It was like watching a cowboy in a movie swing onto his horse. Before Marvin started drinking, he was the best pilot I ever saw. He'd rev up an engine of one of those big four-engine boys and bring her out onto the runway with ease and sit there and play with the stick. He'd like let her bounce a little at first, right before takeoff, then he'd barrel down the runway and pull that nose up and cut through the sky like it was melted butter. He was really something. He'd treat those DC-3s and DC-4s and even DC-7s like they were pieces of clay in the hands of a master sculptor. I really did think he was the best, and I've seen a lot of them come and go through this airport."

Of Dutch descent, Zylstra was born December 26, 1930 in Grand Rapids, Michigan, and after finishing the tenth grade, enlisted in the Army shortly after World War II. Before being sent to Korea he attended the U.S. Air Force Institute from which he received his Government Equivalency Diploma. In 1949 he learned to pilot an airplane and earned an airline transport rating. In Korea he served with the Fifth Regimental combat team on the front line for 145 days without one day of leave. He later told friends in Michigan that it was the toughest time of his life. "After you've looked death in the face every day for nearly five months, you are not afraid of one damn solitary thing in this old world," he was quoted as saying.

Upon returning home, he and his young wife looked the future straight in the eye and decided they could make a living and raise a family in the good old-fashioned American style in their hometown of Grand Rapids. He opened a garage where he worked on trucks and automobiles and had a towing service on the side. His wife joined in the chores, keeping the books and watching the money.

On weekends, Marvin flew. He had several friends who owned planes who wished to be taken to football games and hockey matches and weekend vacations. They paid Marvin a fee and he got to do what he loved best: flying.

Through the years, the flying jobs became more and more frequent. Work at the garage began to fall behind. His wife had her hands full trying to keep the business afloat, and she also became ill and needed rest.

In 1959 he sold the garage and went into flying full time. He did bush-type flying for construction companies. Zylstra flew into field sites and landed on any small strip of flat land. When a company built a highway, Zylstra took the crew out in the mornings and picked them up in the evenings. He chased parts for them. When a part to some piece of equipment broke, he fetched it across great distances. "That's a very important part of the construction business," said a former employer. "If a construction job is down because of a broken piece of machinery, it costs a great deal of money. We always like to have a good pilot who is not afraid to fly in any kind of in-clement weather to make sure our people are working. A pilot like that is money in the bank to us. And I'll say that Marvin was one of the finest we ever had. We could always depend on him. He knew his airplanes. And he didn't know fear."

In late 1960, after he had toyed around with the idea in his spare time, Zylstra moved into airplane sales. Through his contacts with Cessna, he became sales manager at McKinley Airport in Detroit. One-and-one-half years later he was given the opportunity to operate his own aircraft sales business in Muskegon, where he had a big hangar, good bank financing, a large inventory, and twenty persons on his staff.

Zylstra started a travel club, Air Holiday, with a membership that grew to about 500, with each person owning a small percentage in a DC-3 that was lined with seats. At least twice a month Zylstra flew members of Air Holiday to some location in the United States, left them, and came back for them a week or so later.

While operating the travel club, he sold out a trip to New Orleans for the Mardi Gras and filled a second DC-3. He needed someone else to fly a large plane and nobody was available in the immediate vicinity. "I was the only DC-3 captain in western Michigan," he remembered. "Someone put me in touch with Dick Zerbe in another part of the state. I called him after he was recommended. He said he would do it, and that's how I first met him. He worked for me that Mardi Gras weekend, and after that I would see him occasionally if I was in Pontiac. He was flying freight over there. We had occasional contact."

It was during this time, when he attempted to keep up his stable of DC-3s on a shoestring budget, that he was given the nickname Starvin' Marvin.

When the financing of aircraft became difficult in the late 1960s, Zylstra sold his sales company. "We just weren't able to get the business or the airplanes financed," he said.

He kept one of his DC-3s and used it to fly the Milwaukee Bucks basketball team, the Muskegon Mohawks hockey squad, and the Green Bay Blackhawks hockey team to games around the United States and Canada.

Another of the planes that he kept was a converted B-23, an old World War II bomber that had been gutted and refitted with plush interior design fashioned to keep down the noise and make corporate executives comfortable. "It was a real beauty, and I was looking for a home for it when I met George Cassidy, who had a mutual funds company down in Nassau and was looking for an airplane and a pilot. When he saw it, he loved the airplane. It was fast and roomy. And he asked me to fly the airplane for him. The job was good and the pay was so good I couldn't refuse. That's when we moved from Michigan down to the sunny South," he recalled.

Between stints with Cassidy, flying around the Caribbean carrying businessmen and delivering documents, Zylstra joined the CIA as a pilot based in Portugal. Zylstra remembered those as the most exciting days of his life. "The CIA was so undercover, the organization I worked for was called Phoenix Air Transport, located in Portugal, flying over Europe on secret missions.

"There was a revolt in Nigeria, and the Biafrans were revolting against general living conditions and starvation down there, and our government was backing the Biafran cause. I flew out of Portugal, taking arms down there into Biafra, Nigeria, and all over that part of Africa. When we would go down there, we'd pick up some of the refugees—these starving people, these kids—and would bring them back to Portugal where they would be taken care of. I mean, these people were starving to death down there, and they needed help.

"We were flying Constellations. Once I was actually hired to fly the head of the Biafran people in a C-47 they had obtained from the German Air Force. It was that—flying the politicians and also flying freight in and bringing the poor people out," he said.

Before Christmas that year, he told the CIA that he had to take a break from that work. "They gave me a leave," he recalled. "I went home, and I told them I would be back on the 28th, and they said, 'Call before you come back.' The war over there was winding down and they said, 'Don't come back,' and the war ended about three weeks later."

For the following year he flew freight around the islands,

into and out of Central and South America, all the time making valuable contacts among the politicians and business communities of that part of the world. He flew for individuals and for companies. A man wanted a prefabricated home delivered to an island from Miami. He delivered fertilizer, canned goods, furniture, office equipment, and machinery to the Golden Aircraft Farms on Andros Island "because there was nothing on the island that we didn't carry over," he said. And he picked up the harvested crop and brought it back to the United States. "We would just keep going back and forth, back and forth, two and three times a day sometimes," he related.

At the same time, he brokered airplanes on the side. If a person owned a big airplane—"the bigger they are, the better I like them," he said—Zylstra put the word out and looked for a buyer. If he found a buyer, he earned a commission from the sale.

Business as a broker became so good that in the early 1970s he formed his company called Custom Air Limited Inc. in Fort Lauderdale, where he met Rick Thorp and Billy Greenwald.

South Florida in the 1970s was unlike western Michigan in the 1960s. He remembered that there were "more pilots than planes. When you get older fellows who are either retired, semiretired, or have left the airplane companies, they like to keep their fingers in it. If you are a pilot and you are hungry, you are going to start looking around: 'Where can I get a job?' The calls came in all the time," he said.

In federal court in Alton, Illinois, Zylstra said that his only contact with Thorp and Greenwald was when they "asked me about aircraft quite often. They would ask me about different types of aircraft, and before they did anything (bought a certain airplane) they asked what they could expect this airplane to do, what kind of runway did it need, how much runway, what kind of a load could it carry, what kind of range did it have, what kind of crew did it need, what kind of equipment would you need in the airplane, and just the various facts that are a must when somebody is looking at that type of machine.

"This is a very specialized business, dealing with large aircraft. For instance, the DC-3 is a two-engine airplane, sort of the forerunner and backbone of the early aviation industry. It's the most highly produced airplane that has ever been, and I believe it's an airplane every airline in the world has had at one time or other. In the DC-4 we are looking at a World War II development. It is a four-engine airplane. It was made to carry cargo overseas for the military—troops and cargo. It's hard to tell the difference between the DC-4 and the DC-6, but there are a lot of differences. They look basically the same but they are not. The DC-6 has big R-2800 engines while the DC-4 has the smaller engines. The 6 has a bigger fuselage, and the 6 itself evolved from the Baby 6 we call it, the early DC-6. I think America was the leader in going up to the bigger 6s. Your gross weight on the airplane varies from 80,000 pounds up to over 100,000 pounds. But basically they all look the same. You have to be a DC-4 or 6 man to know."

During direct examination from his court-appointed attorney, William Gagen, a well-respected southern Illinois criminal lawyer who had made a name for himself in numerous trials in the area, Zylstra held his own by explaining his situation as a mere bystander who had been caught up in business transactions.

But Cliff Proud, a hard-nosed prosecutor from the tough streets of East St. Louis, where walking down the sidewalk could be taking one's life in one's own hands, and U.S. Assistant Attorney General Greg English took the legal bull by the horns. "They made an excellent trial team, both strong and determined but in two different ways," according to Sarah Gordon, an Alton woman who sat in on most of the trial and wrote a piece about it for a regional magazine. "Cliff Proud was hard as a rock, an assistant U.S. Attorney who absolutely knew his business, short of word and iron-jawed as a champion prizefighter. Greg English was big and baby-faced, with soft eyes that belied his inner depth. He is really a mean prosecutor, although he tends to talk too much," said Ms. Gordon.

With them at the prosecutors' counsel table were Ed Irvin, special agent with the DEA who had led the investigation team, and Dennis Moriarty, DEA intelligence analyst who had worked with Irvin since they had both been reprimanded by their Washington director after the Collinsville and Edwardsville incidents nearly ten years earlier. Irvin was chief of Mobile Task Force 326, Operation Gateway, and Moriarty was his number one assistant in the gargantuan effort.

Greg English explained in simple language the complexities of the indictment charging Zylstra with forty criminal counts. The first count was "what we call a RICO conspiracy, which is simply a conspiracy to perform many different acts of racketeering." The second count charged Zylstra with operating a continuing criminal enterprise. English told the jurors from southern Illinois that "in addition to alleging the defendant is a member of this conspiracy, the continuing criminal enterprise count asserts that he is one of the managers of the conspiracy, one of the top level people in the conspiracy."

For the jury to find the defendant guilty of count two, English explained, they would have to find him guilty of count one first. "In order to find him guilty of that count, you simply must find first that he is a member of the conspiracy as alleged in count one, and secondly that he derived substantial income from that conspiracy," he said, and added succinctly, "and the government will show that he earned a million dollars from his participation in narcotics trafficking."

"Counts three through twenty-eight," he said, "are what we call in this business ITARS or interstate transportation and aid of racketeering, which means simply that someone in the conspiracy went across the state line to do some kind of illegal act. Sometimes this consisted of driving a truck across the state line, sometimes to buy an airplane for smuggling, sometimes to pay off, and distribute proceeds of the illegal activity."

Then, counts twenty-nine through forty, he stated, were separate crimes involving the distribution of marijuana.

Zylstra might not have personally committed every crime, English said. However, the prosecution was operating on a theory known as vicarious liability, which, he said, "refers to the legal rule which says when one member of a conspiracy commits a criminal act, all other members of the conspiracy are criminally responsible for it."

With spring-water clear language that could have been used in a textbook for prosecutors making opening statements, English outlined the evidence that the government would be presenting. First, certain stipulations were made. The defense and the prosecution had agreed that a conspiracy had existed among members of The Company and that more than thirty planeloads with more than 32,000 pounds of marijuana had been brought into the United States by The Company. This was in addition to 24,000 pounds of marijuana the government had seized in Thomson, Georgia; 1,380 pounds it had captured in Darlington, South Carolina; 15,000 pounds grabbed in Atlanta; and 32,000 pounds from a boat brought into Texas and shipped to Henderson, Louisiana. This only amounted to the loads the government could prove, and, the stipulation saved the government the necessity of bringing in the 72,000 pounds of marijuana and stacking it up in front of the jury. "Everyone agrees that the marijuana was brought in; it was seized; it was analyzed by chemists; assigned to the appropriate police agencies, and they determined that the substance really was marijuana," the federal lawyer stated. However, he said, the defense did not agree that Zylstra had anything to do with the conspiracy. Then English told about the crimes that the prosecution planned to prove and how Zylstra fit into the overall picture. English added that the government would prove that Zylstra was responsible for the death of two people, one a DEA informant, who crashed in a plane owned by the defendant. The prosecutor said that testimony and evidence would show Zylstra told two agents, "You had better not doublecross me on this deal. The last person that did was an undercover agent for DEA, who got into me and who got into Thorp, I killed

by sabotaging his plane and causing it to crash while landing."
Staring directly into Zylstra's cold blue eyes, English said, "So
there, by his own admission, we have Marvin J. Zylstra, murderer, as well as a member of a narcotics and trafficking conspiracy."

Gagen refuted English's statement. His evidence would show
that Zylstra was an alcoholic, that he was drunk while being
taped by undercover agents, that "rather than being a manager,
he was really a victim," and that the only reason the plane
crashed with the DEA informant was because "the pilot did
not fly it properly." Gagen added that the jury would discover
from the evidence that Zylstra was far from being the millionaire described by the prosecution, but that he was, instead,
a struggling, hard-working airplane salesman with expertise
in his field.

The first witness for the government was Mike Grassi, who
told of his role as executive assistant to Thorp. He and Thorp
made trips to Florida, he said, to meet with Billy Greenwald
who "ran a shuttling operation which would meet mother
ships off the coast [and] shuttle 2,000 to 3,000 pounds of marijuana to shore." They met to middle the merchandise with
buyers who arrived from New York, Chicago, Detroit, and St.
Louis. "We bought it for $300, we would sell it for three and
a quarter," Grassi stated. Through the work of middling they
made some $25,000 profit with which to start The Company.
After several unsuccessful tries, Thorp obtained the services
of an experienced pilot, Richard Zerbe. The contact was made
through Zylstra, who was to be paid $10,000 after the first
load was brought in, Grassi said.

Then Grassi told about the roles of various individuals involved with The Company and stated Zylstra's "was providing
and procuring and preparing large four-engine aircraft."

On one occasion, when the group was planning to bring
airplanes into Darlington in the winter, they were worried
about windshields becoming iced over, cutting the visibility.
Zylstra came up with the solution of using hair dryers rigged

to an alternate power system to blow onto the windshields and keep them clear.

Grassi said The Company's agreement with Zylstra was to pay him five dollars per pound for all the marijuana for which he was directly or indirectly responsible. He testified that it would have been almost 200,000 pounds with which Zylstra had some connection, although he was paid only about $400,000. Zylstra was told by Thorp that he would not be paid for trips that did not result in off-loading and distribution, Grassi said. And in some instances, Thorp explained that much of the money owed to an individual by The Company would be invested in the next trip, which, if it was successful, would result in double payment.

The Company imported approximately 600,000 pounds, selling it for about $300 a pound after paying about $75 a pound for it in Colombia. The total gross was more than $180 million, he said, and The Company paid all expenses, bought airplanes, boats, trucks, cars, airports, paid all employees for off-loading and truck-driving, and was responsible for legal defenses, all bonds, living expenses of the family while the member went to jail.

Explaining his bookkeeping system, Grassi said, "If we had an average trip, say 10,000 pounds, we were going to sell it at $300 a pound, we were talking approximately $3 million. We would enter this in the ledger on the top sheet. Then we would ledger in the number of bales; each bale had a number starting from one to how many bales you had. Each bale had a weight, and I would enter this in the ledger. Then we would enter in the name of the person the bale went to; then I would have a separate page on cash receivables, listing in payments that were made, as the money came in. We would also have another page listing cash disbursements at the end of the trip. We would balance out the pages. If they came out even, you were through."

On cross examination, Gagen brought out the fact that Grassi had made a deal with the government: if he would cooperate and testify, his five-year sentence for conspiracy and three-year sentence for tax evasion would be served concurrently. He had forfeited personal property, including a Cessna Titan valued at about $380,000 and the South Expressway Airport valued at about $1 million, as well as forfeiting about $250,000 in cash bonds.

Gagen established that Zylstra drank heavily and that he never flew a marijuana trip into the country. However, Grassi added that Zylstra did pick up airplanes on several occasions after they had been off-loaded.

Pushing his questions in an attempt to show Zylstra was never actually paid, Gagen received an answer he had obviously not anticipated. Grassi said, "I questioned why the five dollars a pound was to go to Mr. Zylstra, and I was told because Manny [Viana] was originally Mr. Zylstra's connection, that he introduced Mr. Thorp to Manny, and that was the deal Mr. Thorp made with Mr. Zylstra."

Grassi also said that Thorp had financed most of the cost of Zylstra's Fort Lauderdale business, Custom Air Limited Inc.

The last question asked of Grassi on recross was: "How much money did you make in this operation?" and he answered: "Approximately $2 million."

The next witness was James Anderson Mitchell, who had been convicted of forty-two counts, including continuing conspiracy, RICO, income tax evasion, illegal interstate commerce, and intent to distribute. He had been sentenced to eighty-four years in federal prison. English was not able to get into evidence a telephone conversation Mitchell had had with Zylstra but only the fact that he had once been introduced to him as Marvin.

However, Earl Richard Zerbe, who had pleaded guilty and was awaiting sentencing, told about knowing the defendant since their days in Michigan. He said he had been told to come to Florida to meet Thorp and Greenwald and that through his contact with Zylstra he was hired by The Company.

Zerbe told of several flights to Colombia. After his second, he said, he was given $10,000 in cash in a brown paper sack to deliver to Marvin Zylstra, who thanked him when he handed it over.

Again, on cross, Gagen emphasized Zylstra's drinking. In answer to a question, Zerbe said, "There was a point where Marvin was paid quite a bit of money. And when Marvin was paid quite a bit of money, it seemed like he was drinking all the time. I said to The Company, 'I think it would be a wise idea if we just stopped all Marvin's pay until Marvin goes somewhere, either to a hospital or rehabilitation center, and dries out.' What we effectively did was give an alcoholic the means to become a complete alcoholic."

Bryan O'Neal Sullivan, who had been convicted of forty counts of conspiracy, RICO, and other crimes in the court in Alton, testified that he met Zylstra in Fort Lauderdale with several other members of The Company. "I was instructed by Mr. Zylstra as to what type airstrips to look for that would accommodate large airplanes that would be carrying marijuana from Colombia to come into this country," he said. "Mr. Zylstra said that it would be best to look for airstrips that were not around populated areas, perhaps abandoned army airstrips or something of that type, and that as long as the airplanes could get in and the marijuana could get unloaded, that it didn't matter if you had to burn the airplane—just as long as it could get in and get the merchandise off and be done with it," he continued.

He remembered meeting Zylstra when visiting Rick Thorp's house in Fort Lauderdale and another time when Zylstra and Thorp talked with a third party about bringing marijuana into the United States. "They were haggling over prices," Sullivan said. "And Mr. Zylstra made the statement, 'But I will pay you $250,000, and that's it. I'm not giving you any percentage of poundage.' " The man Zylstra was talking to, Sullivan said, was Jan Louis Brosman, who later flew into Fitzgerald, Georgia, when Sullivan was present.

Asked about Zylstra's friend, attorney George Cassidy, Sullivan answered that "it was my understanding that originally he was working for Mr. Zylstra, and then at a later date became disassociated with Mr. Zylstra and began working totally for Mr. Thorp."

One of Cassidy's functions for The Company "was to place money in a foreign account in the Cayman Islands," Sullivan said. "I have first-hand knowledge of this function because I had some monies that were owed to me, and it was suggested by Mr. Thorp that I allow Mr. Cassidy to open an account in the Cayman Islands in the name of Hayes and the National Corporation."

On cross examination, again Gagen attempted to show that Zylstra was a heavy drinker and drunk during the time he made the statement about giving Jan Brosman $250,000 and that he was basically concerned only with airplanes and the conditions of certain airplanes. However, again it was shown through testimony that Zylstra "had control over procuring airplanes and pilots."

On redirect, English asked: "Was Mr. Zylstra drunk during the meeting with Brosman?"

Gagen objected.

The judge overruled.

English repeated: "Was he drunk?"

SULLIVAN: "He didn't appear to be, sir."

ENGLISH: "Was he steady on his feet?"

SULLIVAN: "Yes, sir."

ENGLISH: "Were his eyes bloodshot?"

SULLIVAN: "Well, they didn't appear to be. I mean, I am not trying to be flippant or anything, but I wasn't looking in his eyes to determine whether or not they were. But the conversation was coherent. And it was very adamant: 'But I will pay you $250,000, and that's it. I am not giving you any percentage of poundage.' So the conversation was very coherent."

Jacques Thomas Delannoy, a twenty-seven-year-old former 727 pilot for American Airlines, testified that he had made at least six trips to South America and back for The Company.

He stated he met Zylstra at the South Expressway Airport when Zylstra flew an Aero Commander in and Delannoy refueled him. On a trip to South America, Delannoy said, he stopped to refuel in George Town, Bahamas, and blew a tire. No one at the Bahamian airport had a spare DC-4 tire, which forced the crew to spend the night. "When we got to our hotel in George Town, I called Mr. Thorp and told him our problems. We were supposed to have been on the way. And he said he was going to call Marvin and have a tire sent out. The following day a DC-3 showed up with two pilots and a mechanic and a DC-4 tire and wheel assembly." Delannoy said the mechanic who fixed the tire worked for Zylstra at Custom Air Limited.

On cross, Gagen was curt and quick.

GAGEN: "You were hired by Grassi?"

DELANNOY: "That's correct."

GAGEN: "You took orders from both him and Mr. Thorp?"

DELANNOY: "That's correct."

GAGEN: "In effect, they were your bosses?"

DELANNOY: "That's correct."

GAGEN: "You weren't employed by Marvin Zylstra, were you?"

DELANNOY: "No."

GAGEN: "Never took any orders from him directly, did you?"

DELANNOY: "No."

GAGEN: "That's all I have."

A flight engineer named Neal Phillip Elve from Carrollton, Texas, testified that he was an expert mechanic on large multi-engine aircraft. A native of Michigan, Elve said that he had first met pilot Earl Richard Zerbe in 1971 after "a real dear friend of mine had been killed in an airplane accident. We took a large aircraft to the funeral in Illinois, and he was the pilot of the aircraft that carried all the people to the funeral."

Since that time, Elve said, they had flown together on many occasions and had become "very good acquaintances."

He had also known Zylstra for "a long, long time," since

they both had been involved in taking people on tours into upper Michigan and into Canada on fishing trips.

His relationship with Zylstra had been "kind of off-again on-again," he said.

In early 1977, Zylstra was in Oklahoma City "and he called me. It was at night. He asked me if I would come to Oklahoma City and do some engine work for him on a Lockheed Lodestar. And I told him I didn't want to go clear to Oklahoma City to work on his airplane, because of a lack of tools and parts and stuff like that. And so he asked me, 'Won't you please come.' I said, 'No, I am not going to do it. But if you want to bring the airplane to Addison, if you figure you can get it down here, I will work on it up here. But not there.' I said I had access to parts that I wouldn't have in Oklahoma City.

"He said, 'Well, the engine is running real bad. I don't know if it will get off the ground with the engine cutting up the way it is.'

"I said, 'Well, if you can't get it down here I am sorry, but I am not coming.'

"He said, 'Well, I will be down there in half an hour.'

"So I got my tools and stuff and drove to the airport. And sure enough, in about a half hour, here he came. And he had, of course, an engine problem. He acted like he was tired. He went over to the hangar and slept for a while.

"I did repairs on the engine. I went and woke him up after I got done, and he paid me $400 and said, 'Thank you.' And he was gone."

About one week later, Elve said, Zylstra called again and said his "airplane was broke down again in Monett, Missouri, and he would very much like to have me jump on an airline and come up there and see if I could fix it. I didn't have any idea where it was at. He just said, 'It's in Monett, Missouri.' I had never been to Monett before, and so I thought about driving up. But then, because of the long distance, I said, 'Well, okay, I will pack my toolbox and I will come up on the airlines.'

"So I caught a flight out of Dallas to Springfield, and a fellow picked me up in Springfield and drove me out to this remote spot outside of Monett, Missouri, where this same Lockheed Lodestar sat, and he [Zylstra] was not there at the time. The fellow said, 'Here is the airplane' and told me what the problems and symptoms were.

"And so I immediately went to work on it. I stayed all night.

"The next day about noon, Dick Zerbe came in. I don't know to this day how he got there. But he came in. And I wanted to take the airlines back to Dallas, but he insisted that he was going to Dallas with this airplane. So he said, 'Why don't you ride to Dallas with me?' So I did. I rode to Dallas with him."

Since "the old airplane was pretty tired," Elve said, Zerbe asked him to spend a week in Dallas working it over "real good," and he said, "All right, I will be happy to tune the thing up for you." Elve said, "I dug into it pretty deep and did quite a bit of work on both engines and got it running for him."

During his years in Texas, Elve had become a member of the Dallas Airwing, "a special group of people connected with the drug enforcement operation. They own and maintain a number of airplanes, ferry airplanes and people to different locations for law enforcement work, and they scrutinize and search out suspected aircraft and stuff of this nature."

In the spring of 1977, Zylstra called and asked if Elve could do him a favor. "What's that?" Elve asked. Zylstra asked if he would put his name into a DEA computer and check to see if Zylstra was a suspected smuggler.

Afterward, Elve said, "I went straight to the DEA."

In April of 1978, Elve said he was in Fort Lauderdale working on a DC-7 when Zylstra took him to dinner. "He told me, 'I am in a new business now. I am making some pretty good money. My company needs a full-time mechanic. We would like to have you go to work for us. I have a DC-4 right now that needs maintaining. And I am buying a DC-7 that will need work.'

"The only company that I knew about was the one that he had which was called Custom Air. That was the company. And I couldn't quite figure out what he meant by this company. But, anyway, while he was talking to me, he said I would need to have a polygraph test before I could go to work for him. And I couldn't figure out why I would need a polygraph test to be a mechanic.

"I told him that I didn't think I would want to go to work full time for his operation but that occasionally I might do some work for him if his airplane was broken down someplace in the Dallas area or anywhere else.

"Just before we got out of the car to go into the restaurant, he gave me an envelope. I took the rubber band off of it and opened it up, and as good as I could tell there were ten packages of $1,000 each which would make a total of $10,000 in this envelope. And he said, 'This is for you.' And, of course, with all this money, I just figured right away that surely this was something that was strictly illegitimate, so I told him, 'No, I don't want to get locked into any operation that is totally against the law.'

"We went in and had dinner. He left the envelope in the car, threw his jacket over it, and we came back out and he gave me the envelope again. I gave it back to him and told him I didn't want any part of it. And that was the end of the meeting with him."

Some time afterward, he said, Zylstra called and asked if he would go to Madrid, Spain, and check out a DC-7 and fly as flight engineer back to the United States. Elve refused, he said, because it was so far away and because he was suspicious of Zylstra and his group.

When Elve read in *The Dallas Morning News* that Zerbe had been arrested in a big drug bust in Colombia, he called Zylstra and asked "the status on Dick."

"He's alive," Zylstra answered. "I'm arranging for him to be back with us soon."

"How's that?" Elve asked.

"I'm personally sending down $300,000 to make sure Dick and the others are broken out of jail."

"Three hundred thousand bucks?"

"He'll be back here soon," Zylstra assured him, Elve testified.

Gagen attempted to show on cross that Zylstra had been incompetent in his dealings with Elve. However, Elve said that he had never been aware of Zylstra's drinking problem.

Elve was dismissed.

It was late in the afternoon of the third day of trial. The government put on for the state William H. "Billy" Shepherd, a supervisor of narcotics intelligence for the Georgia Bureau of Investigation, who was asked by Greg English about Rick Thorp's trial in Georgia. Shepherd said that after the state rested its case, Thorp, who was free on bond, left and did not return.

ENGLISH: "Where, sir, is Mr. Thorp now?"

SHEPHERD: "He is a fugitive."

ENGLISH: "Was he ever seen after that day?"

SHEPHERD: "Not by us, no."

ENGLISH: "What was the jury verdict?"

SHEPHERD: "The jury verdict was guilty."

The judge sentenced Thorp to twenty years in prison, but he never returned, according to Shepherd. After English sat down, the defense attorney said that he did not understand the testimony. Judge William L. Beatty said, "We are just hearing testimony. It's very interesting. I might say I don't know what it's for. I thought we were going to start another case."

English stood. After the jury left the room, he said, "At this time, your honor, the government would like to move that the bond of this defendant revert back to the original $1 million cash bond."

Prior to trial, Judge Beatty had lowered Zylstra's bond to

$100,000 when he was assured the defendant would have to put up all of his cash assets plus the house in which his wife and family were living in Florida.

English added that when bonds were first set for The Company members, it was established that the modus operandi of the organization was to make bond and forfeit bond and to depart before trial ended. "To point out the example of Mr. Thorp who, after sitting in and watching the government's case and seeing that the government had made a strong showing of the evidence in the case, and there was a likelihood he would be convicted, he departed, thus forfeiting a $150,000 cash bond" English stated.

English remarked that, in his opinion, the evidence presented indicated an "overwhelming possibility" that Zylstra would be convicted and would be facing a life sentence on one count and more than 200 years of incarceration on others.

Gagen responded that Zylstra had acted in good faith, that he had driven north from Florida, and that he was presently staying with his wife and daughter at a nearby motel.

Gagen put Zylstra on the stand to testify that he had put up all of his property and his wife's property to make bond and that he would lose it all if he skipped out. "I understand my wife would be sleeping in the street if I ever made a mess of it," Zylstra said. "And I have no intention of not being here when I am supposed to be," he said.

Gagen told the court that Zylstra needed his freedom to be allowed to work with his attorney as the case progressed. In his eight years of practicing law, he said, "This would be unprecedented as far as I have been involved. I have represented people who were charged with murders and facing the death penalty who didn't have their bond revoked in this kind of situation."

Judge Beatty said that obviously Zylstra took a positive view of his case and "seems to be quite confident that [the jury] is going to decide [the government] has made a lousy case and he is going to walk out of here a free man." At the time he originally set the bond at $1 million, he said, "I felt that that was a reasonable bond. I still think it was a reasonable bond. The only reason we lowered the bond was because Mr. Zylstra made a very convincing presentation that there was no way that he could properly prepare his defense if he was in jail up here." Now that Zylstra had had time to prepare his case, he said, "I think that I should now go back to my original position. I thought a reasonable bond was a million, and I still think it is, so I am going to increase his bond to $1 million cash." Then the judge added, "And in no way am I indicating that I share your enthusiasm about your case, Mr. English."

Gagen insisted that his client had appeared promptly and he had always been in touch with the probation officer of the court as he had been instructed.

Judge Beatty shook his head. "I have heard your position here that Mr. Zylstra is an alcoholic, that he drinks a lot. You know, I don't know whether he may have the strongest beliefs in the world in his defense and how well his case is going. Out of sheer joy, he might decide to imbibe a little bit tonight and might not make it tomorrow morning."

Gagen answered that Zylstra could not make bond, and the surprised defendant was taken into custody by the U.S. marshal.

On the following morning, the government opened with Arnold Gene Sims, a forty-year-old Cal Tech graduate in aeronautical engineering who had been in the Air Force astronaut training program and who had flown 457 missions during three years in Southeast Asia. Sims, awarded twenty-two air medals and three Distinguished Flying Crosses for his wartime actions, testified that he had met on numerous occasions with Zylstra to plan his five trips to Colombia to pick up marijuana to bring back to the United States. For Titan loads, he said, he was paid $50,000 each and for DC-type loads he was paid $150,000 each.

Witness Hubert R. "Rick" Coleman, a special agent with the DEA's St. Louis office, told the jury, "When the Drug

Enforcement Administration starts an investigation—and they find out that it's large and it's international in scope and that there are a lot of federal, state, and local law enforcement agencies involved—sometimes we propose a federally funded and federally directed task force. It's actually directed by the Drug Enforcement Administration and funded by us, and that is what a task force is.

"Operation Gateway was a DEA task force and had the objective of immobilizing the marijuana smuggling organization called The Company. It was based in St. Louis, primarily because that's where The Company was based."

In the spring of 1979, Coleman was dispatched to Fort Lauderdale to attempt to infiltrate The Company through Zylstra's Custom Air Limited.

Over the telephone, Coleman told a man who called himself Marv, "I'm looking at airplanes. I'm interested in buying a DC-3."

"I'll be right down there," Zylstra said.

Within fifteen minutes, the two met at a coffee shop near the Fort Lauderdale airport.

While they had coffee, Coleman introduced himself as Rick Johnson from Michigan. He said he was interested in an aircraft that could do three things: had the capability of flying to South America, had auxiliary fuel tanks, and had long-range radio equipment.

Zylstra said, "I think I can help you out." Then he added that he would rather talk in a private place like his office.

Coleman followed Zylstra to a small white house in a neighborhood area close to the airport.

During their talk, Coleman said, "Mr. Zylstra made some conversation about me being in the same business as he is."

Later in the day, Zylstra contacted him at his motel and said there was a plane in Atlanta for sale for $85,000—strictly cash, with only Zylstra, Coleman, and Zylstra's friend who owned the plane knowing about the deal.

Coleman said, "I'll check with my boss and be back in

touch, but I'm sure I'll be ready to go to Atlanta tomorrow."

With their relationship growing more cordial, Coleman began to open up about using the aircraft to smuggle marijuana into the United States.

They flew to Atlanta. Coleman said he liked the plane. Zylstra said he could help obtain anything else needed to make a success of his venture. "I guarantee you, I can be trusted," Zylstra told him. He added that he could find long-range radio equipment at a cheap price and that he knew the right people for Coleman to contact.

At the Carrollton Airport near Atlanta, Zylstra introduced Coleman to a man who assured safe landing of loads of marijuana without interference from law enforcement.

Afterward, Coleman told Zylstra he thought $85,000 was a little too high for the plane but that he might be able to buy it for $80,000.

Coleman told the court, "I was trying to portray the role of a smuggler. I was acting apprehensive to some extent."

After they checked into the Peachtree Plaza Hotel in downtown Atlanta, Zylstra and Coleman went out to eat and had drinks and talked into the late hours. The conversation, Coleman recalled, "became very open. Marvin Zylstra began to tell me about the company he worked for and he referred to it as The Company. He said he had been working for The Company for several years and that his role was basically a troubleshooter and an airplane broker and an all-around man.

"He said that if something would happen in South America to one of the aircraft, on a run where they were getting marijuana, that he would either have to go down there himself or send someone down there to fix the aircraft. If The Company wanted to conceal the purchase of an airplane, he would be the one to handle that. If The Company lost an airplane, he would be the one that handled trying to get it back. If The Company wanted a new airplane, he would be the one to recommend or deny the purchase of a new airplane. He seemed to have a great deal of knowledge about aircraft.

"At that point in time, I portrayed myself as being interested in getting involved with The Company. He said, 'Well, the first thing you will have to do is be polygraphed.' And I said, 'Well, I wouldn't mind having you polygraphed also.'

"After that, he said that The Company had lost two Titans. And I said, 'What is a Titan worth?' And he said, 'A Titan is worth about $350,000, and we lost two of them: one in South Carolina and one in Georgia.'

"I said, 'What happened on that?' And he explained the situation on that particular bust."

Later, Zylstra told him that The Company had lost planes, marijuana, and at least $2 million in bonds later forfeited when defendants did not show up for trial and/or sentencing.

At one time, Zylstra commented, "I notice you don't smoke marijuana or anything like that."

Coleman said, "No, I'm just in it for the money."

"That's the way I am," Zylstra said. "I don't even know marijuana. I wouldn't know it if it hit me in the face. I'm just in it for the money. They'll never bust me because I don't ever get near the stuff."

Coleman pretended to back off, saying he was not really interested in this sort of thing if everybody was getting busted. "The last thing in the world I want is to join an organization that is falling apart," he said.

Zylstra said, "Oh, no, no. We have made certain precautions now. We check out airstrips thoroughly before we land. I take charge of the aircraft. We cover up the purchases of all our aircraft. We won't make the same mistakes we made in South Carolina and in Louisiana."

Coleman told Zylstra that he was originally from Detroit but now lived in St. Louis. Zylstra said, "You probably know my boss. He's from that area."

"Who is he?" Coleman asked.

"I can't tell you right now," Zylstra said. "But you would know him, I bet. He's about your age and is from near St. Louis."

After several more drinks, Zylstra said, "Did you read about a plane getting seized in South America and four people getting arrested? And about the same four guys being broken out of jail?"

Coleman said, "No, I don't recall seeing that."

"Oh, it was in *Time* and a magazine called *High Times*, and I know it was in the newspaper up in Detroit."

"No, I never saw it," Coleman said.

"Well, that was a Company plane."

"I don't believe this," Coleman said. "How is it possible that you can lose all these aircraft and stay in business?"

"We busted them out of jail down there in South America. It cost me $350,000."

"What!" Coleman exclaimed. "How could you bust someone out of jail," he said incredulously.

"Well, there were seven people that got paid $50,000 apiece down there to get our people out."

Coleman told the jury: "I acted naive about almost everything, and I was in need of coaching and I just opened myself to being coached through it." Through the entire conversation, he was "a rookie in smuggling," and Zylstra was the teacher.

Later in the evening, Coleman told Zylstra he had telephoned his boss who said he didn't want to get involved with anyone without their being polygraphed first.

"Hey," Zylstra said, "I will take a polygraph. I've got nothing to hide. I am being truthful. I will take a polygraph that I am a smuggler and that I am not trying to get you busted and that I will help you."

Coleman said, "How about tomorrow? Let's go talk to my boss up in St. Louis and see what he says."

The agent explained that the DEA wanted to lure Zylstra into the Illinois-Missouri area where they could meet principals other than Zylstra.

The next day they flew to St. Louis, drove to Fairview Heights, Illinois, across the Mississippi River and beyond East St. Louis, to a motel where a meeting had been set up with Dick Waber, a group supervisor with DEA, who was playing the role of Coleman's boss, using the name Ed. The three had drinks and talked.

During the conversation, Coleman told the court, Zylstra "indicated The Company had found out that a pilot was a DEA informer. He didn't say when or he didn't say what the guy's name was or anything else. He just said, 'We found out that this pilot was a DEA snitch.' And he said, 'I worked on his airplane a little bit. When the guy took off, he crashed and killed himself [and his passenger]—and it looked like an accident.'

"We said, 'How could he not know that you had tampered with the airplane?' And he said, 'Well, I know enough about aircraft to make it look like it's an accident. I know how to do that.' "

All in all, Coleman said, "It was just solid smuggling the whole afternoon," with Zylstra repeating much of what he had told Coleman in Atlanta. "He talked like The Company had endless money and was an international organization, and that he could get us whatever we needed," the agent said.

"He said, 'I could retire today if I wanted to. I am really not interested in whether or not you buy the airplane. What I am interested in is if you are successful, like on your first trip you hand me a bag of money. Nobody needs to know about it. You can lay some money my way, in case the load comes through. If the load doesn't come through, forget it. You don't owe me anything.' "

On another occasion, when Coleman and Waber went to Fort Lauderdale to see Zylstra, they indicated to Zylstra that they had lost their connection in South America.

Zylstra told them not to worry, he would introduce them to his connection.

Waber said, "We'd have to polygraph him."

"No problem," Zylstra said. "He's a good guy. He'll go with me to St. Louis and we'll be polygraphed together. He is the main source of supply for The Company's marijuana. His name is Manny. He is a Cuban and his wife is from South America. His wife's family has all the marijuana. You don't have to worry about Manny one inch. He's a ten on a scale of ten. I guarantee you can trust him.

"I know he will want to meet you guys, because at present The Company owes him $287,000."

Coleman and Waber appeared astonished. "How can you continue to operate, owing somebody *that* much?" they asked.

"Well, it's been a bad season. Since the last time I saw you guys, we had another bust up in Atlanta and lost 15,000 pounds. Some of our key guys were arrested up there. And, well, you know, things are just real bad right now. We lose a load, we can't pay for it. Manny knows that. We don't pay."

"Well, I don't know . . ." Waber started. He looked at Coleman and they shrugged and said they didn't know if they could do any business under the circumstances. "Everything looks pretty scary with everybody getting caught," he added.

"Everything'll be okay," Zylstra assured them.

Within minutes, a dark-skinned man with a Spanish accent appeared. He and Zylstra walked outside together.

When they came back, Zylstra introduced the man as Manny Viana. Leaving Waber and Viana, Coleman went with Zylstra to another part of the bar where he was introduced to Ligia, Manny Viana's wife, who was very quiet.

After Coleman began asking her questions, she said, "You know, I have to make sure you are not DEA. There has been a lot of stuff going on right now. We cannot afford any mistakes. We have to be very, very careful."

Zylstra intervened, saying, "Now, Ligia, have I ever brought anyone to you that is a DEA agent? Are you kidding? I wouldn't do anything like that. He is good and he is to be trusted."

Then Coleman began asking simple and naive questions. "When our plane lands in South America, are we going to be able to find fuel? How many people will we need to take along to load the plane?"

She said, "Oh, no, no, no, no. The plane is loaded for you

by us. We refuel the plane. We check the plane and make sure
it is okay to fly back to the States. You don't need to worry
about any of that. My husband will work all that out. My
husband works out all the details. He is the main man."

During the summer they had several meetings, and on September 18, 1979, Coleman met Zylstra and Viana at the Lambert International Airport in St. Louis in a borrowed Cadillac.
Again, they drove through East St. Louis to the Ramada Inn
in Fairview Heights. DEA electronics specialist Edward Fergus
had wired a room and had set up his recording equipment in
the adjoining room. While both men from Florida were being
polygraphed by DEA lie detector expert Al Yarbrough, Fergus
taped the proceedings.

These tapes, along with the tapes of telephone conversations between the agents and the suspects, were played for the
judge and jury. Basically, they repeated everything Coleman
and Waber had heard them say earlier. Zylstra bragged about
his situation with The Company, about his sexual prowess,
and about the success he had had. Manny Viana told about
various busts, including Louisiana, where "the guys were mostly
young, around eighteen, and they screwed up. I sent them a
boat [with] 32,000 pounds in the Gulf to Texas, got the thing
through all right, but because of a previous operation, they
were trailed, man, so they took all of the loads to this guy's
house. That's the first number one mistake. They were watching his house and they busted the 32,000 pounds." He said,
"Man, I don't go around like their [Company] guys that go to
a bar with girls every night. They give out $200 tips every
time they go out. They all want to be noticed, you know. I
don't want to be noticed. I don't leave nothing but 50-cent
tips and $1.00 tips that don't bring any attention to you." He
said, "They owe Marvin $400,000. Altogether they owe be-
tween $4 and $5 million." He said his people in South America
"don't want to give them nothing regardless even if they give
them money in advance. They don't want to give them anything 'cause they know they have to pay whatever. See, what

happens over there: if you do something wrong over there, you rip off anybody over there, sooner or later, everybody knows everybody over there. About thirty or forty families doing business. They check with each other: 'You know these people? Are they any good?' So forth. If they don't get paid, they say, 'Okay, your credit line off.' They always check to see who is this guy coming in and if they know that you are the one who doublecrossed . . . This is a business like anything else. It's like having a credit line: if you fool with your credit, it's bad."

Asked about The Company's financial situation, Viana responded, "They got the money somewhere. Right now, they're broke. They owe so much money. Some of the pilots had to lend them money for the previous trip. It's just a crazy situation. I told them I don't want to work with them anymore."

On cross examination, Gagen popped question after question at Agent Coleman in attempts to break down his story. But the succinct answers appeared to strengthen the prosecution's case. The defense attorney attempted again to illustrate Zylstra's drinking problem, and Coleman said they drank in the morning on the plane to St. Louis, during the afternoon at the motel bar, and that night before Zylstra again boarded the plane. It appeared that alcohol had loosened the defendant's tongue.

Richard Waber, supervisor of twelve DEA agents in Operation Gateway, reiterated what Agent Coleman had told the jury. He had played the part of the boss of a small drug smuggling operation based in the Midwest who was very reluctant to talk to any outsiders. Zylstra insisted that he could be trusted, he said, because he was troubleshooter and airplane broker for The Company and he needed new business because The Company was being busted too frequently.

At the restaurant in Fort Lauderdale, after Zylstra and Coleman left Waber and Manny Viana alone, he said, Viana told him he could deliver marijuana to airstrips in Colombia with no problem. "I just want you to know that I can get for you any amount you need. *Any* amount! All I need is a forty-eight-hour notice. You let me know when you're coming down here and when you're taking off to get the stuff. With a forty-eight-hour notice, it's yours.

"My wife's family in Colombia has big plantations. My brother-in-law, he will deliver it in trucks and will load it onto your airplane. All for eighty dollars a pound. You pay me, I take care of them.

"You have to let me have ten dollars a pound in front money before you take off from the States to go down. That's our insurance. Only ten dollars a pound. And when you get ready to go, I give you the radio signals you will need, the location of the landing strip, and the radio frequencies for your pilot.

"One half hour after your airplane leaves the States, I will call over and make sure they know we are on our way. You land, refuel, get loaded, and take off again just like that!" He snapped his fingers. "You go in after 6 P.M. And after you take off, they will call me and let me know that the merchandise has left the area and is on its way.

"Two, three weeks later, after you've sold your product, you pay me the remainder—seventy dollars a pound."

Waber said everything sounded fine, but he was adamant about doing no business without the polygraph test.

Both Viana and Zylstra agreed to take the tests on the following day.

Following Waber's testimony, Greg English stated, "The United States of America rests."

Gagen moved for a directed judgment of acquittal, stating that the evidence was insufficient "to show that my client has done any of the things that he is alleged to have done." The lawyer said the evidence showed only that Zylstra was an airplane broker with a drinking habit.

Gagen continued, "As I said to Mr. English a short time ago, if this was a murder trial, I would have a directed verdict. Unfortunately, it's not."

Judge Beatty interjected that he didn't think the government had evidence in the matter of the deaths. "All you've got are these statements by Zylstra himself, which are vague at best."

English stated: "He said he sabotaged the plane of the informant and caused it to crash. He giggled during the tape, saying it splattered all over the airfield. And he said Tom Gordon would never be testifying against him. So from his own mouth, we have it."

Gagen argued, "I don't think that means that he did it. He said the plane crashed. He also said that this Gordon caused it to crash himself."

After considerable argument on technicalities, Judge Beatty denied the defense's motion.

The first witnesses called by the defense were Zylstra's family. His eighteen-year-old daughter testified that her father would sometimes awaken at five in the morning to drink straight gin and play solitaire. She said that when she was ill her father had taken care of her and had been loving. His wife, Arlene, said that her husband had begun to drink more and more. She added that he had earned barely sufficient amounts of money in the past five years.

In attempting to prove that Zylstra did not tamper with the engine of the plane flown on July 19, 1978, by DEA informant Tom Gordon, Gagen put on the stand Thomas W. Watson, an air safety investigator for the National Transportation Safety Board.

On his final approach to the Jacksonville International Airport, Gordon was cleared for landing. Moments later he called and stated, "I've lost my engines."

Watson said the plane "cut a pretty long swath of about 350 feet through the trees" before it hit the marshy, heavily wooded terrain, going in fairly level. "All of the nose of the aircraft in front of the two seats and the pedestal where the controls are sitting were separated from the aircraft and were found in bits and pieces back down the wreckage path," Watson said.

"When the pilot said, 'I've lost my engines,' the major thrust of my investigation in this case was directed toward why the pilot had lost his engines. This was a twin-engine airplane. Historically, two-engine failures are related to a fuel problem. So, with that background, the major thrust of my investigation was directed at the aircraft's fuel system. I found both of the throttles full forward, which means that the throttle would be full on," Watson continued.

Using technical details, he outlined the situation he discovered in the wreckage. He drew a diagram on a blackboard for the benefit of the jury, explaining how a fuel system works in a twin-engine aircraft and how it controls the flight of such an airplane.

In conclusion, he stated, the National Transportation Safety Board's probable cause was pilot mismanagement of fuel. There was a complete power loss and complete engine failure. He added that "mismanagement of fuel covers any multitude of things that a pilot can do to fix his airplane to where he cannot get the fuel that is in the airplane to his engines where he needs them." The second cause of the accident, he said, was that the pilot failed to follow approved procedures and directives.

Under cross by Cliff Proud, Watson said that the Board investigated approximately 6,000 air crashes annually and that he thoroughly inspected the engines. Again, Proud went over much of the technical details. In conclusion, he asked if certain valves were out of synch with the fuel selector switches, indicating that the pilot could not have synchronized them if he had tried. Watson answered positively.

The valves and switches, Watson answered under redirect, were documented the way he found them in the wreckage after the crash. He did not know if they had been touched before his arrival at the crash site later on the same day.

When the expert witness finished testifying, Marvin Zylstra took the stand on his own behalf. For most of one day and half the next, the tall man with a shock of brown hair falling across his high forehead above gold-rimmed glasses told the jury his background. He stated that he was simply an airplane broker who was trying to buy and sell airplanes. He said he never knew that Rick Thorp, Billy Greenwald, Mike Grassi, and the others were in the marijuana smuggling business. He said that when he discovered one of the planes he had rented to Thorp had been used for smuggling, "I was furious about it."

GAGEN: "What did you tell him?"

ZYLSTRA: "Just exactly that: I didn't want to ever know any of his business, any of his operation. I said that it was so obvious that that airplane had just come in from a smuggling run, and I said, 'You are using me to move an airplane out of a hot area,' and I said that was using me. It was a kind of a fast and furious lecture I gave him, not really an argument. He didn't give me much argument. He just promised not to do it again."

When the undercover agent Rick Coleman came onto the scene, Zylstra said, "I thought he was going to buy that DC-3. I was broke then and needed the money." Asked about conversations he had with Coleman and the other undercover agent, whom he knew as Ed, Zylstra said he could not remember what they had talked about, but "I would imagine airplanes." He said that every time he was around the two he was drinking heavily and did not recall much of the conversations.

Zylstra testified that when he and Manny Viana were flying to St. Louis to be polygraphed was the first time Viana had ever said anything to him about The Company and its smuggling operation. "It was news to me," he said. "I don't know if it was true or not. He told me he had some operation going out of Andros Island. And he had boats running. And he could do this and that. And he was making himself out a big dealer." He added that just during his trial in this courtroom had he begun figuring the great deal of money made on all the thousands of pounds shipped into the United States.

When he told the agents about who paid for the marijuana and who was getting busted, Zylstra said, "I could only give them a little scuttlebutt. I didn't really know how it worked. I was trying to bluff my way through."

Zylstra denied that he had ever conducted any illegal business with Thorp or The Company.

Prosecutor Clifford Proud wasted no time getting straight to the point in his examination of the witness.

PROUD: "Mr. Zylstra, you have just testified here to the jury that you are not a member of The Company. Am I correct?"

ZYLSTRA: "That's correct."

PROUD: "And you also testified if I am correct that you are not associated with The Company in any way. Correct?"

ZYLSTRA: "Correct."

PROUD: "Now, you also just testified, if I am right, that the first time you heard this so-called Company mentioned was when you were on a flight up to St. Louis on the 18th of September, 1979, with Manny Viana, for the purpose of taking a lie detector test. Am I right?"

ZYLSTRA: "No."

PROUD: "I believe you just testified about fifteen minutes ago that the first time you heard this Company stuff was from Manny Viana when he was explaining his operation to you when you were on the plane up here to St. Louis."

Zylstra had quickly taken the stance of a defensive witness attempting to explain every detail of his testimony which contradicted the testimony of almost every prosecution witness. Zylstra said that "what I tried to convey was that Manny filled me in on a lot of his association with The Company and he also filled me in on some other problems. He filled me in on $260,000 that they owed him and so forth. I had heard The Company name all the way through."

PROUD: "You testified yesterday that during all of these meetings that you had with Rick and Billy, there was never any mention of any kind of dope, am I correct?"

ZYLSTRA: "I cannot answer that for sure in a yes or no like you want."

PROUD: "Let me rephrase the question. During your testimony yesterday, you stated that you had dozens of meetings with Rick and Billy and there was never any mention of any dope. Was that your testimony?"

ZYLSTRA: "I had nothing to do with the dope. That is why it was not discussed in front of me."

PROUD: "Now you know Rick and Billy are dope dealers, am I right?"

ZYLSTRA: "Yes."

PROUD: "When did you first figure out that Thorp and Billy were dope dealers?"

ZYLSTRA: "That didn't take long. I couldn't put an exact date on it, but they were pretty much obvious."

Asked if he had had a meeting with Thorp and Bryan O'Neal Sullivan about pinpointing airports in South Carolina for smuggling, Zylstra said he did not.

PROUD: "You heard Mr. Sullivan testify to that here last week, didn't you?"

ZYLSTRA: "Yes."

PROUD: "Are you telling the jury that Mr. Sullivan is mistaken in some manner?"

ZYLSTRA: "No. I am telling you he is a liar."

Asked if he went to Darlington and ferried a plane back to Atlanta, he said that he flew planes out twice. Before and during such trips, he said, he never talked about dope but about airplanes. He said that if he had ever offered Jan Louis Brosman $250,000 to pilot drug trips, "it would have been a joke."

PROUD: "You remember Mr. Elve, don't you? The airplane mechanic?"

ZYLSTRA: "Yes."

PROUD: "He's a pretty good mechanic, isn't he?"

ZYLSTRA: "Yes, he is."

PROUD: "He is the gentleman you described as a born-again Christian?"

ZYLSTRA: "Yes."

PROUD: "Did you ever tell Mr. Elve in a phone conversation

in the middle of 1978 that you and others had helped bust Richard Zerbe out of a Colombian jail for a large sum of money?"

ZYLSTRA: "I don't know. I can't answer that. But it could very well be. I feel I played a part. I kept after Thorp all the time."

PROUD: "Are you saying you could have told Mr. Elve that you helped bust Zerbe out?"

ZYLSTRA: "No, I am saying I don't know."

PROUD: "If you don't know, does that mean that it's possible you told him that?"

ZYLSTRA: "I don't know, sir. I just don't know. It's not in my memory."

Marvin Zylstra was obviously an extremely frustrated man. Sweat popped onto his forehead. He was not the same laidback individual he had been when he was easily rattling off the answers asked by his own attorney. Now he looked as though he was trying to remember what he had said that morning, the day before, three months ago, and two years earlier. He sounded like a man who might have been accustomed to telling untruths.

PROUD: "You heard Mr. Elve testify to that on the witness stand here last week, did you not?"

ZYLSTRA: "I don't know if I did or not. If he said I did, I probably did."

PROUD: "If Mr. Elve told this jury—and I am telling you that he did—then Mr. Elve would be correct?"

ZYLSTRA: "I would say so."

PROUD: "You weren't trying to sell any airplanes to Mr. Elve, were you?"

ZYLSTRA: "No."

PROUD: "Mr. Elve is not the type person that buys airplanes?"

ZYLSTRA: "No."

PROUD: "Are you telling the jury that if you told Elve that you helped bust Zerbe out of a Colombian jail, it was just some small talk?"

ZYLSTRA: "Yes."

PROUD: "Now, in other words, you were kind of just spoofing him, right? You know what the word 'spoof' means?"

ZYLSTRA: "If I said they were broken out of a Colombian jail, it would have been some information that he would have been interested in, as far as my involvement or my support or anything else. I don't know what I would have told him. I know I put no money into it."

PROUD: "You told Mr. Elve that you helped bust Zerbe out of that Colombian jail and that a lot of money changed hands down there and that you had something to do with it. But you were just spoofing Mr. Elve, am I correct?"

ZYLSTRA: "That's correct."

PROUD: "Just playing games with him?"

ZYLSTRA: "Yes."

PROUD: "But you weren't spoofing him to sell an airplane?"

ZYLSTRA: "No."

A moment later, Proud asked if he ever told Elve he was a member of The Company, and Zylstra said he did not. Proud said that if Elve testified that Zylstra told him he was a Company member, would he be mistaken? In utter frustration, Zylstra nodded. "Yeah, yes. I can say things and not know or not remember. I do not see why I would tell him that. I can't believe that I would tell him that."

The same line of questioning continued.

As for Coleman and Waber, Zylstra answered affirmatively that he had been "spoofing" them about his involvement with The Company. He said that Coleman too was mistaken about the contents of their conversation in the lounge at the Peachtree Plaza Hotel in Atlanta. On other occasions, he said he simply didn't remember what he'd said, but if he said he was a member of The Company, he was "just spoofing."

On redirect, Gagen asked, "When you told or if you told Waber and Coleman that you smuggled for retirement, was that true?"

ZYLSTRA: "No."

GAGEN: "Do you smuggle for retirement?"

ZYLSTRA: "No."

GAGEN: "Or for any other reason?"

ZYLSTRA: "No."

GAGEN: "Why did you get the false passport?"

ZYLSTRA: "Thorp called me to the Bahia Mar one day. They had a guy there taking pictures. He took my picture. He said, 'We're going to get you some ID. Then I want you to go get a passport.' They sent me some identification. I went and got the passport. He was a good customer of mine."

GAGEN: "Did you ever use it?"

ZYLSTRA: "No."

GAGEN: "Did you ever intend to use it?"

ZYLSTRA: "No. I don't even have it."

GAGEN: "Did you have any authority from Thorp to hire Elve?"

ZYLSTRA: "No."

GAGEN: "Or anybody else?"

ZYLSTRA: "Thorp did not give me authority over who to hire. I ran my own business."

GAGEN: "Is that because you didn't work for him?"

ZYLSTRA: "That's correct."

GAGEN: "But he was your best customer at that time?"

ZYLSTRA: "He was my best customer, yes."

On recross, Proud said he had several more questions.

PROUD: "Are you saying that at the direction of Richard Dial Thorp, you went to Chicago to get that passport and put your picture on it?"

ZYLSTRA: "At his request."

PROUD: "To put your picture on the passport?"

ZYLSTRA: "Now wait a minute! What is this: to put my picture . . ."

PROUD: "Whose picture is on that passport you are talking about?"

ZYLSTRA: "Oh, yeah. It's a false passport with my picture."

PROUD: "Your picture but not your name?"

ZYLSTRA: "And the name that is on the rest of the ID that they sent me. There was a driver's license and a birth certificate. And he wanted me to go get a passport."

PROUD: "I won't ask the second question, Judge."

The defense rested.

Gagen renewed his request for a directed verdict. He moved for a judgment of acquittal on all counts. English and Proud answered. Judge Beatty stated that he had stricken the subparagraphs dealing with the plane crash which resulted in the deaths of Tom Gordon and his passenger.

In his final argument, Clifford Proud detailed count by count the charges against Marvin Zylstra. He again covered the evidence as it had told the history of The Company from the witness stand. He outlined the specialties of each of the witnesses with each other and with The Company, showing how the pieces of the jigsaw puzzle fit together to make a very clear picture of continuing conspiracy, with Zylstra fitting in as a recruiter and as an airplane broker.

After repeating the names of all the witnesses who had testified that Zylstra was a member of The Company, Proud asked for a guilty verdict.

In his final remarks, Gagen began by praising his opposition. He said that although Greg English had called his client a master criminal, a man who had made a million dollars, and a murderer, he had failed to prove it.

Gagen emphasized that there was no way that a master criminal would make all the errors that the government insisted Zylstra had made. And then he asked, "Did the evidence bear out that Marvin Zylstra was a millionaire?" According to the government witness, Grassi, he said, Zylstra was never paid "anything like that."

"I don't want to make this sound like a detective novel," Gagen said, but he pointed out that to believe the government's case the jurors would need to believe "assumption after assumption."

Gagen asked the jury to question the credibility of the witnesses who were convicted of other crimes and were now testifying for the prosecution.

The defense lawyer also went over the testimony, seeing it from his point of view, questioning the validity of the tapes. He stated that Zylstra was an alcoholic who liked to talk about airplanes and brag about his knowledge of airplanes and all of the business dealing with airplanes.

In closing, he asked that they "consider the evidence carefully." He added, "Thorp was The Company."

The final rebuttal was made by Greg English, who said the DEA agents knew the kind of enterprise they were dealing with and still "risked their lives, went under cover, gained the confidence of this defendant by pretending to be fellow dopers, and lured him" into a taped room where "from his own mouth [came] the perfect government case."

Again, English outlined the bits and pieces of evidence collected against Zylstra. He touched on each of the witnesses and added that it was Zylstra's own character which had finally shown his guilt. "He is so confident of his own ability as a con man, as a former salesman, as a slick person, that he can get on the stand and tell you any kind of story. He can tell you—and he almost did—that the Easter Bunny put the marijuana in those planes."

English ended his summation. Judge Beatty charged the jury.

While the jury was deliberating, English, Proud, Ed Irvin, and Dennis Moriarty retired to Danny's Lounge across the parking lot from the modern courthouse. They drank beer and ate sandwiches in the dark atmosphere beyond the signs reading: Lousy Drinks, Terrible Service, No Entertainment, But We Do Have Fun.

The jury came in twice to ask questions. Finally, the jury said it had reached a verdict. With a slow cadence, each count was read. And to each, the jury responded, "Guilty."

The jury deliberated once again on the question of whether Zylstra's business, Custom Air Limited Inc., should be forfeited to the government. The jury had to find that 100 percent of its proceeds were gained illegally through the crimes for which it had just found him guilty in order for the business to be subject to forfeiture.

After a short deliberation, the jury found that the business was not subject to be taken by the government.

At sentencing on May 29, 1981, Zylstra appeared nervous. He told the judge that his health was okay, but the prisoners in the St. Clair County jail had "tried to steal everything I've got." Zylstra testified that his wife was now confined to bed and that she received about $45 a week disability, about $100 per month from an investment he had made in an oil well, and money from the couple's condominium when it was rented. In short, he said, his wife needed him.

The prosecution put on the stand Dennis Moriarty, the intelligence analyst for Operation Gateway. Moriarty testified that EPIC or the El Paso Intelligence Center reported Zylstra as having three separate classifications, indicating that he had been linked with that many drug trafficking organizations, one of which was The Company.

ENGLISH: "Does the Drug Enforcement Administration make a practice of classifying various narcotics trafficking organizations in terms of their relative culpability as an aid toward prioritizing their targets?"

MORIARTY: "Yes, it does."

ENGLISH: "What rating did The Company receive?"

MORIARTY: "The Company was of the highest priority."

ENGLISH: "How did it compare with other marijuana trafficking organizations?"

MORIARTY: "It was the largest."

Then Ed Irvin, who described himself as a twenty-three-year veteran federal narcotics agent, told the court that his task force had identified more than 200 associates or members of The Company. After reviewing all of the information gathered under Operation Gateway, the supervisor said he had come to the conclusion that Richard Dial Thorp was the number one defendant and that Marvin J. Zylstra was the number two defendant.

Under cross examination, Irvin said he placed Manny Viana as the number three defendant, Billy Greenwald number four, and Richard Zerbe five.

GAGEN: "Where do you put Mr. Michael Grassi?"

IRVIN: "He has kind of shifted a little bit."

GAGEN: "That wouldn't have anything to do with the fact that he has helped the government?"

JUDGE BEATTY: "Where did you put him before he shifted?"

IRVIN: "At one point we had him about number three."

JUDGE BEATTY: "Where do you have him now?"

IRVIN: "In jail."

There was no more testimony.

Asked if he had anything to say on his own behalf before the judge imposed sentence, Zylstra responded, "I was not number two man nor any man in The Company. I had nothing whatsoever to do with supplying or with trafficking of marijuana. The case against me is a trumped-up case of circumstantial evidence. I did not know that my airplanes were being used for that type of business.

"I do not believe I had a fair trial. My rights to a speedy trial were violated by the government. I did not get a speedy trial. The dates were changed several times before I was finally tried.

"It is hard for me to get up here and tell you all the things that I do feel, but I definitely feel that my rights were violated prior to trial. If a trial was to be had, I feel that I should have had a fair trial and it should have been down in Florida where I live.

"I am not guilty."

Gagen stated his client was not a master criminal or a millionaire mobster as he had been characterized by the prosecution. He added that Zylstra needed to be pitied as a lost soul who had gone astray. He pleaded for the judge to exercise compassion in his sentencing.

English called Zylstra a "manipulator, organizer, and corrupter" and asked that the defendant receive the maximum sentence on each of the charges, including life without parole for operating and managing a continuing criminal enterprise.

Judge Beatty said that he felt it was unreasonable for a judge to impose a 945-year sentence on a fifty-year-old man like Marvin Zylstra. He said that the court must strive to be reasonable or "we lose credibility."

"With respect to the life sentence without parole in count two, that is somewhat like the death penalty," the judge said. "I think it has to be reserved for the extreme. I can't think of a word of a magnitude enough to express what I mean. But, once you exercise that, it's like the death penalty. Once you exercise that, you have no further threat."

He added that there "isn't any question in my mind that defendant Zylstra was certainly in the hierarchy of this organization. I am not too sure that I would put him as the number two man from what I have heard. Whether he is number one or number six, I don't know that that is important. He was certainly in the executive suite of this organization."

In one, two, three order, Judge Beatty sentenced Zylstra to fifteen years in prison for conspiracy to perform acts of racketeering, or the RICO charge; ten years for continuing conspiracy, along with a $100,000 fine; five years each on counts three through twenty-five, using interstate transportation for the purpose of racketeering; and five years each on counts twenty-seven through forty, distributing marijuana.

As the judge stated the sentences, a smile formed on Zylstra's face. A bystander said later, "You could see that he was counting to himself, knowing that the longest sentence was fifteen years and realizing that he would be out in three or four years at most."

Apparently Zylstra did not hear Judge Beatty say that the

sentences were to run consecutively, totalling 210 years in prison.

For extra measure, Judge Beatty added, "A special parole term of two years will be imposed to counts twenty-nine through forty," which meant that even if Zylstra happened to get out of prison when he was an old, old man, he would always be watched by an officer of the court.

Zylstra was sent to a medium security prison. Because he did not conform to the relatively lax lifestyle, he was transferred to a maximum security institution in Kansas.

During the winter of 1983, the United States government made cases in the Alton, Illinois, federal court against more members of The Company, these charged with various counts of distributing marijuana. Agents for the DEA said that the investigations were continuing and more arrests in the future were expected. With two of the top leaders, Rick Thorp and Billy Greenwald, still fugitives, drug agents in foreign countries kept their eyes peeled for signs of activities from them.

In 1982 an informant notified the DEA that Thorp was in Norman, Oklahoma, where he had delivered a shipment of cocaine to a local dealer. At the time they received their information the agents were in the company of a police commandante from Mexico who said that he was in the United States on official business. A short time later, when agents surrounded the motel room where Thorp was said to have been staying, they discovered a room with nothing but some of the fugitive's clothes and his dog in a traveling cage. "He had left within minutes before we arrived," said a DEA agent. "He had to have been tipped that we were on our way." Several days later Thorp was spotted south of the Mexican border driving a white Cadillac convertible. A check of the license plates revealed that the car was owned by the commandante who had been with the agents when they heard where Thorp was staying.

According to one of the agents who are constantly on the

watch for Thorp and Greenwald and other fugitive Company members, "Wherever they are, they're operating. We know that. They don't stop that quickly. They know the business. We know them as professional master criminals. Their modus operandi will stay the same until we find them and put them behind bars. We never know when we will be able to catch guys like Thorp and Greenwald. They move around very quickly, very silently, but now and then they show their heads. That is part of the game with them. They cannot stay hidden forever. They have to make it a game. When they make it a game, the odds will shift in our favor. For an instant, we will have our chance."

Author's Notes
and Acknowledgments

This book could not have been written without the cooperation of many people. Many of these were professional lawmen, DEA, FBI, Customs, and state and local narcotics agents who, because of a necessity to remain anonymous in order to work effectively at their jobs, wished to be nameless or disguised under pseudonyms. In all such cases, I followed the wishes of the people who granted interviews, and, as stated in the Foreword, I have indicated where undercover aliases are used.

Foreword
The author had the opportunity to travel with many narcotics agents during the process of collecting material for this book. Several from the Tennessee Bureau of Investigation wished to remain anonymous. Former Investigator James G. Morgan of Memphis was extremely helpful and transported the author via small airplane into several situations similar to the ones described in the Foreword.

Book One: THE INSIDE TRACK

Chapter One: The Good Old Boys
The author interviewed officials of the Alabama Bureau of Investigation, Captain E. B. Taylor, Lieutenant L. N. Bradford, Investigators James G. "Jerry" Ward and William Rhegness,

and State Trooper Pilot Jack Bell in May, June, and August of 1983. Each gave their detailed accounts of the Hurtsboro incident which resulted in the multiple arrests. U.S. Attorney John Bell's office cooperated in allowing the author to study transcripts of the trials of the defendants. Chief Assistant U.S. Attorney Broward Segrest and Assistant Kent Brunson were helpful in providing official documents on file. The dialogue, as it is elsewhere in the book, is lifted directly from official transcripts or recreated from the memory of the participants. Defense attorneys in the court cases described in this chapter included David B. Byrne, Jr., Walter Chandler, Ira DeMent, William Gunter, E. Hamilton Wilson, Jr., Ronald W. Wise, and James Jerry Wood, all of Montgomery, Alabama, and Raymond R. Pines of Tampa, Florida; Jeffrey H. Savlov of Tallahassee, Florida; Richard Gargiulo, Bryan J. McMenimen, and Daniel J. O'Connell III, all of Boston, Massachusetts.

Chapter Two: Bad Bandito

On two occasions in May and June of 1983 the author interviewed the subject of this chapter from locations near Tampico, Mexico, via telephone. In early June he interviewed Andrew Vallejo near Houston, Texas. The author is indebted to his friend Joe Azbell for insights into the character and charisma of Anastasio Somoza. A retired CIA agent living in the panhandle of Florida provided a great deal of information, showed the author charts and relevant documentation backing up some of Vallejo's claims concerning Central America, but because of the touchy political nature of his revelations he wished to remain anonymous. Information was double checked from Anastasio Somoza's autobiography, *Nicaragua Betrayed*, published by Western Islands Publishers in 1980.

Chapter Three: The Money Men

The author talked with Victor Herbert Straus—an alias that the real Straus used in his business of laundering money for a smuggling operation—several times in federal prison at Eglin

Air Force Base near Fort Walton Beach, Florida, and once in
his home near New York City. The dates were Thursday and
Friday, March 17 and 18, 1983, in Florida, and Tuesday, April
19, 1983, near New York.

Assistant U.S. Attorney General Gregory Bruce English met
and talked with the author on Wednesday and Thursday, April
13 and 14, 1983, in Washington, D.C. His files revealed some
of the information used in this chapter as well as newspaper
clippings in his office in the narcotics division of the Justice
Department.

An article by Philip Smith in *The Washington Post* on Sunday, April 17, 1983, outlined the story of Julian Pernell and
Barry Toombs.

On Friday and Saturday, May 6 and 7, 1983, the author was
introduced to the real Benito Lugano. The name was one used
by the smuggler when he operated in Las Vegas to launder
drug money.

Harold Oldham's quotes became public information when
he testified before the Permanent Subcommittee on Investigations of the U.S. Senate Committee on Governmental Affairs on Tuesday, November 17, 1981. The staffs of Senator
William V. Roth, Jr., chairman of the subcommittee, and Senator Sam Nunn, Democrat from Georgia, were very helpful in
providing the author with material and direction when he first
began collecting material to write this book.

Chapter Four: The Glitter Game
In early May of 1983 the author met and interviewed a
number of Drug Enforcement Administration agents in Texas,
Nevada, and California. All wished to remain anonymous. The
agents in turn introduced the author to James C. Stuart, an
alias used in a number of cases when the informant was undercover. The agents expressed concern about their informant.
Although he was no longer working undercover, they stated
that he might be in danger if his real identity was revealed.

On April 16, 1983, a Saturday, the author was taken by

agents in New York to a factory in Queens where narcotics were refined from the raw product brought into the United States illegally from South America, as well as from Turkey through Europe. During this day of driving through the city the agents told the author stories about working "The Glitter Game."

Again, the words of Harold Oldham came from testimony at hearings before the Subcommittee on Investigations.

Special Investigator Lofton Brown was interviewed in Nashville, Tennessee, in October of 1982, when he told about incidents involving country music stars and narcotics.

For their especially candid remarks about politicians in Washington and Capitol Hill, the author wishes to thank several special investigators for Special Counsel Joseph A. Califano, Jr., who investigated narcotics traffic among officeholders for the House Committee on Standards of Official Conduct and reported on May 18, 1983.

Chapter Five: The Florida Phenomenon

The author first heard of the Baron of Baron River, Lowell T. Everett, on a research trip to Jamaica in 1982. Gunter Heinz of Ocho Rios told the author that Everett was the "biggest and smartest trafficker of drugs in the Caribbean Basin." Heinz had worked for the Jamaican government investigating drug smuggling in and around the island.

Several interviews with retired Lieutenant Ralph Chatom of the Tampa Police Department in February and March of 1983 resulted in inside information concerning Lowell Everett and other smuggling operations along the Gulf coast of Florida.

Also, Lawrence Muller of the staff of *The Daily Gleaner* in Kingston not only introduced the author to members of the Ministry of National Security who were helpful and also gave background on Everett.

Reporter Christian Williams's article on July 15, 1983, in *The Washington Post*, was exceptionally thorough and revealing.

The quotes from Charles F. Rinkevich, the coordinator of Vice President George Bush's South Florida Task Force, was taken from his testimony before the Subcommittee on Investigations when it met at the request of Senator Nunn in Savannah on October 25, 1982.

Journalist Bryan Moynahan's article on the Task Force's work in south Florida, first published in *The Sunday Times of London* and later reprinted in *Platinum*, April 1983, was very helpful.

Chapter Six: Yesterday

Since very little has ever been written and published on the history of drug trafficking in the United States, the author searched through the archives of the Library of Congress for bits and pieces of information. The librarians were generous with their time and energy in finding clippings from *The New York Times*, *The Washington Post*, *The Nation*, and other publications.

Horton Heath, Jr., editor of *Drug Enforcement* magazine for the DEA, and his staff were helpful in collecting information and relating facts. Much of the historical background was collected in a special edition of Mr. Heath's magazine in December 1980.

Peter Maas's book, *The Valachi Papers*, published by Putnam, New York, 1968, and Charles Siragusa's autobiography, *The Trail of the Poppy: Behind the Mask of the Mafia*, as told to Robert Wiedrich, Prentice-Hall, Englewood Cliffs, New Jersey, 1966, were most helpful in providing background for Mafia connections with drug smuggling.

Interviews with DEA agent in charge Ed Irvin and Analyst Dennis R. Moriarty filled in many blank spaces and corrected bad information concerning the Collinsville and Edwardsville, Illinois incidents of the early 1970s. The published tapes of President Richard Nixon talking with aides John Ehrlichman, Egil Krogh, and Ronald Ziegler reveal that scapegoats in the form of federal narcotics officers were needed to take the heat off Watergate. And interviews with Justice Department officials and other agents involved show the extent the Nixon people went to to make sure the Midwestern agents were prosecuted.

The DEA's Department of Public Affairs provided facts for this chapter and others.

Book Two: THE COMPANY: OPERATION GATEWAY

Chapter One: The Beginning

On Friday, June 10, 1983, the author visited Alton, Illinois, spent the day talking with townspeople, and interviewed several persons at the federal courthouse including friends of Thorp, Dugan, Mitchell, Smith, and others.

Reporter Don Corrigan's article on The Company in *St. Louis* magazine, June 1982, gave excellent general background.

A number of interviews with Thomas Riley Kimball, access to his notes, and copies of interviews he obtained through the Freedom of Information Act were used in writing all of Book Two. He gave his personal insights into the characters who made up The Company and recalled events in which he was a participant.

Particular thanks are in order for the careful and meticulous and time-consuming work in examining all of Book Two by Tom Kimball and Michael Grassi to make sure the facts concerning the organization were correct.

Chapter Two: Super Pilot

The story of Earl Richard Zerbe was taken basically from his testimony during *United States of America vs. Marvin Zylstra* in U.S. District Court, Alton, Illinois, on April 14 and 15, 1981. The author would like to thank Mrs. Carol May of the James W. May Reporting Service of Edwardsville, Illinois, for promptly providing the 1,000-plus-page transcript of the Zylstra trial.

Chapter Three: Downtime At Darlington

Interviews with South Carolina police officers, Tom Kimball, and reporters for *The Florence Morning News* who covered the story of the Darlington bust helped in the writing of this chapter.

Chapters Three and Four also contain quotes and information provided through interviews with DEA agents in New York, St. Louis, and Chicago.

Chapter Four: The Final Squeeze

Tom Kimball provided much of the information in *The Final Squeeze*, along with interviews of Georgia Bureau of Investigation officers. Dialogue was recreated after hearing tapes and reading notes made by officers.

Chapter Five: The Trial

Almost all of the material for *The Trial* was taken directly from the ten-volume transcript of *United States of America vs. Marvin Zylstra.*

The author traveled to Ft. Lauderdale, Florida, and talked with people who had known Zylstra.

Other information came from other sources. Without the help of friends like Pat Owens and Bob Wyrick of *Newsday*, freelance journalist Claude Duncan of Montgomery, Washington attorney Pam Horowitz, former Sergeant William Carswell of the Houston Police Department, Major John Cloud of the Alabama Peace Officers Association, former Lieutenant James G. Edwards of the Tampa Police Department, Alabama Assistant Attorney General Donald Valeska, and numerous others, this book would have been much more difficult to write.

Staffers on *The Florence Morning News* and *The Columbia Records*, and *The State* of Columbia in South Carolina, the *Alton Telegraph*, *The Bethalto American*, and the *Edwardsville Intelligencer* in Illinois, the *St. Louis Globe-Democrat* and *Post-Dispatch* and the Monett *Times* in Missouri, the *Constitution* and *Journal* in Atlanta, Georgia, *The Miami Herald* and the *St. Petersburg Times* and the Sarasota *Herald-Tribune* in Florida, the Montgomery *Advertiser-Journal*, the Mobile *Press-Register*, and the Birmingham *News* and *Post-Herald* in Alabama, the Houston *Post* and the Dallas *Morning News* in Texas, the Nashville *Tennessean* and *The Chattanooga Times* in Tennessee, *The Los Angeles Times*, the *Detroit Free-Press*, and *The Washington Post* gave assistance in the putting together of facts involving stories that had occurred in their locales.

I want to thank my friend Alabama Lieutenant Governor Bill Baxley, who hired me as his administrative assistant when he was attorney general of the state and gave me an insider's view of law enforcement. His staffers George Beck, George Royer, Don Valeska, and John Yung were especially helpful as was his chief investigator, Jack Shows.

I appreciate very much the tireless help of my editor, Jerry Gross, and encouragement in the beginning from my agent, Chuck Taylor.

And I want to thank my loving wife, Sally, who gave inspiration and guidance.

—Wayne Greenhaw
—*Montgomery, Alabama*

INDEX